BEYOND TEA AND TISSUES

Protecting and promoting mental health at work

First published in 2021.

ISBN: 978-1-86922-889-7 (Printed)
eISBN: 978-1-86922-890-3 (PDF ebook)

Published by KR Publishing
P O Box 3954
Randburg
2125
Republic of South Africa

Tel: (011) 706-6009
Fax: (011) 706-1127
E-mail: orders@knowres.co.za
Website: www.kr.co.za

Typesetting, layout and design: Cia Joubert, cia@knowres.co.za
Cover design: Marlene De Lorme, marlene@knowres.co.za
Editing and Proofreading: Valda Strauss, valda@global.co.za
Project management: Cia Joubert, cia@knowres.co.za

BEYOND TEA AND TISSUES

Protecting and promoting mental health at work

by

Karen Milner
Judith Ancer

kr
publishing

2021

Acknowledgments

We dedicate this book to our beloved parents, Shirley and Bernard Ancer, Miriam and the late Bennie Miller, who long ago laid the foundations for compassion for others, commitment to community and a capacity for critical thinking.

To our families : Laurence, Hannah and Bethia; Andrew and Gabriel who supported us, believed in us and offered coffee (and tea) instead of asking when we would be done – thank you. You make our work and our lives worthwhile.

Thank you to Pierre Brouard and Christiaan Gilliomee for your profoundly knowledgeable contributions, so generously given.

Thank you to Andrew Davies for writing the foreword, your deep knowledge of, and leadership in this field is greatly valued.

Thank you to Cia and Wilhelm and the staff of Knowledge Resources for your patience and for being a pleasure to work with.

Table of contents

About the authors

Prof Karen Milner

Karen Milner is an Associate Professor of Psychology in the School of Human and Community Development at the University of the Witwatersrand, Johannesburg South Africa. She is registered as an Industrial/Organisational Psychologist with the Health Professions Council of South Africa and her teaching and research interests are in the field of employee well-being and mental health at work. Karen has published extensively in the field of health and wellbeing (including mental health) in the work-place in both local and international journals.

Judith Ancer

Judith Ancer is a Clinical Psychologist in private practice in Johannesburg, South Africa. She has worked in both inpatient and outpatient adult psychotherapy settings in both public service and private practice and at Crossroads Remedial School with children and parents. For more than two decades she has worked as a supervisor and trainer of other mental health professionals in clinical, academic and organisational settings. She often gives talks and runs workshops and used to write a weekly column called Letting Grow on parenting and child development issues for the Sunday Times. She is a director of Shrink Rap, a company that offers continuing professional education to healthcare and human resource professionals and provides training and counselling services to small companies.

Foreword by Andrew Davies

A wealth of information has become available during recent times, emanating from many disciplines concerned with workplace health and wellbeing in an increasingly complex and rapidly changing environment. This book is different. It combines the weight of evidence-based research with the extensive real-world experience of two of the brightest and most respected minds in the field of psychology – Karen Milner and Judith Ancer. It is both a comprehensive academic guide to identifying and understanding psychological distress and mental illness in the workplace as well as an excellent treatise on the practical steps needed to prevent and manage such conditions and create a healthy psychological work environment. The critical, and often ignored, influence of socio-economic, cultural, and political factors on the onset, maintenance and perpetuation of mental health problems features prominently throughout the book and serves as an important reminder of the extent to which contextual factors warrant consideration in shaping our understanding and effective management of psychological distress and mental illness.

Wellbeing is now, more than ever, an integral part of the relationship between employer and employee and an employee's emotional wellbeing is, without question, one of the most imperative modifiers to individual performance and organisational productivity. The statistics presented in this book are a sobering reminder of the high incidence of mental illness and the potentially devastating impact of such illness on individuals and society at large. Sadly, despite decades of research demonstrating that investing in the mental health of employees delivers a meaningful return on that investment, government and corporate expenditure on policies, programmes and services aimed at addressing mental health challenges is, in the main, grossly inadequate. As a result of this, far too little has been done to tackle stigma and discrimination or provide support to vulnerable and marginalised employees, leaving those who struggle with mental health challenges to suffer in silence or endure the trauma of neglect or direct and indirect discrimination in the workplace. Pierre Brouard's contribution to the book is a pertinent reminder that a person's mental health and his or her search for care is embedded in and shaped by the interactions of a diverse array of social, political, cultural and environmental factors.

Fortunately, as the COVID-19 driven economic and health challenges of 2020 unfold, there is some indication that workplace attitudes towards mental illness and psychological distress may be starting to change. Recent global events have taught us in the hardest way that employee wellbeing is critical to an organisation's sustained functioning and performance rather than a duty-of-care, 'nice to have' welfare benefit. The COVID-19 crisis abruptly upended normal work routines and caused an acceleration of trends that were already underway, involving the migration of work to online or virtual environments facilitated by the rise of connectivity and communication technologies. It disrupted our way of being in the world and simultaneously generated a wide array of unique psycho-social and economic challenges for employees and employers. Milner and Ancer paint a thought-provoking picture of how the rapid and radical changes in the nature of work influence the mental health of employees and the performance of organisations. Their description of the changing world of work and its multiple impacts on social, occupational and emotional functioning, demonstrates both an excellent grasp of the local environment and their reading of contemporary academic research.

Of course, understanding and managing psychological distress and mental illness is neither simple nor easy and remains one of the greatest challenges of modern history. As the authors point out, not all mental illness can be managed through yoga and meditation and the role of appropriately qualified psychologists and mental health practitioners must not be underestimated. Having said that, the strength of this book lies in the unique framework developed by Milner and Ancer to facilitate an understanding of this complex subject and effectively address its many challenges. Their effort brings some rational order to a complex array of mental disorders and highlights the need for differentiated understanding and intervention based on the type, nature, and severity of the presenting problem. It enables the reader to navigate multiple considerations and details the many issues that those working in the field must aware of in order to provide effective help for those in need.

Having spent more than two decades in the field as both a practitioner and a business leader, I have no doubt that the book will empower and equip a broad mix of academics, students, human resource practitioners, employee assistance professionals and organisational leaders with a set of tools to make sense of the multiple manifestations of psychological distress and mental illness in the workplace while simultaneously outlining practical solutions to address such conditions. As readers will discover, the book's categorisation of mental illness, personality disorders, trauma, loss and crises is superb but the accompanying description of how these manifest in the workplace is what makes the book so useful. The structured recommendations on the steps needed to mitigate and manage these issues is invaluable and reflects the authors' rich experience as active practitioners, consultants and teachers in the field of organisational health and wellness.

A book of this importance would be incomplete without a critical appraisal of the various approaches that have emerged in recent times aimed at empowering individuals and organisations with the tools to become resilient, build psychological capital and thrive in the long-term. Milner and Ancer's work in this area is thought-provoking and exciting. The book expands our understanding of the multiple possibilities that are emerging for intervention aimed at getting in front of this challenge with buffering, bolstering and strengthening initiatives that facilitate the growth and development of an environment in which people can thrive. Without their insight, one stands little chance of having a meaningful and lasting impact on the challenges mental health pose in the workplace. The business case for proactive workplace policies, programmes and interventions that foster the development of a positive, engaging, inclusive and thriving work environment is compelling and well-articulated by the authors. I have no doubt that the most important and meaningful changes in the workplace of the future will come from how leaders 'lean in' and put people and their well-being at the centre of their efforts. Those that do will certainly come out stronger on the other side.

It is hoped that this book will help organisations and those who lead them to understand and embrace their role in helping alleviate psychological distress, amplify existing people frameworks, and implement policies, programmes and evidence-based interventions to reduce the drivers of poor mental health and increase individual and organisational resilience and positivity at work. The cost of doing nothing is too high to bear. Without emotionally healthy and resilient employees, organisational performance will, in all likelihood, be compromised and leaders will be left to grapple with the high financial, legal and reputational cost of a depleted and disengaged workforce. Never has there been more urgency for organizations to view the mental health of employees as both a business necessity and an ethical and societal imperative, and to champion initiatives that assist vulnerable employees and empower the entire workforce to live happier and healthier lives. As seasoned subject matter experts, Milner and Ancer provide a clear and simple roadmap on just how this can be done.

This book is much needed and long overdue and demonstrates the value of combining research findings with practical experience and clinical reflection. Milner and Ancer's work fills a large gap in contemporary academic and business literature and stands in a category of its own when it comes to understanding mental illness in the workplace, appreciating its significance, and, most importantly, managing it effectively. It should become the seminal reference guide for both organisational scholars and practitioners, as well as all those concerned with optimising the health and performance of organisations and their employees. Having known Milner and Ancer for over two decades, I am not surprised that they have managed to produce a book that is a potent mix of academic elegance, social and cultural relevance and practical usefulness.

Andrew Davies
Group CEO, ICAS International
March 2021

Acronyms used

ADHD	Attention Deficit Hyperactivity Disorder
ASD	Autism Spectrum Disorder
AUD	Alcohol Use Disorder
BCEA	Basic Conditions of Employment Act
BMD	Bipolar Mood Disorder
BPD	Borderline Personality Disorder
EMDR	Eye Movement Desensitisation and Reprocessing
DSM	The Diagnostic and Statistical Manual for Mental Disorders
DBT	Dialectical Behaviour Therapy
GAD	Generalised Anxiety Disorder
HERO	Hope, Efficacy, Resilience and Optimism
ICF	International Classification of Functioning, Disability and Health
ID	Intellectual Disability
IPV	Intimate Partner Violence
KPAs	Key Performance Areas
MAOIs	Monoamine Oxidase Inhibitors
MBSR	Mindfulness Based Stress Reduction
MDD	Major Depressive Disorder
MQ	Meaning Quotient
MS	Multiple Sclerosis
NDRI	Norepinephrine–Dopamine Reuptake Inhibitors
OCD	Obsessive-Compulsive Disorder
OCPD	Obsessive-Compulsive Personality Disorder
PD	Personality Disorder
POB	Positive Organisational Behaviour
PPE	Personal Protective Equipment
PTSD	Post-Traumatic Stress Disorder
SADAG	South African Depression and Anxiety Group
SSRIs	Selective Serotonin Reuptake Inhibitors
TQM	Total Quality Management
USPS	United States Postal Service
WHO	World Health Organisation

Chapter 1

Introduction

Mental illness and psychological distress are complicated and often difficult to talk about. They are subjects that most people feel uncomfortable about raising with their friends, their families and particularly within their workplaces. Yet, around the world (including South Africa), one in every four individuals experiences some form of mental ill-health at some point in their lives.[1] The Covid-19 pandemic has highlighted both the vulnerability of our society and our resilience in the context of a sustained and stressful global crisis. Research that is emerging as the pandemic takes its course suggests that there are likely to be very long-term impacts on mental health.[2] As we face a changed world, individuals, families, workplaces and governments will need to be prepared, thoughtful, flexible and compassionate in order to adapt successfully and thrive. Mental illness and psychological distress in the workplace have historically been stigmatised and much neglected. Organisations can no longer afford to minimise or ignore the strategic importance of addressing and supporting mental health issues.

Workplaces and employers have a critical role to play in providing help for individual employees who may be in psychological distress or crisis. Organisations can also play a crucial pro-active role in assisting employees who may be at risk of developing mental health disorders as well as preventing the workplace itself from becoming a source of psychological distress. In addition, the workplace can contribute to enabling all employees to attain optimum mental health. Globally, the workplace is recognised as a crucial setting for health promotion, and more recently, the role of the workplace

---

1   Lund, Kleintjes, Kakuma, Flisher & MHaPP Research Programme Consortium, 2010.

2   Kumar & Nayar, 2020.

1

in promoting mental health is being recognised. In a country with limited resources such as South Africa, where government spending on mental health is extremely low – only 5% of the total South African health budget is spent on mental health[3] – the need for workplace initiatives to promote mental health is even more pressing. Indeed, the costs associated with poor mental health in the workplace are high, for the individual employee and their family; for the employing organisation and for society as a whole. In recognising the costs associated with mental health issues, the ethical, financial and societal imperatives for organisations to engage in this arena become clear. From an individual perspective, the human misery associated with mental health issues is reason enough to intervene. If one of our members is in distress, we, as organisational citizens, need to help. We are often prevented from doing so because we do not have the tools at our disposal to recognise when and how to intervene. One of the key aims of this book is to empower employers and managers to identify and assist employees at risk.

From an organisational perspective, the business case for dealing with mental health and wellbeing in the workplace is absolutely clear. The costs associated with poor mental health are only one element of the business argument for addressing mental health in the workplace. Mental health is not just the absence of mental illness, it is a positive state of being, associated with beneficial business outcomes in its own right. Positive mental health in the workplace, manifested as employee engagement and other positive mental health states, has been found to play a key role in business success.[4]

Given the very high business costs associated with poor mental health in the workplace, together with the positive impact of positive mental health on individual employees and their organisations, the business imperative for addressing this issue at work is evident. Finally there is a significant societal impetus for addressing mental health in the workplace. Being employed is a source of dignity and meaning in people's lives and assisting people to remain in employment even when their mental health may be compromised is a key factor in their recovery. Individuals diagnosed with mental health problems have far better health outcomes if they remain in employment. In an article in the prestigious scientific journal *Nature*' Beddington et al. write about the mental wealth of nations – a societal resource that emanates from the mental capital and wellbeing of a nation's citizens and which has a "significant effect on its economic competitiveness and prosperity".[5]

---

3   Docrat, Besada, Cleary, Daviaud & Lund, 2019.

4   Harter, Schmidt & Hayes, 2002.

5   Beddington, Cooper, Field, Goswami, Huppert, Jenkins, Jones, Kirkwood, Sahakian & Thomas, 2008, p.1057.

This book is the culmination of a collaboration between a Clinical Psychologist (Judith Ancer) and an Organisational Psychologist (Karen Milner) in response to a need we both identified through our respective work. Mental health in the workplace is the juncture at which clinical and organisational psychology meet, yet there is very little collaboration between the two disciplines in either academia or practice. By combining the two disciplines, we are able to focus on assisting individual employees to overcome psychological distress and attain optimum psychological functioning; as well as focus on the organisational context to assist in creating an environment that does the same. Line managers, senior executives, Human Resources departments and even employee wellbeing practitioners often find themselves at a loss when dealing with issues of mental illness. A lack of skills and resources hampers their ability to intervene, leaving them feeling helpless and their employees and the company at risk.

In South Africa, we live in a distressed society with a traumatised past. The employed population spends 30% of their lives at work and the difficulties and challenges we experience as individuals are not left behind when we come to work. Similarly, the way in which work is structured, the interpersonal relationships that are formed, the security of our jobs and the way in which our leaders/bosses treat us, all have a fundamental impact on our non-working lives as well. Both globally and in South Africa, workplaces are in a precarious state of transition, reforming themselves to meet the challenges of the economic and political uncertainty that characterised the 21st century before the Covid-19 pandemic. These challenges have been made more extreme by the pandemic.

"A convergence of forces is reshaping the global economy: emerging regions, such as Africa, Brazil, China, and India, have overtaken economies in the West as engines of global growth; the pace of innovation is increasing exponentially; new technologies have created new industries, disrupted old ones, and spawned communication networks of astonishing speed; and global emergencies seem to erupt at ever-shorter intervals".[6]

This convergence heralds what Klaus Schwab, executive chairperson of the World Economic Forum, terms the "fourth industrial revolution".[7] The fourth industrial revolution is characterised by a fusion of technologies which will blur the demarcations between the physical, digital and biological arenas. This 'revolution' will impact workers, economies and industries and raise the spectre of ever-increasing levels of labour market disruption, displacement of labour through mechanisation on an unparalleled level and associated job insecurity and job loss. Each of these factors has profound implications for organisations and the people who work in them. They

6 Alvertis et al. 2015, p. 195.
7 Schwab, 2017.

impact on the way in which jobs are designed; the types of demands – cognitive, physical and emotional – being made on employees; and the organisational resources available to meet these demands. Some workplaces will manage to meet these challenges in a way that enhances a thriving workforce while others will become increasingly unhealthy places in which to work.

South African workplaces are a microcosm of the society in which we live. The scars of apartheid have not yet healed and individuals enter the workplace with vulnerabilities and sensitivities that stem from our unique and difficult past. The legacy of apartheid remains. We live in a society brutalised by ongoing crime and violence. Our country is still plagued by high levels of inequality and the need to redress these inequalities is a source of conflict, stress, frustration and anxiety for many in the workplace. Given South Africa's history, one of the challenges organisations face is addressing the needs of individuals with differing levels of health and vulnerability. The optimum workplace will manage to contain the stress and distress of the diversity of its employees. The optimum workplace can be shaped to meet the challenge of keeping people healthy and thriving. However, even the best workplace may not be enough to counter the specific vulnerabilities that people bring with them. A responsive workplace will identify, treat and accommodate those with compromised mental health so that they can, wherever possible, continue to lead productive, meaningful lives.

In this book we take a comprehensive view of mental health in the workplace, drawing on theory, research and practice in the fields of both clinical and organisational psychology. In line with the World Health Organisation (WHO)'s perspective on health, we view mental health as not merely the absence of illness but rather a state of complete wellbeing. More specifically, mental health is defined as "… a state of well-being in which the individual realizes his or her own abilities, can cope with the normal stresses of life, can work productively and fruitfully, and is able to make a contribution to his or her community".[8]

The aim of this book is to assist organisations to optimise employee wellbeing and manage distress, trauma and mental illness in a way that promotes and protects the mental health of all employees while preventing as much harm as possible. In pursuit of this aim, the book is structured as follows:

Chapter 2 provides a deep dive into the facts that should shape organisational policy regarding addressing mental health in the workplace. We debunk the fictions, stigma and stereotypes that get in the way of doing this effectively. An essential part of this chapter is the overview of cultural issues that must be considered in the South African context.

---

8   WHO 2001, p.1.

In Chapter 3, we look at the psychiatric illnesses that cause people to feel excessively sad, worried and bewildered and to possibly behave bizarrely. We consider the major mood disorders (depression, and bipolar illnesses); anxiety disorders (including general anxiety disorder, panic disorder, social anxiety, obsessive compulsive disorder and phobias); and psychosis (schizophrenia and other causes). We provide a brief description of each of these conditions and how they may manifest in the South African workplace. A helpful and comprehensive review of possible treatment options is provided.

Chapter 4 considers the realities of dealing with people who have personality disorders. We have titled this chapter 'Some we love, some we hate' because those with personality disorders wreak havoc in the workplace through either 'hooking' managers and colleagues into their destructive behavioural patterns or through alienating managers and colleagues as a result of negative interpersonal interactions creating heightened levels of conflict and stress for all concerned. We will describe and explain the three clusters of personality disorders (Cluster A – paranoid, schizoid and schizotypal disorders; Cluster B – antisocial, borderline, histrionic and narcissistic disorders; Cluster C – avoidant, dependent and obsessive-compulsive personality disorders). We focus specifically on the personality problems that are most prevalent within the workplace context.

Difficult, challenging and destructive behaviours are addressed in Chapter 5 – workplaces gone wild. Bullying, harassment, violence and various forms of addiction that impact on the workplace and employees are discussed. Best practices for managing these issues are explored.

In Chapter 6 we move on to look at what happens when people are faced with difficult, and typically unavoidable, stressful life experiences. Stress, burnout and trauma are not always considered within an array of mental disorders or mental illnesses but they are a significant source of mental distress, and, if not managed effectively, constitute a threat to mental health. Similarly we consider the impact on the employee and the workplace of bereavement, loss and relationship problems as well as loneliness. Clinical psychologist and diversity and inclusion researcher, Pierre Brouard, explores the topical and challenging issue of marginalised identities and the workplace.

Having identified the individual mental health issues that can manifest in organisations, Chapter 7 deals with mental health crises and emergencies at work. We provide practical interventions for acute crises and longer-term individual mental health problems, ranging from how to talk to a psychotic employee through to a mental health first aid guide for helping people in mental health crises or in the early stages of mental health problems. The legal issues and ethical implications of dealing with mental health issues in the workplace are addressed and resources related to workplace accommodations and further referrals are provided. Experienced attorney Christiaan Gilliomee provides a clear summary of the legal considerations in relation to mental illness, incapacity, duty of care and the employer, which is included as an Appendix to this chapter.

In Chapter 8 we identify the psycho-social conditions that contribute to a healthy organisation. Through this chapter we show that mental health at work is not the responsibility of the individual employee alone. We argue that it is essential that we recognise the role organisations themselves play in the mental health of their members so that a holistic approach to worker mental health and wellbeing can be achieved.

The book concludes on the positive end of the mental health spectrum. Chapter 9 focusses on thriving. We briefly review the origins of positive organisational scholarship and spend some time describing Psychological Capital at work with its HERO (Hope, Efficacy, Resilience and Optimism) components. Other practical interventions, including mindfulness and gratitude, are explored and the evidence of their effectiveness is evaluated.

Conclusion

When faced with a mental illness or issue in the workplace it is important to offer more than just tissues and tea, sympathy and clichés. Our intention in writing this book is to empower and educate managers, HR practitioners, and employers across the spectrum with the insights, evidence and practical tools to protect their employees, prevent harm and promote thriving. The book is driven by the theory and research available in this area and we also hope that it will serve as a base and impetus for researchers to generate additional, much needed research in this field. There are no quick fixes and no easy answers. The challenges of mental health, exacerbated by Coronavirus are an existential threat to our society but also provide an opportunity to find meaning and transcendence.

Chapter 2

Mental illness: fact, fiction, stigma and stereotypes

Work and health are considered universal human rights.[1] The South African Bill of Rights, which is part of our Constitution, sets out a number of principles with regard to equality, dignity, fair labour practices and health, including the right to have access to health care.[2] In addition to the ethical, legal and humanitarian imperative to facilitate the rights of people to work and to have access to health care, mental illness costs the workplace a great deal of money. There is a growing awareness of the global prevalence and significant negative impact of mental illness on society in general, and the workplace in particular.[3] Mental illness as a category encompasses a broad range of difficult, painful and often life-threatening conditions that need to be taken as seriously and given as much care and consideration as physical illness. The workplace can be seen as the place where "the human and economic dimensions of mental health and mental illness come together most evidently".[4]

Mental illness and psychological distress in the workplace are associated with decreases in productivity, increased physical illness, absenteeism, poor work quality, wasted materials and compromised workplace safety. Despite the significant financial loss to employers and the country's economy, mental illness is under-acknowledged, under-treated and employers have not given the issue the consideration needed in

---

1 UN General Assembly, 1948.
2 Constitution of the Republic of South Africa, 1996.
3 Evans-Lacko & Knapp, 2016.
4 The Standing Senate Committee on Social Affairs 2006, p.171).

terms of policies, processes and funding. A more proactive approach for managing mental illness in the workplace is a strategic imperative for all employers.

In this chapter we will define and clarify what constitutes a mental illness, and look at the myths, stigma and stereotypes surrounding mental illness. An overview of cultural considerations and the global and local prevalence of mental illness and its impact will make a powerful case for why all workplaces should take this issue seriously.

What is mental illness?

Crazy muttering people locked away in asylums, straight-jacketed, knife-wielding serial killers or dishevelled people living on the streets, sleeping rough because they have become homeless. These are some of the common stereotypes of mental illness. But these dramatic, exaggerated images in no way represent the realities of the vast majority of people who are living, and working, and creating, and earning, and loving, and raising families and contributing to society, and who happen to have mental illnesses.

> "Mental health is defined as: ... a state of well-being in which the individual realizes his or her own abilities, can cope with the normal stresses of life, can work productively and fruitfully, and is able to make a contribution to his or her community."[5]

Good mental health[6] involves a subjective sense of wellbeing, resilience in the face of ordinary obstacles and adverse events, a capacity to persist despite these, and the ability to further develop one's own abilities. Mental ill-health, on the other hand, can be conceptualised as falling into two broad categories: psychological distress and mental disorders.

Psychological distress is something that is likely to affect us all at some stage of our lives. This may be the expected and often appropriate response to difficult life events such as transition, loss or trauma. The stress and distress experienced by many people as a response to the Covid-19 pandemic is an example of an expected (and often normal) reaction to such abnormal circumstances. In Chapter 6 we elaborate on these "normal but difficult" experiences. People who are in a state of psychological distress typically do not reach the threshold for a clinical diagnosis of mental illness. This does not mean that they are not in need of assistance and support, and indeed they may become significantly compromised in terms of their work performance and interpersonal functioning. Sometimes these experiences may be so severe as to precipitate a full-scale mental illness. And some people who have pre-existing vulnerabilities may

---

5   WHO, 2004, p. 10.
6   WHO, 2014 p.1.

manifest with mental illness in response to fairly minor life stressors. Untreated or poorly managed psychological distress, especially in a high-stress or low-satisfaction job environment, may develop into a mental illness. The frequent fatigue, physical ailments and consequent presenteeism and absenteeism typically associated with psychological distress are a significant cost to employers and the economy.

Mental disorders or mental illnesses, on the other hand, are health conditions involving "changes in thinking, emotion or behaviour (or a combination of these). Mental illnesses are associated with distress and/or problems functioning in social, work or family activities".[7] People with mental illnesses meet the criteria for a formal medical or psychiatric diagnosis. Some forms of mental illness may be classified as severe (for example, schizophrenia) or, much more frequently, some as moderate or mild (sometimes called common mental disorders). While mental disorders are frequently disabling and tend to compromise an individual's functioning, they are illnesses that can be treated. It is vital to debunk the harmful and inaccurate stereotype that people with mental illnesses cannot function at all and need to be locked away in an asylum. Most individuals with mental illness continue to function in their daily lives even though many mental illnesses have some degree of chronicity; that is, they are unlikely to be permanently curable, and relapse is a real and common phenomenon.

To understand mental illness, it is important to understand the issue of *comorbidity* – people with mental illness may present with more than one diagnosed psychiatric or psychological condition. A 2006 population-based study conducted in Canada found that 18% of workers had one diagnosis of a mental disorder, while 7% had two diagnoses and 8% had three or more diagnoses. There is also often comorbidity of mental and physical illnesses.[8] Physical pain and disease may cause psychological distress or precipitate a mental illness (particularly depression and anxiety) and psychological distress and mental illness can cause or trigger physical symptoms and illnesses. Comorbid physical and mental disorders also significantly increase the likelihood of ongoing functional impairment and incapacity processes. This does not necessarily mean that mental illnesses always constitute a disability. The World Health Organisation (WHO) defines disability in the ICF (International Classification of Functioning, Disability and Health)[9] as "an umbrella term for impairments, activity limitations and participation restrictions. It denotes the negative aspects of the interaction between a person's health condition(s) and that individual's contextual factors (environmental and personal factors)". To assess whether any condition (mental or physical) constitutes a disability, professionals focus on the person's level of functioning rather than on the physical or mental condition that is causing the

---

7   APA, 2017.

8   Buist-Bouwman et al., 2005.

9   WHO 2001, p.8.

impairment. To evaluate disability, the person's level of functioning relative to the demands of the environment (work/ home/ social/activity) must be considered. There is no absolute or final line between "no disability" and "disability". This does make the job of managers, HR practitioners and incapacity panels challenging, as decisions about the level of incapacity need to be made and have legal, financial, psychological and social implications for individuals, workplaces, and the wider community.

Formal classification of mental illness

In order to classify and research mental illness, the American Psychiatric Association publishes a system called *The Diagnostic and Statistical Manual for Mental Disorders* (DSM). In 2013 they issued the fifth edition, the DSM-5. In South Africa, mental health professionals rely on the DSM-5 to make formal diagnoses of mental illness and to classify their severity and impact. There are nearly 300 mental disorders listed in the DSM-5.

The DSM distinguishes between mental illnesses that appear to have a "biological" or "neurological" basis and those that are related to environmental events such as stress, trauma or loss, and those that are related to personality (or habitual ways of being in the world). Another classification system that is used in South Africa, particularly by insurers and medical aids, is the ICD-10, the *International Classification of Diseases*, published by the WHO.

Table 2.1: Overview of psychiatric diagnostic categories

Neurodevelopmental disorders	Specific learning disorders (involving reading, writing, and arithmetic), motor disorders, communication disorders, autism spectrum disorder (ASD), attention deficit/hyperactivity disorder (ADHD), intellectual disability (ID) and tic disorders are all placed in a neurodevelopmental cluster.
	Symptoms can include:
	• Inattention or hyperactivity • Deficits in social interaction and communication • Learning deficits in areas of reading, writing, and mathematics
	Some examples of neurodevelopmental disorders include:
	• Autism spectrum disorder (ASD) • Attention deficit hyperactivity disorder (ADHD) • Learning disorders

Schizophrenia spectrum and other psychotic disorders	Psychotic disorders are serious illnesses that make it hard for someone to think clearly, make good judgements, respond emotionally, and communicate effectively, among other effects. Some of the common symptoms are: • Delusions • Hallucinations • Disorganised thinking and speech
Bipolar and related disorders	Bipolar disorder, otherwise known as manic-depressive illness, is a brain disorder that causes unusual shifts in mood, energy, activity levels, and the ability to carry out day-to-day tasks. Some of the symptoms can include: • Mania or hypomania, such as periods of excessive activity and energy • Major depressive episodes • Mood swings Some of the types of bipolar disorders are: • Bipolar I • Bipolar II • Cyclothymia
Depressive disorders	Also known as clinical depression, depressive disorders involve a sense of constant hopelessness and despair. This may make it difficult to eat, sleep, work, and enjoy friends and activities. Some of the symptoms may include: • Fatigue or loss of energy almost every day • Insomnia or hypersomnia (excessive sleeping) almost every day • Impaired concentration, indecisiveness Some of the common depressive disorders include: • Major depressive disorder • Persistent depressive disorder (Dysthymia) • Post Partum depression
Substance-related and disorders	Diagnosis of a substance abuse disorder is based on evidence of impaired control, social impairment, risky use, and pharmacological criteria. Some of the symptoms include: • Craving the substance or activity • Developing a tolerance, which requires more of the substance • Experiencing withdrawal symptoms after stopping Some of the types of substance-related disorders are: • Alcohol use disorder (AUD) • Cannabis use disorder • Gambling disorder

Obsessive-compulsive disorders	Formerly classified as a type of anxiety disorder, obsessive-compulsive disorder is now regarded as a unique condition that traps people in endless cycles of thoughts and behaviours.
	Some of the symptoms include:
	• Having things symmetrical or in a perfect order • Excessive cleaning and/or handwashing • Usually spends at least one hour a day on these thoughts or behaviours
	Some of the types of these disorders include:
	• Obsessive-compulsive disorder • Hoarding disorder • Hairpulling disorder (trichotillomania)
Trauma- and stressor-related disorders	Usually, trauma- and stressor-related disorders occur in people after they have experienced a shocking, scary, or dangerous event.
	This also includes those who experience recurring disturbing events, such as first aid responders. It can even include those who experience a sudden, unexpected death of a loved one.
	To be diagnosed with PTSD, one of the types of stressor-related disorders, an adult must experience all of the following for at least one month:
	• One re-experiencing symptom • One avoidance symptom • Two arousal and reactivity symptoms • Two cognition and mood symptoms
	Some of the types are:
	• Post-traumatic stress syndrome • Acute stress disorder • Adjustment disorders
Personality disorders	Because those who suffer from a personality disorder have trouble perceiving and relating to situations and people, they typically suffer from significant problems and limitations in relationships, social activities, work, and school.
	Some of the symptoms are:
	• Persistent lying, stealing, using aliases, conning others • Unstable and intense relationships • Failure to recognise others' needs and feelings
	Some of the types of personality disorders are:
	• Borderline personality disorder • Antisocial personality disorder • Narcissistic personality disorder

Anxiety disorders	While we all experience anxiety at some point in our lives, those with an anxiety disorder face this excessive worry or fear every day. These symptoms can get worse over time and interfere with daily activities.
	Some of the symptoms include:
	• Restlessness • Muscle tension • Sudden and repeated attacks of intense fear
	Some of the types of anxiety disorder include:
	• Generalised anxiety disorder • Panic disorder • Phobia

These disorders, specifically those that have relevance for the workplace, are discussed in more detail in Chapter 3. Intellectual disabilities (such as learning difficulties, mental retardation, or problems as a result of brain injuries or neurodegenerative conditions such as Huntington's chorea or dementias) are not included in our definition of mental illness. However, managers in the workplace need to be in a position to recognise and deal with the possible accompanying psychological and behavioural difficulties associated with these conditions should they arise.

Cultural issues in mental health

Each culture defines what is considered a normal or appropriate expression of emotions. Parents teach children what is an acceptable way to behave and what expression of feelings will be tolerated or encouraged or punished in different contexts. These rules get reinforced at school and via the media. We are all taught how and when we should show emotion, when we should dramatise or exaggerate our feelings, and when we should hide or block them.

Mental illness does not discriminate on the basis of race or culture. The way any person experiences, describes, expresses and interprets their psychological difficulties is, however, shaped by the norms and traditions of their culture.

Mental health practitioners and employers need to be particularly mindful of the spiritual and cultural context of the person's behaviours, as what is considered a symptom of mental illness in one culture may be considered normal in another.

This is particularly relevant in the South African context as our workplaces encompass a wide variety of people of different cultures and religions.

Mental illness in a South African context is typically researched, treated and understood from a Western, allopathic medicine framework (as described earlier in this chapter). Amongst faith-based communities mental illnesses may be explained as the result of a spiritual crisis and from the perspective of traditional African medicine they are understood in the same context as physical illnesses as deriving from disrupted social relationships,[10] bewitchment,[11] and the person having displeased their ancestors.[12]

'Amafufunyana' and 'ukuthwasa' are two culture-specific descriptive terms used by Zulu and Xhosa traditional healers to explain unusual behavioural and psychological phenomena. There is clearly some overlap between these conditions and schizophrenia.

> "When an individual in the Zulu culture has an ancestral calling, he/she sometimes presents with symptoms and signs that are similar to those of a person with a mental illness/ psychosis. The individual needs to go through the process of ukuthwasa in order to be healed from the signs and symptoms of ancestral possession and to become a traditional healer".[13]

Ukuthwasa is a calling to serve the ancestors as a traditional healer, a special, but normal, event. If the person follows this 'divine calling' from the ancestors, this will confer special powers on them. However, resisting this calling may lead to illness called 'ukuphambana' or madness.[14] Among the amaZulu specifically, there is also the belief that a "horde of spirits" from multiple ethnic groups come together to take over a person's body. The typical cultural treatment for this condition is for one of the traditional healers, often ukuthwasa themselves, to conduct an exorcism ritual.[15]

Amafufunyana directly translated from isiXhosa means "nerves" and symptoms include hearing "voices from their stomachs", speaking in another language or in a disturbing tone, and general agitation and possible violence. The affected person may shout, sob, become paralysed or temporarily blind, lose consciousness, appear "out of it" or in a trance-like state (dissociated). There have been reports of attempted suicide. One of the cultural beliefs for this is that the individual is cursed, possessed by evil spirits or demons or bewitchment.[16] Recorded incidents of amafufunyana are found from early in the 20th century and researchers have suggested that its emergence may be related to the impact of colonisation and migration of indigenous peoples

---

10 Hewson, 1998.

11 Crawford & Lipsedge, 2004.

12 Ngubane, 2005.

13 Kubeka, 2016.

14 Niehaus et, al. 2004.

15 Helman, 2007.

16 Train, 2007.

away from their homes. There have also been widespread outbreaks of the condition, similar to events involving the contagious spread of mass hysteria.[17]

Developing the cultural literacy of employers and managers will go a long way to empower organisations to deal ethically, sensitively and appropriately with their staff. Sensitivity to different cultural manifestations of mental illness will assist employees of all races and from a variety of cultural and faith backgrounds get help when necessary.

Difference and discrimination: stigma and shame

Throughout history, people who are different in some way from the dominant group or majority have been treated differently, excluded and even brutalised. In Chapter 6, we address the mental health implications of having a "different", marginalised identity in the context of the workplace (such as being black, female, gay, transgender or disabled). Some of the social consequences of difference are stigma and discrimination. In this section we will look at how public and personal assumptions and attitudes exacerbate the problems faced by people with mental ill-health.

"Stigma is typically a social process, experienced or anticipated, characterised by exclusion, rejection, blame or devaluation that results from experience or reasonable anticipation of an adverse social judgment about a person or group".[18] Stigma, the result of fear, ignorance and prejudice, is a significant reason that mental illness is both underreported, under-recognised and under-treated.

There are two forms of stigma that impact on mental health: social stigma and self-stigma (internalised or perceived stigma.)

Social stigma is characterized by prejudicial attitudes and discriminating behaviours directed towards people with mental health problems as a result of the psychiatric label they have been given. Internationally, studies demonstrate that prejudicial attitudes towards people with mental health problems are widespread and commonly held.[19, 20, 21, 22, 23]

---

17 Sinason, 2002.
18 Weiss & Ramakrishna, 2006, p.536.
19 Bryne, 1999.
20 Crisp, Gelder, Rix, Meltzer & Rowlands, 2000.
21 Heginbotham, 1998.
22 Wang & Lai, 2008.
23 Reavley & Jorm, 2011.

Below are some of the commonly held beliefs about mental illness:[24]

Table 2.2: Some common fictions about people with mental illness

- People with mental health problems are dangerous – especially those with schizophrenia, alcoholism and drug dependence.
- Some mental health problems such as eating disorders and substance abuse are self-inflicted.
- You can tell who is mentally ill by looking at them.
- People with mental health problems are generally hard to talk to.
- They "act crazy" or behave weirdly.
- They need to be locked away.
- They are dangerous and unpredictable.
- They cannot be expected or trusted to work.
- They need to be protected from themselves.
- They can't ever cope with or manage any stress.
- Once someone has had one episode of mental illness they should never go back to work.
- Mental illness is a result of personal inadequacy or weakness.
- Severe mental illnesses are easy to identify.
- Severe mental illnesses are more of a problem for the workplace than common mental disorders or psychological distress.

The media, especially the entertainment media, play a role in perpetuating stigmatising stereotypes of people with mental health problems. For example, movie depictions of schizophrenia are often stereotypic and characterised by misinformation about symptoms, causes and treatment. In an analysis of English-language movies released between 1990 and 2010 that depicted at least one character with schizophrenia, Owen[25] found that most schizophrenic characters displayed violent behaviour; one-third of these characters engaged in homicidal behaviour and a quarter died by suicide. These portrayals are certainly not true of the reality of the behaviour of the vast majority of people with schizophrenia (see chapter 3). Negative portrayals of schizophrenia in contemporary movies are thus common and serve to reinforce biased beliefs and stigmatising attitudes towards people with mental health problems.

Research indicates that people tend to hold negative and incorrect beliefs about mental illness regardless of their age, the knowledge they have of mental health problems, and whether they know someone who had a mental health problem. Recent studies of attitudes to individuals with a diagnosis of schizophrenia or major depression found that a significant proportion of members of the public considered

---

24 Crisp, et al., 2000.
25 Owen, 2012.

that people with mental health problems such as depression or schizophrenia were unpredictable, dangerous and they would be less likely to employ someone with a mental health problem.[26]

In this way we see how stigma leads to discrimination including loss of status, rejection, exclusion, avoidance, hostility and withholding of help. The process of stigmatisation with regard to psychological difficulties usually begins with diagnosing and labelling someone with mental illness. Diagnostic labels are an effective shorthand for doctors to use in order to understand the needs of the client, possible cause of the condition, and most appropriate treatments to try. Unfortunately, labelling someone with mental illness can also lead to associating the person with the negative stereotypes and fictions that are associated with that label. In that way people distance themselves from those who have symptoms of mental illness and can maintain the false sense that mental illness is something that happens only to people who are different or "other". Those who are stigmatised are rejected and isolated from others.

In contrast, perceived stigma or self-stigma occurs when people internalise these negative attitudes and endorse the publicly held stereotypes about themselves. As a result they suffer numerous problematic consequences. Internalised stigma causes negative emotional reactions, such as low self-esteem and poor self-efficacy, feelings of shame, a need for secrecy and leads to poorer treatment outcomes.[27]

Mental ill-health is often hidden, in part because people themselves are often not fully aware of their own illness, because the illness is not disclosed by the employee, or because the environment is such that there is an unwillingness to take note of the problem. But, even once people have been diagnosed by their GP or mental health professional as having a psychiatric condition, many hide this knowledge from employers and colleagues as they fear the negative consequences of disclosing this information, such as being labelled a problem or experiencing loss of promotional opportunities. The fear of victimisation, being the subject of gossip and the pity or judgement of others leads many people to feel they would rather die than admit they have a mental illness.

Internalised stigma, or the shame people feel about themselves because they have a psychological problem or diagnosed mental illness, involves the absorption of negative attitudes and is one of the greatest barriers to effective management of mental illness. This is a problem that is more pronounced in work settings. The stigma of mental illness can be more difficult to overcome and create more difficulties than the mental illness itself.[28]

---

26 Reavly & Jorm, 2011.

27 Watson, Corrigan, Larson & Sells, 2007.

28 Day, Edgren & Eshleman, 2007.

At some point, many people who have been diagnosed with a mental illness or psychological problem are faced with the challenge of who to tell, when to tell and how to tell. With regard to the workplace, disclosure of mental ill-health is complicated. Non-disclosure prevents employees from getting the assistance they need. Notably, many employees choose not to disclose their diagnosis or the fact that they are in crisis as they are afraid of stigma and discrimination. They worry that they will be overlooked for promotion as a result of this disclosure, labelled as defective or weak or incompetent. On the other hand, in order for an employee to be able to be assisted in the workplace, reasonable accommodations may need to be made to allow for treatment, management and non-exacerbation of the problem in the work context. These can only be made if the organisation is informed of the problem. Historically, workplaces have ignored the challenges posed by acknowledging the realities and impact of mental illness amongst workers. This denial allowed employers and managers to hide behind the misperception that mental health issues are a rarity, so not of concern to employers. Employees are afraid to disclose in case their jobs or work opportunities are compromised. Employers are afraid or reluctant to acknowledge the problem. There is a conspiracy of silent suffering, resentment and frustration that contributes to a worsening of mental health in the affected individual, and longer-term damage to health and career paths.

In Chapter 7 we cover the ways workplaces can assist people with mental illness to make disclosures that allow them to be appropriately accommodated in the workplace, and how to reduce stigma, gossip, anxiety and shame about mental illness. In addition, we will highlight the legal framework that covers mental illness in the context of work.

Why should workplaces care about mental illness?

Aside from the immense personal costs associated with mental illness at work, and the duty of care employers have towards their employees, poor mental health is extremely costly for the organisation as well. The following statistics provide some indication of the extent of the problem for society as a whole, and the workplace.

- Global Burden of Disease statistics show that depression ranks as a leading cause of disability worldwide,[29] affecting 350 million people.[30]

- Approximately 1 in 5 adults in the U.S., 18.5% of the population, experiences mental illness a year.

---

29 Murray et al., 2012.
30 WHO Depression factsheet, 2013.

- Approximately 1 in 25 adults in the U.S., 9.8 million people, experiences a serious mental illness per year that substantially interferes with or limits one or more major life activities.[31]

- Individuals living with serious mental illness face an increased risk of having chronic medical conditions. Adults in the U.S. living with serious mental illness die on average 25 years earlier than others, largely owing to treatable medical conditions.[32]

- Serious mental illness costs America $193.2 billion in lost earnings per year.[33]

- Mental health disorders cost the global economy $1 trillion in lost productivity a year, with depression being the leading cause of ill-health and disability, according to the World Health Organisation.[34]

- While absenteeism (unscheduled absence from work) is a problem for all employers, it is increasingly evident that presenteeism (attending work despite illness, injury, anxiety, depression etc. often resulting in reduced productivity) is even more costly. Internationally, costs associated with presenteeism tended to be 5 to 10 times higher than those associated with absenteeism.[35]

In South Africa research conducted by The Mental Health and Poverty Project found that psychiatric conditions are ranked third, after HIV, AIDS and other infectious diseases, in their contribution to the burden of disease in this country.[36]

Evans-Lacko and Knapp[37] reported that depression was collectively costing the nations of Brazil, Canada, China, Japan, South Korea, Mexico, South Africa and the US more than $246 billion a year. In that study, nearly twice as many South African employees reported a previous diagnosis of depression (25.6%) in comparison to the average (15.7%) reported across these countries. This is in line with a previous South African study by Professor Crick Lund and others[38] that found mental health problems affected one in four South Africans – with only 15%–25% of affected individuals seeking and receiving help.

Historically, many employers have underestimated the financial impact of mental illness on their businesses. But in 2016 the loss of earnings owing to major depression

---

31 National Alliance on Mental Illness, 2019.Date is 2020 on reference list
32 Parks et al., 2006.
33 Insel, 2008.
34 WHO, 2014.
35 Evans-Lacko & Knapp, 2016.
36 Flisher et al., 2007.
37 Evans-Lacko and Knapp, 2016.
38 Lund et al., 2010.

and anxiety disorders was estimated at R54,121 per affected adult per year. The total annual cost to the South African economy amounted to more than R40-billion which is 2.2% of the country's GDP.

Presenteeism, which is frequently linked to mental illness and psychological distress, poses significant challenges to all workplaces. In South Africa the annual cost of presenteeism is estimated at $14.8 billion (more than the total value of South Africa's tourism industry), while absenteeism costs around $2.2 billion.[39] Substance abuse is another area of mental illness that has a huge impact on organisations. Smook et al. estimate that half of all workplace accidents in South Africa are related to substance misuse or abuse.[40] They emphasise that an unrecognised, untreated substance abuser can cost the employer 25% of that person's wages.

The South African state spends only 5% of its health budget on mental health. The impact of this patterns of spending and care is reflected in the tragic outcome of the Life-Esidimeni case, when in order to cut costs at a provincial level, long-term psychiatric patients were moved to low-cost (often unregistered) care facilities. The resultant deaths of more than 155 patients highlighted the lack of investment and care in the most vulnerable of individuals in this under-resourced sector.[41] Political leaders, policymakers and employers cannot afford to ignore the situation and hope for the best. It is simply too costly and too damaging.

The relationship between the workplace and mental illness

In light of the growing prevalence and huge social and economic impact of mental illness in society, it is imperative to consider how mental health issues intersect with organisational practice. It is also important to distinguish between mental health policies and "wellness" initiatives. Many large companies proudly offer wellness initiatives such as meditation workshops and onsite gyms. Google, for example, is famous for the quality and range of gourmet foods, coffee and juice bars freely available to staff on their campus. It is big business to supply corporate wellness initiatives to big businesses.

Wellness is important, and in corporate settings is often understood to be a set of lifestyle benefits or perks that enhance well-being. However, if wellness becomes conflated with mental health there is a huge risk that we minimise the seriousness and significance of mental health issues. "The reality is that mental health is not getting a massage or eating salads for lunch; for many, it's a matter of life or death. Mental

---

39 Schoeman, 2017.

40 Smook et al., 2014.

41 Durojaye & Agaba ,2018.

health is not an indulgence."[42] Neither is mental illness a choice you make because you did not take advantage of the onsite yoga classes or monthly massages on offer. Mental health is infinitely more important than wellness, and it should take priority as much as any other potentially fatal issue.

There is a complex and very important interplay between psychologically vulnerable individuals, the nature and demands of the workplace and social circumstances that highlight the role workplaces have in either minimising or exacerbating mental illness.

Job stress and burnout as a result of workplace demands are frequently highlighted as precipitating and perpetuating psychological distress. In this way employers may be understood to be causing, or failing to prevent, mental illness. Health professionals are growing more aware that the mental health concerns of their adult clients are affected by their experiences at work and that treatment without regard to what happens in the workplace is inadequate.

Research in the USA suggests that some of the blame for depression and poor mental health is based on the experiences employees have in the workplace. A study in 2017 by Mental Health America of 17,000 employees across 19 industries indicates that a lack of employer support contributes to higher levels of workplace stress and isolation. Workplace stress continues to contribute to increased mental and physical impairments: 80% of employees stated that workplace stress affected their personal relationships and 35% of employees "always" miss 3-5 days a month because of workplace stress.[43]

Researchers at Harvard Business School and Stanford University in the United States gathered data from over 200 studies and found that stress at work can be as harmful to health as passive smoking – the exposure to a considerable amount of smoke from other people's cigarettes.[44]

Internationally, and in South Africa, employment opportunities for people with psychiatric illnesses are limited and many of those who are already employed struggle in their jobs. Workplaces can provide meaningful and appropriate jobs and career pathways for people with diagnosed mental illnesses. In light of the pervasiveness of mental illness in society, it is in the interests of all organisations to have policies and protocols in place to pro-actively recognise and address this. In the past employers might simply dismiss an ill employee or "work out" a difficult or disruptive staff member. However, current labour laws, an increasingly nuanced understanding of the

---

42 Frank, 2017, p.1.
43 Mental Health America, 2018.
44 Richardson et al., 2012.

nature of mental illness, as well as a growing pragmatism have changed the options for employers (see Chapter 7).

It is clearly in the interests of employers to address mental health issues, both with regard to attempting to accommodate the individual needs of individuals experiencing psychological distress or suffering from a clinically diagnosable illness, as well as to consider the broader needs of the organisation as a whole (see Chapter 8 on the healthy organisation).

Conclusion

Given the enormous, and growing, impact of mental illness on society at large, and the workplace in particular, it is no surprise that tackling mental ill-health among the working-age population is becoming a key issue for labour market and social policies. The impact of Covid-19 on mental health will add to the importance of addressing this issue.

Despite increased awareness and a legislative framework that attempts to protect people with mental illnesses, those affected still have to manage stigma, a lack of accessible, accurate information and a broken healthcare system, all of which compromise the possibilities for recovery and integration of mentally ill people in our society. Before any systemic changes can take effect to help destigmatise mental health and expand access to affordable, proper care, we need to re-prioritise mental health – wholeheartedly, across the board, as a society, in and out of the workplace.

Chapter 3

Sad, Worried, Bewildered and Bizarre – Psychiatric Conditions

Introduction

In this chapter we will consider the following common psychiatric conditions that have implications for the workplace: mood disorders, anxiety disorders and psychosis – being out of touch with reality. Substance abuse and addictions, including behavioural addictions, are also psychiatric illnesses and these are covered in detail in Chapter 5 where we look at destructive behaviours in organisations.

By knowing what to look out for and how to understand what is happening, a manager or organisation is better equipped to manage mental illness in the workplace. We are not suggesting that managers or human resources practitioners or even workplace-based health practitioners should engage in diagnosing employees with mental illnesses; but understanding the basis for some problematic and difficult behaviours is important as this will allow for more effective, pragmatic and ethical crisis interventions, conflict resolution, problem-solving and forward planning.

Mood disorders

The category of Mood Disorders incorporates a number of different conditions including Major Depressive Disorder, Bipolar Mood Disorder and Persistent Depressive Disorder. Each condition may have different ways of presenting, and different underlying causes and different treatment needs. But what they have in common is a disturbance of mood, thinking patterns, energy and activity levels. These disturbances all impact significantly on work performance and relationships.

In Chapter 2 we reported the huge cost of mental illness both internationally and locally. Major Depressive Disorder stands out above all other psychiatric conditions as having the greatest negative impact on the workplace. This is because of the prevalence of depression (it is the most common of all psychiatric illnesses) and the fact that it primarily affects workers in their most productive years, between 20 and 50 years of age.

Major Depressive Disorder

It happens to all of us. We have bad days, we might feel down, unhappy, lethargic, irritable and unable to concentrate and certainly unable to function at our best. People might notice we are not quite ourselves and we may feel unproductive and miserable at work. We are irritable with our family and friends and are unsure what the point of it all is. Now imagine feeling like that for weeks, or even months, on end. And that's what clinical depression, more properly called Major Depressive Disorder (MDD), feels like. The hallmark of major depression is an inability to get pleasure or satisfaction from anything (the professional jargon for this is anhedonia). Someone with clinical depression feels the same low mood, unhappiness, sense of personal worthlessness, lack of drive and anhedonia whether they are at work, at home or on the most beautiful tropical island dream holiday. This is to say the depression is not context bound, it does not simply lift because something the depressed person has always wanted or hoped for, like getting married, or having a baby, or going on that dream holiday to the Seychelles, is happening.

It is this that distinguishes burnout from depression. Burnout is considered to be work related and situation-specific, whereas depression presents irrespective of circumstances.[1] This distinction can be confusing as depression in its first stages might be circumstance-specific[2] starting with work-related stress or burnout and evolving into a full clinical depression. For a full discussion of burnout please refer to Chapter 6.

---

1   Freudenberger & Richelson, 1981.; Iacovides et al., 2003.

2   Rydmark et al., 2006.

Depression is often called the common cold of mental illness. In 2015 a global study found that approximately 216 million people, 3% of the world's population, were affected by MDD.[3] The American Psychiatric Association indicates that 10% to 25% of women and 5% to 12% of men will suffer from MDD at some point in their lifetime. Additionally, roughly half of all people who get diagnosed with MDD are likely to experience a second episode, and even a third or fourth. Depression is common, widespread and has a significant impact on the workplace. Research emerging during the period of the Covid-19 pandemic has indicated a rise in rates of diagnosable MDD.[4]

The DSM-5[5] divides depression into Major Depressive Disorder and Persistent Depressive Disorder, also called dysthymia. Mental health professionals often see and deal with people who do not meet the full diagnostic criteria for MDD, but who have difficulties that warrant defining them as having a sub-clinical depression. Depression affects feelings, doing and thinking. Many people make the mistake of assuming that depression is simply a bad mood, and that it only impacts on emotions. However major depression has a significant negative impact on thinking, concentrating, energy levels and behaviour.

Table 3.1: Symptoms of Major Depressive Disorder

A person having a depressive episode may:
Have a depressed mood most of the day, nearly every day
Have diminished interest or pleasure in all, or almost all, activities most of the day, nearly every day, have difficulty enjoying anything (anhedonia)
Feel very sad, down, empty, or hopeless and be tearful or cry easily
Have very little energy with decreased activity levels, feel tired and slowed down
Have disturbed sleep – they may sleep too little or too much
Feel irrationally worried and anxious
Feel agitated and nervous
Be irritable, have a quick temper
Have trouble concentrating, feel like their thinking has slowed down
Forget things a lot, be indecisive
Have significant weight loss when not dieting or weight gain, or decrease or increase in appetite
Feel worthless or excessive or inappropriate guilt
Think often about death or suicide

---

3   GBD, 2015.

4   Gallagher et.al., 2020.

5   APA, 2013.

A depressive episode can be diagnosed after two weeks of symptoms and, according to the DSM-5, must include either a depressed mood or loss of interest or pleasure. To receive a diagnosis of depression, these symptoms must cause the individual clinically significant distress or impairment in social, occupational, or other important areas of functioning. The symptoms must also not be a result of substance abuse or another medical condition.

On average, untreated episodes of depression last several months. However, episodes of major depression can last any length of time, even up to a year. And symptoms can vary in intensity during an episode. If depression is not treated, it can become chronic (long-lasting). Treatment can shorten the length and severity of a depressive episode.

Causes of Major Depressive Disorder

Factors such as personality characteristics, genetic vulnerabilities, life stressors, pregnancy and childbirth, trauma, loss, burnout and coping styles have all been implicated as possible triggers for depression.

Many workplace factors have also been identified as possible catalysts for depression. Workplace stress (see Chapter 6) for example, has been shown to have an impact on emotional well-being as it is related to depression,[6] physical illness,[7] and somatic complaints.[8]

There is also a great deal of thinking currently about the link between social disconnection and depression. In Chapter 6 we address the impact of loneliness on the workplace.

An important factor to keep in mind is that the directionality of causal factors is challenging to pinpoint. It is often unclear whether difficulties at work are the result or the cause of depression. In fact, they may be exacerbating each other. Furthermore, individual characteristics may interact with both workplace environments and non-workplace circumstances and lead to even more complications.

Informally, many people talk about depression as being caused by a "chemical imbalance", but this is not strictly accurate. While it is known that some of the brain chemicals such as serotonin and noradrenalin and dopamine are involved in how we feel and behave, it is not yet clear what the exact link is between depression and our biochemistry. In fact, we do not know if low levels of serotonin are a cause or a result of being depressed.

---

6   Tennant, 2001.; Gray-Stanley et al., 2010.; Blackmore et al., 2007.

7   Ganster & Rosen, 2013.

8   Shirom, Westman, & Melamed, 1999.

What is well established however is that chemicals in the form of medications have an important and useful role to play in treating depression and anxiety.[9]

Impact of depression on the workplace

The obvious primary risk that depression poses to workplaces is a loss of productivity due to absenteeism, presenteeism and reduced performance.[10] Research by the South African Depression and Anxiety Group (SADAG) found that during a depressive episode, South African employees took an average of 18 days off work due to the condition.[11] That is a significant number of people hours directly lost.

Of those who did take time off work because of depression, 80% did not tell their employer the reason. This reflects the problem of stigma and shame as well as the anxiety people feel about disclosing honestly to their employers. And people's anxiety is for good reason, because most managers or workplaces do not feel adequately prepared to assist or manage a person with depression. The primary findings of Stander's study indicate that only 25% of managers interviewed felt they had good support in dealing with an employee with depression, more than one in ten didn't know how to react or what to say to someone with depression. Half of the managers studied did not know how many sick days are a result of employees' depression. Most worrying is that only half of employees diagnosed with depression did actually take time off work because of their condition. This must make us wonder about the work performance of those depressed people who continued working, especially when considering the fact that depressed people make significantly more mistakes, and are much slower and less productive as a result of the commonly experienced cognitive symptoms of poor concentration, forgetfulness and indecisiveness.[12] Depressed people are often excessively self-critical and doubt their own abilities to the extent that it interferes with work production. Their increased sensitivity to criticism means that depressed people will often not ask for clarification if they do not understand an instruction, and may not ask for help if they are not managing with a project or for feedback about their performance.

The excessive negativity and lowering of morale in depressed individuals can decrease team morale.[13] In some contexts, especially in safety-sensitive jobs, there is increased risk due to lowered efficiency, decreased awareness, poor attention to detail as a

---

9   Penninx, 2019.

10   Lerner et al., 2010.

11   Stander et al., 2016.

12   Hammar & Guro, 2009.

13   Rajgopal, 2010.

result of the sleep and energy disturbances associated with MDD as well as possible self-medication through alcohol and other substances.[14]

Bipolar Mood Disorder

> "There is a particular kind of pain, elation, loneliness, and terror involved in this kind of madness. When you're high it's tremendous. The ideas and feelings are fast and frequent like shooting stars, and you follow them until you find better and brighter ones. Shyness goes, the right words and gestures are suddenly there, the power to captivate others a felt certainty. There are interests found in uninteresting people. Sensuality is pervasive and the desire to seduce and be seduced irresistible. Feelings of ease, intensity, power, well-being, financial omnipotence, and euphoria pervade one's marrow. But, somewhere, this changes. The fast ideas are far too fast, and there are far too many; overwhelming confusion replaces clarity. Memory goes. Humor and absorption on friends' faces are replaced by fear and concern. Everything previously moving with the grain is now against – you are irritable, angry, frightened, uncontrollable, and enmeshed totally in the blackest caves of the mind. You never knew those caves were there. It will never end, for madness carves its own reality."[15]

In her powerful 1996 memoir, the psychologist Kay Redfield Jamison describes the intensity of her own experience of having severe Bipolar Mood Disorder (BMD Type I). These are no ordinary mood swings and the shifts in energy, activity and mood are unusual and out of proportion with the person's usual pattern. BMD, what used to be called Manic Depression, is a disease that can wreak havoc on the life of the patient and their family.

According to the WHO, BMD is one of the leading causes of disability in the world[16] and the National Institute of Mental Health reports that BMD affects approximately 2.6% of the adult U.S. population.[17] There is not much research on how many South Africans are diagnosed as Bipolar, with a 2006 study suggesting a prevalence of 1%.[18]

There is evidence that Bipolar diagnoses are increasing internationally.[19] Some people argue that this is a result of third-party funders (like medical aids) covering BMD (for example, it is one of the few Prescribed Minimum Benefits conditions that South African medical aids have to fund) rather than conditions that may present with

---

14 Haslam et.al., 2005.

15 Jamison, 1996. p.66.

16 Ferrari et al., 2016.

17 Merikangas et al., 2011.

18 Williams et al., 2008.

19 Yutzy et al., 2012.

similar symptoms, but are not as well covered by medical aids or third-party funders, such as personality disorders, complex trauma or anxiety disorders.[20]

SADAG found in a 2017 survey that 69% of BMD patients reported an initial misdiagnosis. BMD is a complex and serious condition and is often comorbid (occurs together with) substance abuse and anxiety disorders and there is a high rate of attempted suicide (30%) amongst people diagnosed with Bipolar Type 1.[21] Although the illness can start in childhood or early adolescence, typically people are only properly diagnosed in their mid-twenties. Initial episodes of the illness may be thought to be related to the mood swings of puberty, or teenage rebelliousness or simply depression. Many people who have it may suffer needlessly for years or even decades

BMD affects all classes, races, cultures and genders equally. More than two-thirds of people with BMD have at least one close relative with the illness or with Major Depressive Disorder, suggesting that there is some inherited vulnerability to the disease. As with MDD, the exact cause of BMD is unknown, but it is most likely to be a combination of biochemical, genetic and psychological factors. A particularly stressful life event such as bereavement, job loss, relationship problems, or a trauma may trigger an episode of mania or depression. At other times, episodes occur for no apparent reason. Mania and depression can occur in cycles, sometimes at particular times of the year with a seasonal pattern.

At least 40% of people with BMD also have a substance abuse problem, particularly alcohol and cannabis use.[22] Many people will use substances when they are in a manic phase to slow themselves down or to improve their mood when they are depressed.

Bipolar Mood Disorder Types I and II

BMD is divided into two types. Bipolar I is a very serious condition characterised by marked and significant mood changes between the low and high ends of the mood and energy spectrum. When a person is in the manic or "up" end of the illness, they have a great deal of energy. They sleep less, if at all, think, move and talk quickly (often too quickly) and generally, at least initially, feel "high" – euphoric, expansive and ecstatic. Some people feel irritable, agitated and physically aggressive when they are manic (this is sometimes referred to as a mixed episode). Extremes of impulsivity and optimism, uncontained by common sense or caution, fuel the behaviour of the person who is manic. Spending sprees, disinhibited behaviour and sexual acting out

---

20 Child, 2013.
21 SADAG, 2017.
22 Hunt et al., 2016.

are typical components of mania, sometimes accompanied with excess alcohol or drug use. As mania progresses, people may become increasingly psychotic and delusional in grandiose or paranoid ways; their thoughts and speech may become disorganised and incoherent. They may claim to have special powers, or be an important person with a special mission, and may even have hallucinations.

Mania should be considered a psychiatric emergency and is ultimately a very treatable condition with medication and psychotherapy. Not surprisingly, the manic individual's sense of euphoria and grandiosity makes them reluctant to accept treatment. These periods of mania (which untreated may last up to three months) are typically followed by a crash and a period of depression, which is the "low" pole of the illness. The symptoms of this phase of the condition are the same as major depressive disorder but can be long lasting and severe. The contrast between the "feel good" mania and the depression is very hard to deal with, and people may have to come to terms with the often negative consequences of their manic behaviour. Between these extremes, people with BMD can have periods of ordinary moods and these times can last for anything from days, weeks, months or even years. Bipolar individuals can, and have had, great job and career successes.

Mania comes in degrees of severity and, while a very little amount may be pleasant and productive, even the less severe form known as hypomania can be problematic and cause social and occupational difficulties.

Bipolar II is diagnosed if the patient has never had a full manic episode but has had at least one episode of clinical depression and periods of hypomania. Hypo is a prefix that means "beneath" or "below," or "less than normal," in this case less manic behaviour than a typical manic episode. During a hypomanic episode, a person may feel very good, be highly productive, and function well. The individual may not feel that anything is wrong, but family and friends may recognise the mood swings and/or changes in activity levels. Without proper treatment, people with hypomania may develop severe mania or depression.

Bipolar II disorder is not a milder form of Bipolar I disorder, but a separate diagnosis. While the manic episodes of Bipolar I can be severe and dangerous, people with Bipolar II disorder can be depressed for longer periods, which can also cause significant impairment.

BMD (especially Type I) can be extremely disabling, but it also responds well to treatment. It is important to have a thorough medical evaluation as soon as possible. Bipolar disorder is a chronic illness like diabetes or hypertension, and while it cannot be "cured," it can definitely be managed successfully. With the right kinds of treatment most patients will return to productive lives. On the other hand, if not diagnosed and not treated, the impact of the illness can be devastating to the individual, significant others, and society in general. Between 73% and 90% of people who have a first episode of Bipolar Type 1 will have another.[23] Because of this, maintenance treatment is essential in this illness.

Table 3.2: Symptoms of Mania

A person having a manic episode may:

- feel very "up," "high," or elated
- feel very energetic
- be much more active than usual
- feel "jumpy" or "wired"
- have trouble sleeping – sleeping much less than usual
- talk really fast about lots of different things
- be agitated, irritable, or "touchy"
- feel like their thoughts are racing and that they are not always able to control their thoughts
- believe they can do a lot of things at once but often not finish things they have started
- make very poor decisions such as making foolish investments, ending or starting new relationships or jobs without much planning or forethought do risky and impulsive things, like spend a lot of money or have reckless sex

Impact of Bipolar disorders on the workplace

Because the diagnosis of BMD is often only made more than ten years after the initial symptomatic episodes, by the time people with BMD are diagnosed they are typically already working. Their mood and behaviour symptoms often lead to trouble on the job. Lost productivity due to BMD imposes a significant economic burden on employers. Studies analysing data from six large US corporations found BMD to be the most expensive mental health condition in terms of medical care and lost productivity.[24] The cost of chronic maintenance of Bipolar employees was 2.5 times greater than the cost of the next most expensive mental health condition, depression. Indirect costs of BMD related to work absences by not only the ill employee but the family members responsible for taking care of a person with BMD, as well as short-term disability losses are also significant. Individuals with BMD also incur substantial

---

23 Sajatovic, 2005.
24 Goetzel et al., 2003.

general medical costs associated with multiple comorbid conditions, both mental, such as anxiety, ADHD, personality disorder, substance use, and physical, including endocrine, metabolic, immunity, and circulatory disorders.[25]

A 2005 study in the USA reported that when present at work, the average hourly productivity of employees with BMD was similar to that of employees without BMD. However, because of their high rates of absenteeism, on an annual basis, the overall productivity loss was significantly different, with an annual output 20% lower than that of employees without BMD.[26] Unlike anxiety and depression, productivity loss from BMD appears to be mainly attributable to absenteeism rather than presenteeism.

In a 2007 study, many employees with BMD felt that the effects of cycling between manic and depressive episodes affected the continuity and consistency of their work because of lost work time, decreased job prospects and financial loss. The majority of interviewees had experienced stigma in the workplace and believed this had resulted in their being dismissed from positions, denied promotions, demoted, or held back in their career in other ways. Interpersonal problems in the workplace were also an issue, arising from a perceived lack of education about BMD.[27]

As a consequence of their illness, up to 60% of people with BMD do not have paid employment.[28] People with BMD can be very valuable and productive employees, bringing creativity, energy, and passion to the workplace, and it is important to identify ways to help these employees find appropriate and fulfilling work.

How to recognise or assess mood disorders in the workplace

Signs of Depression in the workplace

Many people do not know they are in fact depressed. They may ascribe their negative feelings and disturbed activity and energy levels to physical illness, burnout or to personal weakness or incompetence. Below are some signals that should indicate that an employee may be suffering from depression:

- **Absence and sick leave**. Is the employee taking more sick leave than usual? Are they seeking medical attention, but reluctant to disclose what the issue is? The problem may be a major depression.

---

25 Rajagopalan, 2006.
26 Kleinman et al., 2005.
27 Michalak et al., 2007.
28 Bowden, 2005.

- **Increased symptoms of physical illness and pain**. Physical illness is often a symptom of stress, depression and anxiety. This is both because depressed people appear to have less resilience to everyday ailments (like colds, stomach aches, minor but generalised infections and pain conditions) and that some people struggle to identify or articulate difficult feelings and that these are then expressed somatically (i.e. through the body). Some cultures are more comfortable reporting depressive symptoms that are physical in nature rather than mental. For example, Chinese people with depression often report bodily discomfort, feelings of inner pressure, and symptoms of pain, dizziness, and fatigue.[29] Even in cultures where depressive disorders are understood as psychological illnesses, researchers have suggested that some conditions (such as chronic pain, fibromyalgia, and chronic fatigue syndrome) may be more physical manifestations of a mood disorder rather than primarily physical illnesses. At the same time, a depressive disorder may be the result of suffering from ongoing pain, discomfort and fatigue.

- **Decreased motivation**. Is the employee more reluctant than usual to take on new tasks, are they slower to meet deadlines, or in fact not completing work? Depressed people struggle to take initiative because of the low energy, pessimism and self-doubt associated with the condition.

- **Changes in behaviour and social interactions**. Is the employee more socially withdrawn than they used to be? Many depressed people become increasingly isolated and avoid other people or social situations. Persistent irritability and aggression may also indicate a mood problem. Depressed people seem "thin skinned", over-sensitive to any criticism (real or perceived) and are easily upset or insulted. Depressed people also struggle with increased self-doubt and uncertainty about their abilities, relationships and judgement. They tend to have ruminative anxiety (that Is repetitive anxious thoughts that loop over and over in their minds) and are often very pessimistic and negative, even hopeless. Depressed people may also be excessively tearful or quick to cry.

- **Substance misuse/abuse**. Regular or excessive substance and alcohol use worsens mood disorders but may also be a way that depressed people try to self-medicate in order to try to manage or numb the distress or anxiety they feel. Notice if people seem excessively sedated or "out of it", smell of alcohol, or come late to work, or miss work particularly on a Monday or after a holiday.

- **Fatigue**. Along with increased physical complaints, a significant problem with depressed people is lethargy, very low energy reserves, frequent yawning, chronic fatigue (sometimes worsened by problems with insomnia and poor sleep quality), and a feeling of chronic exhaustion.

---

29 Ryder et al, 2008.

- **Diminished work output**. Poor concentration and memory as a result of depression will start to impact on the employee's output and the quality of their work. They may start missing deadlines, not completing tasks, being more disorganised or scatty.

There are also gender differences in how depression is expressed,[30] probably due to both physiological differences and significant differences in the way men and women are socialised. Women, in general, may be more anxious, or panicky and more easily tearful while men tend to express their depression through aggression and anger. Women more often have increased appetite, while men more often have a comorbid substance or alcohol misuse problem.[31] While these gender differences are often noted in clinical practice, many depressed men become tearful, and many depressed women do abuse alcohol or substances.

Signs of Mania in the workplace

Because the disorder varies in severity, initially manic or hypomanic symptoms can be ascribed to moodiness or trouble at work or tiredness. But over time these symptoms create difficulty in the workplace because they can interfere with an individual's ability to show up for work, do their job, and interact productively with others.

- **Poor task completion, distractibility**. People who can harness their energy when they are in a hypomanic phase can be really productive. Those who cannot, often go from task to task, planning grand, unrealistic projects that are never finished before moving on to something else. Because of high levels of distractibility and poor judgement, the employee who is becoming manic may volunteer for, or propose, new tasks and projects, but typically never finish them. The desk or office or workshop (or home) full of half-completed projects is a hallmark of bipolar disorder.

- **Interpersonal difficulties, irritability, grandiosity, euphoria.** In addition to having problems completing tasks, a manic person may have interpersonal difficulties at work, become irritable and aggressive to co-workers (and even managers), and irritate and provoke others with their inflated, unrealistic sense of their own abilities and importance.

- **Changes in speech, thinking and behaviour.** Manic people stop sleeping properly and feel as if they are full of energy. They may appear jumpy or restless, and struggle to sit through meetings. People who are manic speak and think too fast; they have what is known as pressure of speech. They may jump from idea to idea.

---

30 Romans et al., 2007.
31 Schuch et al., 2014.

- **Losing touch with reality.** As mania continues the individual becomes increasingly unrealistic – whether in their speech or ideas. Their judgement is impaired, and they may behave inappropriately, for example excessive emailing or messaging others, including managers. They may believe, without any evidence, that they have made a ground-breaking discovery, or have solved a significant problem.

Anxiety disorders

The world is a scary and unpredictable place, so some level of anxiety or worry at home and at work is not only expected, it is probably completely warranted. However, anxiety disorders are persistent, excessive and irrational experiences of fear and worry, either about the past, present or future that interfere with everyday functioning.[32] Anxiety is a symptom of depression and trauma, a side effect of some medications, the result of withdrawal from substances like alcohol, or the over-indulgence in substances like caffeine. Anxiety also refers to a group of disorders that can be diagnosed in their own right. The context of the Covid-19 pandemic exacerbates ordinary anxieties and worries and rates of all anxiety-related psychiatric conditions have increased considerably over the course of the Covid-19 pandemic.[33]

In 2010 approximately 273 million (4.5% of the world's population) had an anxiety disorder.[34] Women are diagnosed more often with anxiety disorders than men,[35] and in Europe, Africa and Asia, lifetime rates of anxiety disorders are between 9 and 16%, in contrast with the United States, which has a lifetime prevalence of anxiety disorders of about 29%.[36] This difference probably reflects the different ways in which diverse cultures interpret anxiety symptoms and what they consider to be normal or appropriate behaviour.

There are several different anxiety disorders that can be diagnosed including Generalised Anxiety Disorder (GAD), Phobias, Social Anxiety Disorder, and Panic Disorder. People can suffer from more than one anxiety disorder. Anxiety disorders frequently manifest with significant physical symptoms such as a racing heartbeat, difficulty breathing, chest pains, dizziness, shakiness, stomach aches and physical pain. In fact the physical symptoms of anxiety can be so overwhelming that many people who are having a panic attack or severe anxiety will initially seek medical treatment for a suspected heart attack. Panic attacks remain the reason for a significant number of people seeking treatment for non-cardiac chest pain at hospital casualty departments.[37]

---

32 APA, 2013.
33 Czeisler et al.,2020.
34 APA 2013.
35 Vesga-López et al., 2008.
36 Ruscio et al., 2017.
37 Foldes-Busque et al., 2019.

Generalised Anxiety Disorder

People with Generalised Anxiety Disorder (GAD) experience non-specific persistent fear and worry and become overly concerned with everyday matters. GAD can be diagnosed when a person has been excessively worried about an everyday problem for six months or more. To be diagnosed the person has to also have three or more of the following symptoms: restlessness, fatigue, concentration problems, irritability, muscle tension, and sleep disturbance.

Panic Disorder

Panic disorder sufferers have brief episodes of intense terror and apprehension, typically involving marked physical symptoms such as trembling, shaking, confusion, dizziness, nausea, and/or difficulty breathing. These panic attacks often seem to arise suddenly, and they peak in less than ten minutes, although they can last for several hours. Panic attacks can be triggered by stress, irrational thoughts or general fear. However sometimes the trigger is unclear, and the attacks can arise without warning. People with panic disorder are preoccupied with fear of future attacks and worry about the attacks' potential negative implications. As a result, they become avoidant of possible triggers (including such everyday activities as entering a shopping mall or driving on the highway), and hypervigilant about any bodily signs which may be interpreted as evidence of an impending panic attack. They may begin to become depressed or show signs of generalised anxiety.

Specific Phobias

Fear and anxiety that are triggered by a specific stimulus or situation are called Specific Phobias. Between 3% and 10% of the population worldwide suffer from these,[38] typically anticipating terrifying consequences from encountering the object of their fear, which can be anything from an animal to a location to a bodily fluid to a particular situation. Common phobias are flying, blood, birds, highway driving, and tunnels. In response to the coronavirus epidemic, a condition researchers have called "coronaphobia" is manifesting with associated fears of death and illness.[39] When people are exposed to their phobia, they may experience panic symptoms. Phobic people understand that their fear is not proportional to the actual potential danger but still are overwhelmed by it.

---

38 Wardenaar et al., 2017.

39 Lee et. al., 2020.

Social Anxiety Disorder

Social Anxiety Disorder used to be known as social phobia and involves an intense fear and avoidance of negative public scrutiny, public embarrassment, humiliation, or social interaction. The fear can be specific to particular types of social situations (such as public speaking and/or presenting to colleagues or clients) or, more typically, is experienced in most (or all) social interactions. Social anxiety is often associated with physical symptoms including blushing, sweating, dry mouth and difficulty speaking. As with all phobic disorders, those suffering from social anxiety often try to avoid the source of their anxiety; in the case of social anxiety this is particularly problematic, and in severe cases can lead to complete social isolation.

Obsessive-Compulsive Disorder

Obsessive-Compulsive Disorder (OCD) is a complex and long-lasting disorder in which a person has uncontrollable, recurring unwanted intrusive thoughts or ideas (obsessions) that typically make them feel driven to do something repetitively (compulsions). Typical obsessions include excessive concerns about contamination or harm, the need for symmetry or exactness, or forbidden sexual or religious thoughts. The repetitive behaviours, such as hand washing, checking on things, cleaning or repeating behaviours, are aimed at preventing or reducing distress or a feared situation. Perfectionism or having a systematic approach to life is not the same as OCD. To be diagnosed with OCD the obsessions and compulsions must be time consuming (more than an hour a day), cause significant distress, and impact negatively on work, social and relationship functioning. Although most adults with OCD recognise that what they are doing does not make sense, some adults and most children may not realise that their behaviour is out of the ordinary.

Other conditions that share some features of OCD occur more frequently in family members of OCD patients. These include hoarding disorder, body dysmorphic disorder (preoccupation with imagined ugliness), illness anxiety disorder (hypochondriasis – preoccupation with physical illness), trichotillomania (hair pulling), excoriation (skin picking disorder), some eating disorders such as binge eating disorder, and neurologically based disorders such as Tourette's syndrome. OCD has a lifetime prevalence of 2 – 3% in both developed and developing countries and among adults slightly more women than man are affected.[40] OCD can begin in childhood, adolescence or early adulthood. The average age symptoms appear is 19 years old. In South Africa OCD is significantly under-reported, especially in the Black community.[41] It is one of the most disabling psychiatric conditions, and has a negative impact on the

---

40 Ruscio et al., 2010.

41 Stein et al., 1996.

quality of life of both patients and those close to them. The WHO ranks OCD as one of the 10 most disabling conditions in terms of lost income and decreased quality of life. However when correctly recognised and diagnosed, it can be successfully treated.

The presence of an anxiety disorder is the single strongest risk factor for development of depression and this comorbidity predicts a very poor outcome. As depression is a huge risk to any workplace, active treatment of clinical anxiety as it emerges should be a priority.

How to recognise anxiety disorders in the workplace

As with MDD, the employee with a clinical anxiety disorder may appear nervous, worried, distracted, distressed, fatigued, tense, irritable, physically unwell, withdrawn or excessively needy and self-doubting. At work they may have difficulties with everyday decision making and remembering or fulfilling commitments as a result of their lack of focus and poor confidence. Like depressed people, anxious people may avoid coming to work when they feel overwhelmed, but some anxious people, in an attempt to compensate for their anxiety, may become overly perfectionistic, controlling and then vulnerable to burning out. Some forms of anxiety may be a result of the conditions of the workplace itself. The employee who feels excessively pressurised by their manager, or is unable to cope with the pressure of the workplace may be vulnerable to developing an anxiety disorder.

Out of touch with reality: psychotic disorders

What is psychosis?

Psychosis refers to a state of having an impaired experience of reality, in terms of irrational or idiosyncratic thoughts or ideas or perceptions that are contrary to actual evidence. These experiences may lead to bizarre and dysfunctional beliefs, behaviour and speech and associated problems with judgement and decision making. Psychotic states tend to be very frightening and there is also some risk that these psychotic experiences may cause the affected person to hurt themselves or someone else.

Typically, psychotic individuals may have hallucinations which are sensory experiences that occur in the absence of an actual stimulus. For example, auditory hallucinations involve hearing voices when there is nobody around, visual hallucinations include seeing things or people who are not actually present. Hallucinations can also be tactile (feeling things crawling on one's skin) and olfactory (smelling things that are not present). Delusions are systems of irrational thoughts/beliefs that have become entrenched and tend to be very difficult to challenge or change. Paranoid delusions, the conviction a person may have that other people are plotting or scheming against them, are particularly difficult to treat or shift. An individual may be acutely psychotic and dysfunctional, or have ongoing psychotic beliefs but otherwise be fairly functional and organised in their everyday lives.

Psychosis is a symptom, not a diagnosis in itself. Psychosis may be a transient effect of an extreme reaction to medication, drugs, alcohol, steroids, sleep deprivation, or significant trauma. Brain disease such as Parkinson's Disease, Huntington's Disease, brain tumours or cysts, delirium, dementias caused by Alzheimer's Disease, AIDS, syphilis, or other brain infections may lead to psychosis.

Psychosis may also be a manifestation of an underlying epileptic condition or a severe psychiatric disorder, including schizophrenia, extreme mania or deep depression or as the result of a severe post-natal depression.

Schizophrenia is a psychiatric condition involving delusions (fixed and false beliefs), hallucinations, disorganised speech, deterioration in personal hygiene, and social withdrawal. Schizophrenia can result in significantly impaired general functioning. It is thought that unemployment rates amongst people with Schizophrenia are between 70 to 90%.[42]

Delusional Disorders are characterised by false, fixed beliefs based on incorrect assumptions about external reality despite what virtually everyone else believes. The beliefs are firmly held despite obvious proof or evidence to the contrary and involve situations that could occur in real life, such as being followed, poisoned, loved at a distance, or deceived by a spouse or lover. Functioning may not be obviously impaired for a long time, which makes this disorder particularly complex to manage in the workplace. For instance, an individual with a paranoid delusional disorder, the most common sub-type, may only come to the attention of Human Resources when they demand an investigation because they think they are being harassed or unfairly treated by co-workers or managers. On investigation it becomes clear that their accusations have no basis in reality. Delusional disorders do not typically respond well to treatments and can be very disruptive at work, and potentially even the source of violence (see more on the violence-prone personality, Chapter 5).

Psychosis and the workplace

Typically, people who have psychosis that is associated with severe mental disorders tend to drop out of formal employment so they are a problem for the community as a whole but usually only an indirect problem for the workplace. The impact may be felt when an employee becomes psychotic for the first time when they are already employed and considerations such as incapacity processes may become necessary.

---

42 Marwaha & Johnson, 2004

There is also the indirect impact on the family members who take care of the psychotic person who may need time off work to deal with some of the practical issues, but will also experience increased emotional, relationship and financial stress as a result of their ill family member.

It is very useful to have some idea of the early warning signs of psychosis to be in a position to recognise when someone may be developing a psychosis. Although these signs may not be very clear or dramatic on their own, when considered together, they may suggest something is not quite right. It is essential not to ignore or dismiss such warning signs, even if they appear gradually and are unclear. Do not assume the person is just going through a phase or misusing alcohol or other drugs, or that the symptoms will go away on their own.

Table 3.3: Recognising Psychosis

Depression, anxiety, irritability, suspiciousness, blunted, flat or inappropriate emotion, change in appetite, reduced energy and motivation
Changes in thinking and perception
Evidence of anxiety (or attempts to hide anxiety)
Difficulties with concentration or attention, sense of alteration of self, others or the outside world (e.g. feeling that self or others have changed or are acting differently in some way), odd ideas, unusual perceptual experiences (e.g. a reduction or greater intensity of smell, sound or colour)
Suspiciousness
Changes in behaviour
Sleep disturbances – either too much or too little sleep
Withdrawal from family, friends, peers and work colleagues
Social isolation
Reduced ability to carry out work or social roles
Disorganised speech, such as switching topics erratically

Symptoms of psychosis may vary from person to person, culture to culture and can change over time. For this reason managers, medical and mental health practitioners need to be educated about and sensitive to issues of religious, national and cultural diversity. For more on this, please refer back to Chapter 2.

Typical treatments of mental illness

Who can assess and treat a psychiatrically ill person? A psychiatrist is a medical doctor who specialises in mental illness and a psychologist is a mental health professional who specialises in counselling and psychotherapy as well as psychometric assessments. Psychologists cannot prescribe medication; this must be done by a medical doctor (psychiatrist, family physician or general practitioner). In addition, counselling services may be offered by clinical social workers, registered counsellors and psychiatric nurses. Psychiatrically trained occupational therapists can assist with assessment of functionality and fitness for work. Psychological treatments can include individual, group, couple and family counselling

The most effective treatments of mood and anxiety disorders are considered to be a combination of medication with some kind of counselling or psychotherapy as well as lifestyle interventions. But every person is different, and each person will respond differently to treatment.[43] Meaningful treatment must be able to accommodate the individual's needs and capacities. Some people are more sensitive to the effects and side effects of medication so may need medication types and dosages adjusted by their GP or psychiatrist. Some people prefer individual to group therapies, and some people respond best to counselling that addresses their relationships and support structure, a more systemic approach.

Lifestyle changes can make a significant difference to help relieve and manage depression and anxiety. Useful techniques include relaxation exercises, deep breathing practice, and meditation.[44] Exercise, regularising sleep patterns, reducing caffeine intake, and stopping smoking[45] are all helpful in reducing anxiety.

Medical treatments of mental health conditions

See Appendix 1 for a list of medications commonly prescribed in SA.

A medical doctor (usually a general practitioner or a psychiatrist) may prescribe medication (pills) for someone who is struggling with mental health difficulties. This may be short-term medication aimed at assisting the person to remain calm in the face of panic or extreme and unmanageable anxiety or to assist someone to sleep who is currently overwhelmed and insomniac. More typically, psychiatric medication focuses on longer-term treatment of underlying depression, anxiety, mood instability or psychosis. This may mean that the person has to take medication for six months

---

43 Sugarman, 2016.
44 Dinsmoor & Odle, 2015.
45 Taylor et. al., 2014.

to a year or more. For some people full recovery may entail taking medication for the rest of their lives.

Table 3.4: List of medical treatments

Antidepressant medications: lift depression and anxiety by increasing levels of serotonin (one of the chemical messengers – neurotransmitters – that carry signals between brain cells).	
<ul><li>May be used to treat conditions other than depression, such as anxiety disorders</li><li>Not addictive</li><li>Don't work immediately – take up to a few weeks to build to a therapeutic dose</li><li>Better to start on a low dose and gradually increase so any negative side effects can be better tolerated</li><li>Don't stop taking medication without consulting doctor</li><li>Medication should be gradually stopped to prevent getting unpleasant discontinuation (or withdrawal) effects such as dizziness, irritability, nausea</li><li>Different groups of antidepressants all work equally well, prescription depends on individual response and sensitivity</li></ul>	
Tricyclics (e.g. Anafranil and Tofranil) significant side effects: weight gain, increased appetite, sedation, dry mouth, constipation, blurred vision (especially when first taking meds)	Selective serotonin reuptake inhibitors – **SSRIs** (e.g. Prozac, Cipramil) and Serotonin and Norepinephrine reuptake inhibitors – **SNRIs** (e.g. Effexor) = most widely used meds globally
Mood stabilisers: used long term to manage mood swings, intense and sustained mood shifts. Also to augment (or promote) the effect of antidepressants. Includes Lamictin, Neurontin, Convulex and Tegretol – all also used to treat epilepsy. Lithium = naturally occurring mineral, only used to prevent mania in diagnosed Bipolar Type 1.	
Benzodiazepines (BZD) or tranquillisers: work on central nervous system to create sedation, muscle relaxation, reduce experience of anxiety, treat insomnia, panic, alcohol withdrawal, and high levels of agitation. Commonly prescribed, also commonly abused as they are addictive. Long-term use of benzodiazepines creates the potential for tolerance, dependence, and other negative effects. If used for short periods of time, under care of a medical doctor, they are safe and effective. Side effects can include dizziness, drowsiness, poor co-ordination, low mood.	

Can be toxic in overdose, and taking them together with alcohol or other substances can be fatal.

If someone is dependent on benzodiazepines, it is crucial not to suddenly stop medication without medical advice. Like alcohol, stopping "cold turkey" can lead to tremors, muscle cramps, life-threatening seizures.

Taper off benzodiazepines slowly with professional help.

Short acting BZDs e.g. Ativan, Xanax and Urbanol.	**Middle acting BZDs** e.g. Valium, Librium
For panic attacks, relief from extreme anxiety	For generalised anxiety, insomnia, seizures, restless leg syndrome, alcohol withdrawal
Do not make person excessively sleepy, work quickly	

Sleeping tablets = range of drugs including BZDs, older antidepressants, even antihistamines to treat sleep disturbances.

Should only be used short term, lifestyle changes needed to address insomnia. Can cause drowsiness, and impair ability to drive or be fully alert the morning after.

Antipsychotics: Treat psychosis and severe anxiety associated with schizophrenia, Bipolar mania. Used short term to manage severe anxiety or agitation, or even insomnia.

Patients need to be carefully monitored because of possibly problematic side effects including: blurred vision, dry mouth, constipation, drowsiness, muscle spasms or tremors, skin and blood reactions and weight gain.

Symptoms may take a few weeks to ease after starting medication, dose of meds should usually build up gradually to minimise side-effects.

Atypical antipsychotics (such as Abilify, Clozapine, Risperdal, Seroquel and Zyprexa)	**Older antipsychotics** (such as Fluanxol, Haloperidol and Thorazine)

Electro Convulsive Therapy (or ECT): under general anaesthetic and involves small electric currents being passed through the brain, intentionally producing a very quick seizure. Believed to cause changes in brain chemistry that may quickly reverse symptoms of severe mental health conditions.

In the past lack of anaesthesia /sedation and high levels of electricity would lead to memory loss, fractured bones and other serious side effects.

ECT as a modern psychiatric treatment is now considered fairly safe and effective, used when other treatments haven't worked or in situations where some medications cannot be used such as during pregnancy and with older adults who cannot tolerate drug side effects.

Ketamine: anaesthetic, mild pain killer and historically used recreationally. Recently some evidence has been found for its use as a rapid-acting antidepressant. This is, however, a very controversial treatment, must only be administered by a medical professional.
Ibogaine, Ayahuasca, microdosing with hallucinogenic drugs

Over The Counter Medications and Herbal Medication

Many people feel that while medications from a pharmacy are processed and artificial, herbs are in some way a more natural alternative. It is certainly true that a range of plant products can be useful for mood and anxiety symptoms. However, the contrast of processed medications and natural herbs is too simplistic. For one thing, many medications were in fact originally developed from plants. And conversely, many herbs work in very similar ways to medications, and so have similar benefits and side effects.

Psychological and counselling treatments

Psychological treatments in the form of psychotherapy and counselling services (i.e. talk therapies) may be sought out by people who have an interest in personal growth or self-development and are curious about their internal world, their patterns of behaviour, the origins of their feelings and beliefs and to enhance interpersonal relationships, choose healthier coping strategies and build resilience. These services also help people who have ordinary or extraordinary life stressors (see Chapter 6 for an overview of the normal, but difficult experiences that can impact on us). And of course, psychological and psychosocial treatments are an essential part of assisting and supporting the person who has a mental illness.

Importantly, research shows that medication alone is not nearly as effective in the treatment of psychiatric illnesses as the combination of medication with psychological and psychosocial support services.[46]

There are a number of different psychological treatments that may be used, depending on the needs, capacities and resources of the individual. These may happen one-on-one or in a group setting, and may happen in person (face-to-face) or via teletherapy, online or telephonically. In general all psychological treatments aim to help the person become more functional and less symptomatic, to help them learn healthy coping techniques and problem-solving skills and regain a sense of control and pleasure in life.

---

46 Cuijpers et al., 2014.

Table 3.5: List of psychological treatments

Supportive counselling and psychoeducation, including:		
Crisis Intervention This includes "psychological first aid" and is indicated for people who have been or are currently in crisis or in immediate distress and unable to access ordinary coping strategies. This is often provided by Employee Assistance programmes either telephonically or face to face and is a short-term, emergency intervention. This is not typically an intervention that can address longer standing mental health issues or environmental stressors.	**Bereavement or Trauma counselling (see Chapter 6)**	**Support Groups** Groups for people dealing with similar issues can be a powerful source of social support. These include groups for people with similar medical conditions, parenting groups, divorce groups, formally organised groups for bereaved parents (such as those offered by Compassionate Friends), and groups such as Alcoholics or Narcotics Anonymous that address addiction or Al-Anon groups, for the families of addicts.
Psychotherapy:		
Psychodynamic, explorative, relational therapies More explorative therapies aim to help the person understand the behaviours, emotions, and ideas that contribute to his or her illness and learn how to modify them. Understanding and identifying the life problems or events, like a major illness, a death in the family, a loss of a job, or a divorce, that may contribute to their illness will help the patient understand which aspects of those problems they may be able to solve or improve. These therapies may be short or long term.	**Cognitive Behavioural Therapies** are excellent for helping people gain control of the symptoms associated with anxiety, panic disorder, obsessive compulsive disorders, phobias and other conditions that involve distorted thoughts and negative ideas. This helps people with mental illness to identify and change inaccurate perceptions that they may have of themselves and the world around them. This kind of intervention is often helpful in the short-term with people who are able to co-operate with their own treatment.	**Technique Driven Therapies** Technique driven therapies such as BWRT, EMDR and hypnotherapy need to be used judiciously by healthcare professionals who have the necessary training. They can be very powerful in the short-term if appropriately used, but for the most part are not well supported by acceptable scientific evidence. There is a fair amount of research evidence for the value of Eye Movement Desensitisation and Reprocessing (EMDR) in treating trauma and PTSD , although it remains controversial and the mechanisms of change are not fully understood.

Other psychotherapies:		
Couples/Marital Therapy (see Chapter 6) This intervention is indicated if the person involved has relationship difficulties that are interfering with their functioning. While some issues can be dealt with in the immediate short term, most relationship difficulties take a while to resolve and sometimes the impacted individuals may be unsettled in the short term.	**Family Therapy** This is a specialised intervention that can assist when the issues are manifesting within the employee's family system.	**Group Therapy** Unlike support groups, which have a psycho-educational, information and resource-sharing focus, and may be related to a specific issue (such as divorce or eating issues), group therapy is an in-depth psychotherapy intervention conducted by a mental health professional. This can be a powerful form of personal discovery and growth. A form of group therapy that has grown in popularity recently is called DBT (Dialectical Behaviour Therapy) – an integrative and fairly intensive process of group and individual therapies to address difficulties with affect regulation, distress tolerance, self-harm and aims to enhance coping skills. DBT was initially designed to treat people with suicidal behaviour and borderline personality disorder (see Chapter 4). But it has been adapted for other mental health problems that threaten a person's safety, relationships, work, and emotional well-being.

Psychiatric Hospitalisations and Rehabilitation

The primary function of psychiatric hospitalisation to ensure the safety of the ill individual (and possibly of other people who may be threatened by an aggressive or violent person), and to ensure immediate and more intensive treatment. Private psychiatric hospitals typically offer a 2 - 3 week admission (aligned to what private medical aids will pay for). Similarly they may pay for 21 days admission for substance rehabilitation.

Table 3.6: Hospital treatments

Short-term admissions usually focus on trying to reduce an acute mental health crisis, avert suicidal or homicidal behaviours, and contain someone who is feeling overwhelmed and unable to cope in their ordinary lives.	Slightly longer admissions (a week or more) may introduce, change or reduce medication, help the person establish a better sleep pattern, ensure the patient is feeling calmer and more in control of themselves. Allow time to attend individual and group psychotherapy sessions.	Long term admissions (more than 6 weeks)
Hospitalisations for substance addictions:		
Short-term admissions into rehab facilities tend to focus on medically managed withdrawal from substances and initial treatment. These typically last up to 1 month.	Longer inpatient rehab programmes (sometimes these last for 2-3 months) for significant substance addiction followed by ongoing Outpatient treatment programmes.	Secondary or step down facility (or halfway house)
Specialist State Psychiatric facilities		
Some may offer longer hospital admissions. For example, Tara Hospital in Johannesburg runs an eight-week inpatient Psychotherapy programme. They also have a specialist Eating Disorders unit that admits patients for long-term treatment of their illness. These admissions may last several months. Finally, some State Psychiatric facilities offer long-term admissions for chronically ill people, those people whose mental illness is resistant to treatment and for those people who are an ongoing threat to themselves or others.		
Chronic hospitalisation is offered for people whose illness and symptoms are severe and do not respond well to treatment. Usually, someone who needs chronic hospitalisation is likely to qualify for either temporary or permanent incapacity.		

Conclusion

People developing a mental health condition do not often reach out for help in the early phases of their illness. For a depressed person this may be because the changes are subtle and because the person has not realised that their symptoms are part of a psychiatric condition. Someone who is experiencing profound and frightening changes such as psychotic symptoms will often try to keep them a secret. It is for this reason that it is important for employers, managers and HR staff to be able to identify and assist employees who are showing signs of mental illness.

Chapter 4

Some we love, some we hate –
Personality Disorders at work

Introduction

This chapter deals with the challenge of working with people who have personality difficulties and personality disorders. We have titled this chapter 'Some we love, some we hate' because those people with personality disorders can wreak havoc in the workplace through either 'hooking' managers and colleagues into their negative behavioural patterns or through alienating managers and colleagues as a result of destructive interpersonal interactions creating heightened levels of conflict and stress for all concerned.

We will touch briefly on the three clusters of personality disorders (Cluster A – paranoid, schizoid and schizotypal disorders; Cluster B – antisocial, borderline, histrionic and narcissistic disorders; Cluster C – avoidant, dependent and obsessive-compulsive personality disorders) but we will focus specifically on the clinical and sub-clinical personality problems that are most prevalent within the workplace context. We will also consider how best to understand and accommodate people on the Autism Spectrum in the workplace. Finally we will discuss the impact of disruptive behaviours related to personality pathology at work, and how to deal with these. Issues such as bullying, harassment, threats or incidents of workplace violence and co-worker conflict can pose significant risks to individual safety and wellbeing, but also to workplace functioning and productivity.

What is a personality disorder and who is a difficult person?

Not everyone who you do not like or is difficult to deal with has a personality disorder. But some of them do. So how do we distinguish a person with a personality disorder from a difficult person?

Personality disorders are, in essence, what happens when a person's way of being in the world causes **significant and ongoing** problems to themselves and to other people. It is important to note, however, that clinical diagnosis of personality disorders is fairly controversial and open to abuse. Both the American Psychiatric Association's DSM-5 and the WHO ICD-10 diagnostic frameworks provide very broad and vague diagnostic criteria. Many ordinarily functional people, can, and will, under stress, behave in unhealthy or maladaptive ways. That is not enough to diagnose someone as having a Personality Disorder (PD). To make a diagnosis of a PD the DSM-5 emphasises that there must be evidence that the pattern of unhealthy behaviour and relationships is dysfunctional, pervasive (across all contexts of the person's life), persistent (it's been an enduring way of being since late teens) and inflexible (the maladaptive patterns are not significantly improved or changed by external inducements).

In general personality disorders are "ego syntonic" conditions. This means that the person who has the disorder is unaware of the problem and the disorder feels part of themselves and is consistent with their self-image. This makes treatment difficult as they may not perceive anything wrong and view their perceptions and behaviour as reasonable and appropriate. In contrast, the majority of mental illnesses discussed in Chapter 3 are understood to be "ego dystonic" or "ego alien" conditions, in that the symptoms (thoughts, perceptions and behaviours) are unwanted and cause distress and are in conflict with the person's sense of self.

No-one is only borderline at home or antisocial at work or paranoid in their position as head of the neighbourhood watch. And nobody suddenly develops a narcissistic personality disorder because they got promoted. While previous editions of the DSM suggested that PDs were an either/or category (that is, you either had one or you didn't), current thinking sees personality as operating on a continuum. Importantly, to be diagnosed with a personality disorder, these ways of behaving must cause significant impairment in the person's functioning and/or distress to the individual or those who know them.

It is not helpful (or ethical) to label someone as having a personality disorder simply because they frustrate or worry you or because you don't understand them. Personality disorders are not a result of defiance, or laziness, or a moral defect; and no-one chooses to have a personality disorder any more than a person can choose their birth parents. These are the result of biological, social and cultural influences interacting with individual developmental experiences. Both genetic and physiological factors play a role, but these are mediated and shaped by the nature of each person's life experiences, starting from in the womb. Childhood experiences of trauma, abuse, neglect and parenting disturbances appear to play a significant role in the development of personality disorders.[1]

Currently researchers are finding evidence of genetic links to aggression, impulsivity, anxiety and fear, all traits that could be influential in the later development of a personality disorder. Twin studies provide fascinating evidence for the power of these biological forces. Markon et.al.[2], reported on 128 twin pairs who had been raised apart. This study found that the identical twins (who share exactly the same genetic material) were more similar in personality traits than the fraternal twins.

Personality disorders are diagnosed across nationalities, race and gender, although cultural factors may certainly influence the expression and acceptability (or not) of certain behaviours. For example, some cultures affirm the "stiff upper lip... don't let them see that you are hurting" approach when people are distressed, so in these communities people who cry openly or discuss their problems with strangers may be seen to be overly emotional or uncontained and unhealthy. On the other hand, cultures that value and foster open expression of emotions, may see the person who does not cry at a funerals or talk loudly in social situations as being repressed and uptight and unhealthy.

A general comment about dealing with someone with a personality disorder at work:

Under each heading we list some suggestions for how workplaces can best manage someone with significant personality difficulties. These lists are not comprehensive and none of these strategies offer fool-proof quick fixes. Rather think of these coping strategies as "mini-experiments". Some ideas may work, while others may not, or you may need to modify using a trial-and-error approach in order to bring about the

---

1   Gunderson et al., 2000.

2   Markon et.al., 2002.

best results. But be aware that even with intensive psychotherapy, it is exceptionally difficult to bring about sustained personality and behaviour change and this kind of change occurs only when the person concerned is truly motivated to address their difficulties. So, rather than expecting massive personality change, it is more helpful to see these "mini-experiments" as ways in which you can help the person with a personality disorder to function better or, at the very least, to refrain from creating chaos.

Personality disorder clusters

Formal classification of Personality Disorders divides them into three clusters. This is a fairly artificial classification but is a helpful way of starting to get to grips with this topic.

Table 4.1: List of Personality Disorders

Cluster A	Paranoid, Schizoid and Schizotypal personalities	Socially withdrawn, eccentric and odd people
Cluster B	Borderline, Histrionic personalities	Emotionally needy and intense personality types, unstable, sensitive, dramatic, manipulative and unpredictable people
	Narcissistic and Antisocial personalities	Selfish, grandiose, aggressive, manipulative, scheming, entitled, disruptive people
Cluster C	Avoidant, Dependent and Obsessive-Compulsive personalities	Anxious, fearful and rigid people

Cluster A: Socially withdrawn, eccentric and odd people

This cluster includes people with Schizoid/Schizotypal and Paranoid personality disorders. People with these disorders tend to be socially awkward and seem introverted and socially withdrawn. Their thinking can be distorted by eccentric ideas and rigid beliefs. These types of PDs used to be thought of as fairly uncommon conditions and as such have not historically been seen as a significant problem in the workplace. However, research by Hengartner et.al.[3] found that PDs within cluster A were significantly associated with occupational dysfunction. This illustrates that these

---

3   Hengartner et.al., 2014.

PDs are indeed a concern for the workplace. Table 4.2 describes the characteristic features of the different Cluster A PDs, followed by a discussion on what they can add to the workplace, the problems they pose to organisations and how best they can be managed. This format is followed throughout this chapter.

Due to the overlap in presentation, behaviour and interpersonal issues between Cluster A personality disorders and people on the high functioning end of the Autism Spectrum, further ideas and strategies for dealing with odd, idiosyncratic people may be found at the end of this section when we discuss Autism Spectrum Disorder in the workplace.

Table 4.2: Characteristics of Cluster A Personality Disorders

Paranoid Personality Disorder is characterised by:	Schizoid Personality Disorder is characterised by:	Schizotypal Personality Disorder is characterised by:
• pervasive distrust and suspiciousness of other people • a belief that other people intend to harm, take advantage, or humiliate them in some way • a need to protect themselves and minimise engagement with others • possible pre-emptive attacks on those perceived to be a threat • a tendency to hold grudges, litigiousness (resorting to suing people often), and pathological jealousy • seeing malevolent intentions in harmless, inoffensive comments or actions • reluctance to confide in others or to develop close relationships, an emotional life dominated by distrust and hostility • the absence of systematised delusions or psychosis	• a pervasive pattern of social detachment and a restricted range of emotional expression • being a loner, preferring social isolation • reluctance to seek out or allow or enjoy close relationships • typically engaging in solitary activities, seem to take little pleasure in life • apparent indifference to both criticism and praise • appearing detached and aloof • obliviousness to social nuance and social cues causing them to appear socially incompetent • a restricted emotional range and failure to reciprocate gestures or facial expressions (such as smiles or nods of agreement) which causes them to appear rather dull, bland, or inattentive	• a pervasive pattern of social and interpersonal limitations • acute discomfort in social settings and a limited capacity for close relationships • social isolation, reserved, and distant manner, and/or eccentric behaviour • perceptual abnormalities such as noticing flashes of light no one else can see, or seeing objects or shadows in the corner of their eyes and then realising that nothing is there • cognitive distortions and unusual beliefs and fantasies that are inconsistent with their cultural norms. For example, they may believe they can read other people's thoughts, or that that their own thoughts have been stolen from their minds

What can people who are socially withdrawn, odd or eccentric add to the workplace?

People who are eccentric are able to provide unusual perspectives and may be able to add fresh, unexpected ways of seeing or understanding issues. They can offer high levels of productivity when engaged and interested in the tasks or projects in which they are involved. They pay attention to detail, are good at working on their own or at their own pace and are unlikely to be distracted by social relationships at work.

Particular problems people who are socially withdrawn, odd or eccentric may pose to the workplace

Their eccentricity may lead to social difficulties and interpersonal misunderstandings. They may be a poor fit for a very fluid or fast changing work environment. Because of their tendency to rigidity and need for interpersonal space they can also be irritating to colleagues and managers and challenging of authority they do not respect.

How best to manage people in the workplace who are socially withdrawn, odd or eccentric?

Communicate clearly and directly. These are not people who will "get your hint" or understand nuance easily. Treat these employees with empathy and show a professional interest in their lives, but keep in mind that they do not respond well to intrusiveness or excessive curiosity. These are the kinds of staff members who do not necessarily appreciate or respond well to compulsory group team-building events or work-based socialising, especially if the nature of the events is unfamiliar, anxiety provoking or uncomfortable for them.

Here are some mini-experiments to try:

- These individuals do not respond very well to being micromanaged and giving these employees personal space (both physically and psychologically) and some autonomy over decision making tends to optimise their performance.

- Flexibility about work hours, leave periods and dress codes can also facilitate better work engagement and output for people who have Cluster A traits.

Autism Spectrum Disorders and the Workplace

"What would happen if the autism gene was eliminated from the gene pool? You would have a bunch of people standing around in a cave, chatting and socializing and not getting anything done." [4]

Autism is best understood as a group of developmental disorders that together make up autism spectrum disorder, known as ASD. People with autism tend to have difficulty with social interaction, communication and behaviour.[5] The historical image of the autistic person as being someone who is unable to communicate at all and needs institutional care has been shaken by the current understanding that Autism is a spectrum disorder. This means that at the one, extreme end of the spectrum are those people who are unable to function independently at all. At the other end are those people with High Functioning Autism (sometimes called Asperger's Syndrome) who are often extremely productive and may even be exceptional in some of their talents. Some of the famous people who have high functioning autism are Professor Temple Grandin who is a scientist and advocate for the humane treatment of livestock for slaughter, and Greta Thunberg, the young Swedish climate change activist, *Time* Person of the year 2019 and two-time Nobel Peace Prize nominee. Autistic people are of varying intelligences, abilities, skills and interests. Many of them are part of the workplace and there is benefit in identifying and understanding their specific assets.[6]

The current prevalence of Autism Spectrum Disorders (ASD) is estimated to be at least 1.5% in developed countries.[7] ASD is considered a global public health concern, yet little is known about its prevalence and presentation in sub-Saharan Africa.[8] There is some controversy as to whether people with ASD can be categorised as having personality disorders.[9] Both ASD (considered to be a neurodevelopmental disorder) and personality disorders imply lifelong impairment. There is a considerable overlap in symptoms between High Functioning Autism and certain personality disorders, especially those in Clusters A and C.

Adults on the milder end of the Autism Spectrum are difficult to diagnose but may be characterised by:

---

4   Grandin, 2011, p.37.
5   American Psychiatric Association, 2013.
6   Rutter, 2005.
7   Lyall et al., 2017.
8   Franz et.al.,. 2017.
9   Lugnegård, Hallerbäck, & Gillberg, 2012.

- average or above-average intelligence
- problems with understanding another person's point of view
- difficulties engaging in social routines such as conversations and 'small talk'
- problems with controlling feelings such as anger, depression and anxiety and a vulnerability to having "meltdowns" when under stress
- a preference for routines and schedules which can result in stress or anxiety if a routine is disrupted
- restricted and/or repetitive fields of interest
- problems with social interaction, establishing relationships, lack of emotional reciprocity (which can give an impression of indifference)
- difficulty with flexibility of thought, forward planning and thinking in abstract ways

These people may be so high functioning that their difficulties remain undiagnosed in childhood and they only receive a diagnosis in adulthood.

Just 16% of adults with autism in the United Kingdom have full-time jobs;[10] only 32% have some form of part-time work and more than a quarter of all graduates with autism are unemployed, the highest rate of any disability group.[11] There are no equivalent figures available for South Africa, but with our significant unemployment rates and a general lack of awareness of the condition, it is likely that the vast majority of people disabled by Autism Spectrum conditions are excluded from formal employment.

Job interviews are a huge barrier to employment for those with ASD because of the requirement for good communications skills. By definition autistic adults may communicate and interact differently from their neurotypical counterparts. Traditional recruitment methods are often biased towards individuals with well-developed interpersonal and communication skills. As a result many talented autistic individuals remain unemployed or underemployed.

What can people on the Autism Spectrum contribute to the workplace?

Employing people on the Autism spectrum is not simply part of corporate social responsibility but can be of real benefit to employers. Individuals with autism, while often challenged by social and communication difficulties, have many critical skills that can be of benefit to any job. These skills include (but are not limited to) attention

---

10 Office for National Statistics, 2016.
11 Hedley, Uljarević, & Hedley, 2017.

to detail, superior pattern recognition, high diligence, perseverance, good memory and a low tolerance for mistakes. People with autism tend to be very reliable and punctual. They like routine, and most will not mind doing repetitive tasks. Many are very good with maps, figures, computer programming and engineering. They can be scrupulously honest, and they are generally not effective liars.

Despite the reluctance of some organisations to hire high functioning autistic adults (possibly due to a lack of understanding of the adult presentation of autism), these employees will thrive given understanding and inclusion.

Particular problems people on the Autism Spectrum may pose to the workplace

People on the spectrum may frustrate managers and coworkers with their tendency to be rigid and obsessive. Communications that are ambiguous or nuanced tend to lead to misunderstandings as the autistic person may interpret these literally. They may perseverate and go on and on and on and on, in a way that can be excruciatingly boring to other people, about a subject which is their particular interest. If you have ever been trapped at a work cocktail party with a high functioning autist with a passion for trainspotting (or pigeon racing or medieval poetry) you may understand the challenge this poses. When overwhelmed, people on the spectrum may become distressed and anxious and then either withdraw significantly or meltdown.

How best to manage people on the Autism Spectrum in the workplace

The management of people on the Autism Spectrum will depend on the nature of the person's abilities and skills. Individuals on the lower functioning side of the Autism Spectrum may have more limited social communication and poorer cognitive skills. They will need clear rules, consistent monitoring and evaluation and explicit instructions such as "don't call customers fat". These employees do not need subtlety; they respond best to direct specific instructions. Often minimal accommodations are needed for an employee on the spectrum, and changes made to accommodate autistic employees (such as unambiguous consistent instructions) are commonly reported to be of benefit to all employees in the workplace.

All workplaces have unspoken office rules about things like how people are addressed or greeted, who gets coffees for whom, when and where it's appropriate to interrupt someone, and it is helpful to go through these with the autistic employee. These rules vary greatly between organisations, and sometimes even between different teams in the same organisation, so it is important to talk them through. It can be really helpful to allocate a workplace mentor, or a named person to assist the person on the spectrum.

Mini-experiments to try with the autistic person:

- Write down instructions and tasks

- Give short, clear instructions

- Break down large tasks into smaller components

- Have a regular timetable of tasks to add structure to their working day

The strengths and interests of autistic employees may align well with some, but not all parts, of traditional roles. Being flexible around job expectations and descriptions may allow autistic employees to thrive by engaging in roles they both excel at and enjoy. As a manager it is useful to be reminded not to take offence at the bluntness or social awkwardness typical of people on the Autism Spectrum.

Cluster B: Unstable, disruptive, manipulative, emotionally needy and unpredictable people

This cluster includes people with Borderline, Narcissistic, Histrionic and Antisocial personality disorders. People with these disorders tend to be unpredictable and can be unreliable. They may be charming and likeable, but also self-centred and excessively sensitive to being criticised. They are often involved in relationship dramas and workplace conflicts. People with these personality styles can be a huge challenge to their colleagues and employers and create significant difficulties in the workplace.

For practical (and clinical) reasons it is useful to separate out the highly emotional, overly dramatic, needy part of Cluster B (Borderline and Histrionic) from the more manipulative, exploitative types of individual (Narcissistic and Antisocial). There is an interesting gender divide in that more women are diagnosed with Histrionic and Borderline PDs and more men with Antisocial PDs. This is likely related to gender biases and cultural stereotyping and as societies become more equal, we will be better able to recognise the presentation of borderline traits in men and antisocial traits in women.[12]

---

12 Sansone & Sansone, 2011.

Table 4.3: Cluster B: The Emotionally Needy and Intense Personality

Histrionic Personality Disorder is characterised by:	Borderline Personality Disorder is characterised by:
<ul><li>self-centeredness, egocentrism and a need to be the centre of attention</li><li>dramatic emotional expression</li><li>flirtatiousness or seductiveness</li><li>constantly seeking reassurance or approval</li><li>suggestibility, being easily influenced by other people's ideas and opinions</li><li>rapidly shifting emotional states that appear shallow to others, giving the appearance of being fickle and insincere</li><li>being overly concerned with physical appearance, and using physical appearance to draw attention to self</li><li>a craving for novelty and excitement which may lead to engaging in risky situations</li><li>low tolerance for frustration or disappointment, easily hurt feelings</li><li>persistent manipulative behaviour to try to get needs for attention, comfort and appreciation met</li><li>lack of consideration for others</li><li>a tendency to believe that relationships are more intimate than they actually are.</li></ul>	<ul><li>unstable sense of self, unstable emotions and unstable relationships</li><li>frantic efforts to avoid real or imagined abandonment</li><li>emotional instability in reaction to day-to-day events (e.g., intense episodic sadness, irritability, or anxiety usually lasting a few hours and only rarely more than a few days)</li><li>intense emotional reactions and difficulties in regulating these intense emotions</li><li>inappropriate, intense anger or difficulty controlling anger</li><li>a tendency to see the world in polarised, over-simplified, all-or-nothing terms. The tendency to see the world in black-or-white (polarised) terms makes it easy for them to misinterpret the actions and motivations of others</li><li>a pattern of unstable and intense interpersonal relationships characterised by extremes between idealisation and devaluation (also known as "splitting")</li><li>high levels of impulsivity and impulsive behaviour in at least two areas that are potentially self-damaging (e.g., spending, sex, substance abuse, reckless driving, binge eating)</li><li>recurrent suicidal behaviour, gestures, or threats, or self-harming behaviour</li><li>chronic feelings of emptiness</li><li>transient, stress-related paranoid thinking or severe dissociative symptoms (such as an ongoing and unsettling feeling of emotional and social detachment, being "zoned out", familiar things feeling strange or unreal, emotional numbness.[13]</li><li>frequent changes in careers, relationships, life goals, or residences.</li></ul>

13 Korzekwa et al., 2009.

Histrionic Personality Disorder

People with Histrionic Personality Disorder may initially come across as very warm and attractive, but over time their behaviour may seem increasingly unpredictable, insincere and untrustworthy. Their behavioural style often gets in the way of truly intimate relationships; however, they are extremely uncomfortable being alone and long for interpersonal attention and connection. They tend to feel depressed when they are not the centre of attention. Histrionic people may embarrass friends and acquaintances by greeting and hugging a relative stranger with excessive intensity or weeping uncontrollably over some minor loss or sentimental moment.

Individuals with Histrionic PD are usually able to function at a high level and can do well in social and occupational environments. They may seek treatment for depression when their romantic relationships end. They often fail to see their own situation realistically, instead tending to overdramatise and exaggerate. Instead of taking responsibility for failure or disappointment, they typically cast blame on others.

Borderline Personality Disorder

Borderline Personality Disorder (BPD) is one of the most widely studied personality disorders. The term "borderline" can be misunderstood. It refers to a specific and serious diagnosis and despite the word "borderline", it does not imply that the person is in-between two different diagnoses or has a mild version of a personality disorder. People with BPD tend to experience intense and unstable emotions and moods that can shift fairly quickly. They generally have a hard time calming down once they have become upset. As a result, they frequently have angry outbursts and engage in impulsive behaviours such as substance abuse, risky sexual encounters, self-injury, overspending, or binge eating. These behaviours function to soothe in the short-term, but harm in the longer term. They characteristically experience great distress which they cannot easily control. Self-destructive behaviours such as cutting or suicide attempts are maladaptive strategies used to cope.

What can people with emotionally needy/intense personality types contribute to the workplace?

When in an emotionally regulated (stable) state, and engaged with their task, people with these personality styles can be enthusiastic, creative and productive. They can feel a great deal of empathy for others and can work hard for managers they believe in and feel believe in them. However, this sense of positivity may unfortunately come to be replaced with negative, critical thoughts as the person with BPD gets dysregulated, bored or feels criticised or hurt.

Particular problems emotionally needy/intense personality types may pose to the workplace

Although there can sometimes be obvious evidence of impulsive or disruptive behaviour, problems are more often manifested in more subtle ways. Histrionic and borderline personality traits create the appearance of immaturity and entitlement. There may be conscious and unconscious manipulations designed to attract attention and approval from those in authority. As a result of this neediness there may frequently be issues with the maintenance of appropriate and healthy relationship boundaries at work. Histrionic and borderline people often evoke a desire to rescue and save on the part of caring and compassionate managers and HR personnel. This has a tendency to result in situations where managers (or other co-workers) become over-involved (or enmeshed) in the personal lives and dramas of the borderline and histrionic employee. This is a form of enabling (or co-dependency) on the part of the rescuer.

Without even being conscious of this, the employee can have a divisive influence on co-workers, for example, by positioning one manager as all good and helpful, and another as all bad and critical. This dynamic (the result of splitting) may lead the "good" supervisor (who might be drawn into a rescuing role) into conflict with the "bad" or critical supervisor as the one tries to convince the other of their view.

Erratic levels of functioning and unpredictability when under stress make these employees less productive and hard to manage. They are prone to anxiety and depression and sudden shifts in mood. In addition, relationship crises both within the workplace and from outside of work may spill over into work hours. Their intense emotional neediness means they seek high levels of reassurance, and are oversensitive to perceived criticism, making feedback and performance appraisals a treacherous process. Behaviour patterns like these lead to more one-on-one engagement with managers, taking up time and energy. This can be very frustrating for managers and colleagues, as it arouses feelings of jealousy and competitiveness in teams. Colleagues of the emotionally needy employee may resent the extra attention, time, and accommodations that managers seem to make for them.

Because these individuals are exquisitely sensitive to rejection (real or perceived), they tend to over-react negatively when they believe that a manager or colleague is being critical or is disengaged from them. This can trigger feelings of abandonment which may lead to intense emotions and behavioural meltdowns, panic attacks, inappropriate anger and threats of, or actual, self-harm. This spill-over of stress and drama into the workplace may lead co-workers and managers to feel that they are walking on eggshells around the troubled employee. Overall stress levels rise and productivity may suffer.

Goldman's[14] research illustrates how senior managers with BPD represent "high toxicity leadership" which can contaminate an entire organisation. They provide a case study analysis of Favio Burnstein – Senior Manager of the Creative Designs R&D Division at Sergio Mondo Fashion House:

> *"As a leader, Favio was obviously flamboyant, dramatic, deeply troubled and enigmatic. He engulfed, lifted and confused his workforce. In the final analysis, Favio took his employees on a wild, steeplechase ride, through praise, hyper compassion and wild success, to depression, anger and despair."[15]*

Favio's career path began extremely successfully as he was talented and innovative. However, the instability and stress of the fashion industry seemed to trigger the worst symptoms of his BPD and he became volatile in his decisions and abusive to his staff. Company morale plummeted, productivity was negatively affected and expensive labour lawsuits were launched against the company. Sergio Mondo Fashion House executives were, however, loathe to lose Favio as they relied on his enormous talent and creativity. They took the decision to support and assist Favio in dealing with his condition, overcoming the initial stigma and reluctance he felt and providing him with coaching with a psychotherapist. A co-leadership model was implemented followed by six months of team consultations and conflict resolution meetings:

> *"Favio showed strong signs of improvement. He realized that this company was in it for the long haul. Half of his healing was due to the fact that his CEO and his company were committed to him. A fatally flawed Favio was reinvented as a merely flawed and 'mildly toxic' Favio. He was brilliant and innovative and even learned how to share the stage and stress of leadership (with his co leader)."[16]*

The case of Favio and Sergio Mondo Fashion House illustrates the complex interplay of personal and workplace factors in individual mental health and organisational performance that forms the premise of this book. Individual vulnerabilities can be exacerbated or ameliorated by organisational demands, stress, and levels and types of support.

How best to manage the emotionally needy/intense employees in the workplace

Initially, management should help to set boundaries by providing all employees with clear rules, expectations, feedback and modelling. This is particularly helpful for emotionally dysregulated people. They need consistent, predictable, firm but reasonable limits to be set.

---

14 Goldman, 2006.

15 Ibid, p. 735.

16 Ibid, p. 742.

Early identification and management are helpful. As with other personality disorders, emotionally needy employees may believe that their problems are caused by other people. It may be especially difficult in the workplace to address any problems of inappropriate relationships, personal dress or seductive style.

Here are a few mini-experiments to try:

- Appropriate limit setting is essential, with a focus on proper workplace conduct, completion of assigned tasks, and due consideration of co-worker feelings.

- An explanation of the appropriate time and place for different types of interactions may be necessary.

- Supervisors may need to remind the individual with the disorder to focus on finishing assigned work.

- The supervisor must also be ready for angry protests and even tolerant of the possibility that the employee will be angry at them.

- Problems and complaints should be discussed specifically and with particular suggestions for improvement. Supervisory meetings should not deteriorate into arguments. Stay polite and do not cross boundaries. If possible, document everything.

- Referral for consultation to an employee wellbeing programme can be useful when problems persist. The recommended form of treatment for histrionic and borderline PD is psychotherapy, although medication is also a useful way to assist managing the mood and anxiety issues. Therapy for people with this diagnosis is often challenging because they may exaggerate their symptoms or ability to function. They may also be emotionally needy and challenge the behavioural boundaries set up by the therapist. The prognosis is quite good when there are strengths that can enhance social and work activities and a capacity to develop introspection and change.

- Workplaces can assist by supporting attendance in long-term or ongoing individual counselling and group psychotherapies.

Consistency is helpful for employees with unstable personality styles because they experience so much chaos in their personal lives. Above all, try to maintain an understanding of, and some empathy around, the difficulty of living with Borderline or Histrionic PD. While these individuals may be a challenge to deal with, a workplace environment can actually provide them a degree of much-needed stability and goal-orientation in their lives.

Cluster B: The grandiose, aggressive, manipulative, scheming, entitled, disruptive and unpredictable personality types

Many very successful people have narcissistic or even mildly psychopathic (antisocial) traits. While they can be a significant interpersonal challenge to those close to them, they are nowhere near as problematic as individuals who meet the full diagnosis of Narcissistic or Antisocial Personality Disorder. People who are interpersonally exploitative, entitled and lack empathy for others are also often the kinds of managers or employees who create problems in organisations related to bullying, harassment and even violence.

Table 4.4: Cluster B: The grandiose, aggressive, manipulative, scheming, entitled, disruptive and unpredictable personality types

Narcissistic Personality Disorder is characterised by:	Antisocial Personality Disorder is characterised by:
<ul><li>a grandiose sense of self-importance and a belief in their own "specialness" and uniqueness</li><li>a sense of entitlement and the expectation of special treatment from others</li><li>a preoccupation with fantasies of success, power, brilliance, attractiveness or ideal love</li><li>a need for excessive admiration from others</li><li>a lack of empathy or consideration toward the feelings and needs of others and taking advantage/exploitation of others to achieve one's own goals</li><li>extreme envy of others, and the belief that others are equally envious of them</li><li>arrogance and controlling behaviours (this can include bullying and belittling others</li><li>an obsession with status, associating with famous and special people provides a sense of importance</li><li>a tendency to move from over-idealising others to devaluing them</li></ul>	<ul><li>a pervasive pattern of disregard for the rights of other people that often manifests as hostility and/or aggression</li><li>deceit and manipulation</li><li>impulsivity without thinking of consequences, often resulting in loss of employment, accidents, legal difficulties and incarceration</li><li>failure to feel genuine remorse for the harm they cause others. (However, they can pretend to feel regret or remorse when it is in their best interest to do so)</li><li>inability to take appropriate responsibility for their actions and a tendency to blame their victims for "causing" their wrong actions or deserving of their fate</li><li>aggression</li></ul>

The Dark Triad

The Dark Triad[17] comprises people who have high levels of narcissism together with psychopathy and Machiavellianism (characterised by manipulation and exploitation of others, an absence of morality, and a high level of self-interest). This presents a significant problem in the workplace (and in society in general) as people with this callous-manipulative interpersonal style are more likely to commit crimes, cause social distress and create severe problems for an organisation, especially if they are in leadership positions.[18] Recent research confirms that destructive leadership, characterised by aggressive, authoritarian and manipulative behaviours, has a strong negative effect on employees' psychological wellbeing.[19]

Narcissistic Personality Disorder

Narcissism is a term used to describe an extreme pre-occupation with oneself, and one's own wants, needs, and desires as well as a great need to be admired by others. The word "narcissism" has its origins in the Greek myth of a beautiful young man called Narcissus who falls in love with his reflection, unaware that the image he adores is actually his own.

Clinically there are two main types of narcissists – the grandiose, overt or thick-skinned narcissist and the covert or thin-skinned narcissist.[20] Both types are extraordinarily self-absorbed people, but they present in seemingly opposite ways. "Thin-skinned" narcissists are fragile, vulnerable, easily hurt, hypersensitive to the judgements and opinions of others and find it very difficult to deal with any trauma or failure. Interpersonally they may be shy, seem outwardly self-effacing, but protect an inner secret grandiosity. In contrast, "thick-skinned" narcissists have an effective defensive armour that they use to protect themselves from any experiences that might reveal any flaws or deficits in themselves. They refuse to acknowledge or absorb criticism at all, so they remain in a bubble where they are blameless and invulnerable. They have little obvious anxiety or shame and tend to be attention seeking and arrogant. They can be socially charming, despite being oblivious to the needs of others, and are interpersonally exploitative. Some people with narcissistic personality disorder shift between grandiose and vulnerable states, depending on life circumstances, while others may present with mixed features.

---

17 James, 2013.

18 Kaufman et al., 2019.

19 Montano et al., 2017.

20 Bernardi & Eidlin, 2018.

In addition to the grandiose and vulnerable subtypes, there is a more functional group of individuals with Narcissistic PD, that have been described as "high-functioning," or "productive" narcissists.[21] These individuals are grandiose, competitive, attention seeking, and sexually provocative, while demonstrating adaptive functioning and using their narcissistic traits to succeed. Because of their high level of functioning, at first glance individuals in this group may not appear to have a personality disorder, and the narcissistic personality disorder diagnosis may be overlooked on diagnostic assessment.[22]

The experience of relating to a narcissistic partner, parent, colleague or boss is well described in thousands of internet articles. But in general, this can be summarised in the comment that there is nowhere as warm as in the glow of the narcissist's sun, and nowhere as cold as in their shade.

Particular problems narcissistic personality types may pose to the workplace

At work narcissists may present initially as very motivated, ambitious and even charming and likeable, at first. In fact, narcissistically inclined people are often very impressive during the recruitment phase and in selection interviews.[23] However, research indicates that narcissism is not related in any way to job performance.[24] Over time it becomes apparent that their ambition is self-centred, rather than aligned with the needs and focus of the organisation, and that in fact they are selfish and very poor team players. They have strong needs for control and therefore struggle with accepting other people's authority and may openly or passive aggressively undermine managers or supervisors.

They may get so caught up in their fantasies of achievement that they don't put any real effort into their daily life and don't direct their energies toward accomplishing their goals. This means that people with NPD, despite talent and ability, may be underachievers, promising much more than they end up delivering.

The narcissist's need for admiration means that they may take credit for the work or ideas of other people and struggle to admit that someone else has done something well. They have difficulty with saying "thank you" or "sorry". This creates a lot of conflict with other co-workers who feel exploited and who dislike being treated in a patronising fashion.

---

21 Crompton, 2014.

22 Caligor, Levy, & Yeomans, 2015.

23 Grijalva & Harms, 2014.

24 Campbell et al., 2011.

Studies have suggested that the colleagues of narcissists experience high levels of stress, manifesting in increased staff absenteeism and a reduction in staff retention.[25] Among the many reasons for this may be that narcissism has been found to be positively related to problematic workplace behaviours such as interpersonal aggression, sabotaging the work of others, finding excuses to waste other people's time and resources, and spreading rumours.[26]

Narcissists are often initially extremely successful in organisations – their psychological strategies to secure admiration and recognition work to gain them promotion and power. Unfortunately it's often only once narcissists have ascended to the C-suites or upper management of organisations that their pathological personality styles are revealed. As leaders they are notoriously poor at consulting with others and tend to make unilateral decisions. Unfortunately, this is allied with a refusal to take responsibility for any mistakes or errors. They typically manipulate situations so that other people take responsibility for their failures and incompetence.

People with Narcissistic Personality Disorder often feel devastated when they realise that they have normal, average human limitations; that they are not as special as they think, or that others don't admire them as much as they would like. These realisations are often accompanied by feelings of intense anger or shame that they sometimes take out on other people. However, the same is true of their self-judgments. They tend to vacillate between feeling like they have unlimited abilities, and then feeling deflated, worthless and devastated when they encounter their normal, average human limitations. Despite their bravado, people with Narcissistic Personality Disorder require a lot of admiration from other people in order to bolster their own fragile self-esteem. They can be quite manipulative in extracting the necessary attention from those people around them.

What can people with narcissistic personality types contribute to the workplace?

The so-called productive narcissists may still be over-sensitive to criticism, over-competitive, isolated and grandiose, but appear to have a sense of freedom to do whatever they want rather than feeling constantly constrained by circumstances, and through their charisma they are able to draw people into their vision, and may be able to inspire a team, or even a whole organisation to pursue their dream.[27]

---

25 Colligan & Higgins, 2006.
26 Penney & Spector, 2002.
27 Maccoby, 2003.

How best to manage the narcissistic employee, manager or CEO in the workplace

- Assess the nature of the relationship realistically and try to understand the limitations of the narcissistic person. If possible, remind yourself that beneath the narcissist's veneer of competence, specialness and power, there is a frightened and vulnerable person hiding behind a mask that shields them from being seen for who they really are.

- It may be helpful to understand that narcissists are suffering from a type of chronic emotional pain; denying this pain by holding onto the deluded belief that being admired or getting praise or having celebrity friends or making a fortune from the next big thing will cure them. We can know that these "fixes" will never work, but it may be helpful to develop some realistic compassion for the narcissist.

- Maintain your professionalism and your emotional distance. Try to imagine how it must be to have a desperate, constant need to hear that the world holds you in high regard, knowing you will collapse if your self-deceptions are not supported and validated. This does not mean you should try and befriend them and lower your personal and professional boundaries. In fact, getting too close to a narcissist in the longer term can create significant problems as closeness triggers their vulnerability and they are unable to tolerate this state. So they will then lash out and devalue or attack you emotionally.

Here are a few mini-experiments to try:

- In order to manage narcissists' over-promising, keep your expectations of what they will deliver as low as possible, and understand they will give you only what they need to maintain their own self-esteem

- If you have an issue with a narcissist avoid direct blame. Any accusation will cause them to feel shame, and nothing wounds a narcissist more than humiliation. Confront them when necessary gently and tactfully.

- Try not to directly criticise a narcissistic person because regardless of how accurate you are, you run the risk of inflicting a "narcissistic injury" and becoming the recipient of their "narcissistic rage". Instead, if possible, share constructive feedback by trying to share some mild praise initially, and then offering the feedback: *"Thank you for emailing me the slides, they look very professional. There are just some minor grammar corrections needed, I am sure you will be able to make the changes very easily."*

- If you repeat a request often enough, using measured words in a calm manner, you may elicit an awareness of their obligation.

If you are working for a narcissistic boss:

- Document your accomplishments because your narcissistic manager is unlikely to hold them in mind.

- Seek mentoring and support elsewhere. Narcissistic people are not good mentors because they often lack the ability to offer praise or reinforcement for a job well done. It's better to seek advice, support and mentoring from others whether it be within your organisation or from without.

- Be willing to accept criticism, but don't take it personally. It's important to stay grounded and realistic and to avoid basing your self-worth on a narcissist's approval.

- Enjoy the praise when they are pleased with you (which is likely because you have made them look good) but don't take it personally and remind yourself that when you no longer serve a function in their life, they'll move on and you may end up feeling disregarded.

Here are a few mini-experiments to try:

- If your boss is being hypercritical instead of defending yourself or defending something you did, agree with the criticism, but then ask what your boss what like you to do differently. This conveys that you are willing to learn and that you are open to their mentoring you.

- Over-respond to what you know the manager's pet/ trigger issues are and anticipate how you can prevent them being triggered

- Never ignore a narcissistic boss or manager. It helps to keep the peace by quickly responding when they demand attention. If you do react as desired, what can save you from psychic torment is learning to temper the narcissist's demands without incurring their anger. Responses such as, "Sounds good to me" calm down the needy child inside the narcissist by affirming their belief systems while limiting your involvement in actualising it.

If you cannot manage the demands and emotional impact of working for a narcissist it may be necessary to consider changing jobs. Document any unreasonable requests, behaviour or comments from your boss. If you do need to lodge a grievance you will need to back this up with concrete evidence. Maintain a strong network of supports and connections in other parts of your company or professional world. This allows you the option of getting some outside reality testing, feedback and the opportunity to move out if things become intolerable.

Antisocial personality and psychopathy in the workplace

This is an extremely controversial and muddled field, with no universally agreed on definitions. The DSM-5 does not have a category for psychopathic personality and instead incorporates this into the much broader diagnosis of Antisocial Personality Disorder. This has been criticised by experts in the field as being unhelpful[28] as it overemphasises criminal and physically aggressive behaviours and may lead people to miss signs of psychopathy in higher functioning people, especially in the workplace. The term "sociopath" has sometimes been used interchangeably with "psychopath". Psychopathy is not the same as psychosis. The majority of psychopaths are not psychotic (or out of touch with reality) but if they are psychotic then they can be very dangerous indeed.

Psychopaths demonstrate persistent antisocial behaviour, impaired empathy and remorse, and bold, disinhibited, and egotistical traits. Psychopathy has been described as an extreme variant of narcissistic personality disorder.[29] "(M)ost psychopaths are .... preoccupied by interpersonal power (rather than relationships), with a range of manifestations which may include manipulativeness, being charming, minimised affect and anxiety, high stimulation thresholds, emotional indifference toward others, and absence of guilt or moral values."[30]

We tend to think of psychopaths as killers, criminals outside the bounds of society, but not all psychopaths are physically aggressive or violent or serial killers or sexual offenders and there are many high functioning psychopaths who have what the psychiatrist and researcher, Hervey Cleckley[31] called the Mask of Sanity. In an article by Chivers[32] on 'How to spot a psychopath', British neuroscientist David Eagleman states "...because of their glibness and charm and willingness to ride roughshod over the people in their way, [they] become quite successful. They become CEOs, professional athletes, soldiers. These people are revered for their courage and their straight talk and their willingness to crush obstacles in their way. Merely having psychopathy doesn't tell us that a person will go off and commit a crime".[33]

---

28 Blackburn, 2007.
29 Meloy, 1988.
30 Juni, 2014, p. 78.
31 Cleckley 1951.
32 Chivers, 2014.
33 Chivers, 2014, p. 4.

Online articles that reference the notion of workplace psychopathy provide lists of diagnostic criteria and appear to encourage the perception that it is common. Regarding a coworker as a psychopath is highly stigmatising and given the relatively low prevalence of psychopathy in the community, online diagnosing is probably wrong. However if there are people with significant psychopathic and antisocial traits in an organisation it is essential that management is able to recognise and deal with the issues as effectively as possible.

What can people with antisocial and psychopathic personality types contribute to the workplace?

People who have psychopathic or antisocial traits can be extremely ambitious and achievement oriented. Their ruthlessness can be an asset in some situations that demand decisive action and unemotional decision making. There is some evidence that people with these kinds of personalities can do well in structured hierarchical organisations with clear rules such as armies, prisons and organised criminal gangs.

Particular problems antisocial and psychopathic personality types may pose to the workplace

Typically the longer-term problems these people pose are more significant than the short-term value they may add to an organisation. Their ruthlessness, willingness to take advantage of others and manipulate the system for their own selfish purposes, their callousness and need to feel in control inevitably leads to unhappy coworkers, frustrated managers and frightened and powerless employees. The major risks they pose to the workplace include violations of workplace ethical codes including breaches of confidentiality, corporate espionage, lying, dishonesty and bullying as well as criminal behaviour such as theft, fraud, sabotage, extortion, harassment and violence. For an excellent overview of this issue we recommend you read Robert Hare and Paul Babiak's book on psychopathy in the workplace: *Snakes in Suits: When Psychopaths Go to Work.*[34]

How best to manage the antisocial or psychopathic employee, manager or boss

- Establish good recruitment and screening practices when hiring. Make sure that CVs, qualifications and references are all checked.

- It is good practice to ask for police clearances if you are hiring people to work with children, in positions where they will have access to weapons or access to an organisation's money.

---

34 Hare & Babiak, 2006.

- Keep records and document all complaints made against that person. When investigating complaints keep notes of any excuses and ensure you get corroboration of the reasons the employee may give for their behaviour.

- Try to hold the problematic employee accountable as quickly as possible for any problematic workplace behaviour. Excusing their outbursts or small dishonesties or failure to produce the work they promise will embolden them in future and will lead to greater problems.

- Because many people who are antisocial or psychopathic can be initially charming and manipulative, it is tempting to excuse or minimise the complaints and concerns.

- Once you have assessed someone's personality style to be this problematic and potentially destructive it is useful to approach any issues arising from a position of emotional detachment, distance and scepticism rather than empathy or advocacy. This allows you to evaluate situations without getting sucked into their stories and distortions.

Cluster C: Anxious, Fearful and Rigid people

This cluster includes people with Avoidant, Dependent, and Obsessive-Compulsive personality disorders. People with these disorders all have very high levels of anxiety and are prone to depression. Their thinking can be distorted by eccentric ideas and rigid beliefs. These are fairly common conditions and are not typically significant or intractable problems in the workplace, but they are problematic enough to be the reason that individuals may fail to achieve to their potential or that they become problematic in a team as a result of their self-doubt, social insecurity and interpersonal difficulties.

Table 4.5: Characteristics of Cluster C Personality Disorders

Avoidant Personality Disorder is characterised by:	Dependent Personality Disorder is characterised by:	Obsessive-Compulsive Personality Disorder is characterised by:
• a pervasive belief that they are not good enough, and that others don't like them, feelings of inadequacy, and a hypersensitivity to negative evaluation	• a strong need to be taken care of by other people	• a persistent pattern of preoccupation with order, perfectionism, and control of self, others, and situations at the expense of flexibility, openness, and efficiency

Avoidant Personality Disorder is characterised by:	Dependent Personality Disorder is characterised by:	Obsessive-Compulsive Personality Disorder is characterised by:
• an intense fear of ridicule, rejection and criticism • avoidance of social situations in order to avoid interactions with others (and minimise the risk of rejection) • a limited social world with a small circle of friends • difficulties with public performance such as giving presentations at work or speaking up in meetings • appearing to others as distant, aloof, shy, stiff or restricted • not being easily able to make friends, or progress professionally	• a fear of losing the support of others leading to "clinginess" and a tendency to submit to the desires of other people • fear of conflict and great difficulty standing up for themselves • vulnerability to manipulation and abuse • difficulty expressing disagreement or making independent decisions • difficulty initiating a task when nobody is available to assist them. • intolerance of being alone	• preoccupation with details, rules, schedules, organisation, and lists • a striving to do something perfectly that interferes with completion of the task • excessive devotion to work and productivity (not due to financial necessity) • excessive conscientiousness, fastidiousness, and inflexibility regarding ethical and moral issues and values • reluctance to delegate or work with other people unless those people agree to do things exactly as the person wants, anxiety and resistance to delegating tasks for fear that another person will not "get it right" • a tendency to be miserly with both themselves and others because they see money as something to be saved in case of future disasters.

Avoidant Personality Disorder

There is some overlap between the behavioural characteristics of what DSM-5 defines as an avoidant personality style and introversion. Importantly, introversion is not a personality disorder, rather it is a preference and choice. Introverts[35] are not

---

35 For an excellent overview of Introversion we recommend Susan Cain's book : Quiet: The Power of Introverts in a World That Can't Stop Talking. (2012)

necessarily anxious or shy, and they may be socially confident. However, they may feel uncomfortable or drained by social gatherings and situations involving groups of people. Extroverts feel recharged by social engagement and introverts feel drained by the same situations. Conversely, introverts need time alone, or solitude, in order to energise themselves and extroverts struggle with too much social isolation. The disposition of an introvert is frequently misconstrued as shyness, social phobia or even avoidant personality disorder. However, many introverts are completely capable – and even skilled – at socialising; they just frequently prefer not to do so. Instead, they simply choose to be alone to enjoy their own thoughts and introspection. On the other hand, avoidant people are distressed by their difficulties and plagued by their high levels of social anxiety (see Chapter 3 for more information on Social Anxiety Disorder).

Obsessive-Compulsive Personality Disorder

People with OCPD find it hard to express their feelings and have difficulty forming and maintaining close relationships with others. They often feel self-righteous, indignant and angry, and often face social isolation. They may also be anxious and get depressed.

Obsessive-compulsive personality disorder (OCPD) is not the same thing as Obsessive-Compulsive Disorder (described in Chapter 3). OCD is characterised by obsessive thoughts and compulsive rituals. OCD is considered to be ego-dystonic as the thoughts and compulsions experienced or expressed are not consistent with the individual's self-perception. The OCD patient generally realises that their obsessions and compulsions are unreasonable and is typically distressed by their inability to manage these. In contrast, people with OCPD, like the majority of people with personality disorders, tend to be unaware that they are the problem in relationships. OCPD is ego-syntonic, as the individual generally perceives their obsession with orderliness, perfectionism, and control to be reasonable and even desirable.

Our work with Johanna provides a useful case of how someone with OCPD presents in the workplace and the advantages and disadvantages that this personality disorder presents for those who have to work with individuals with this disorder. Johanna is the head of an NGO that does advocacy work in Johannesburg. She is widely praised as being exceptionally good at her job, tireless and fearless in her advocacy. Her role is one which often places her in highly conflictual situations. She 'speaks truth to power' as she holds public officials, organisations and private individuals accountable for their words and deeds. Some of her OCDP traits are extremely valuable in these interactions. She is always meticulously prepared for all encounters, unflinching in her moral judgement and in her demands for justice. She is most demanding of herself – travelling long distances and available at all hours.

But, Johanna is excessively demanding of her subordinates and is extremely controlling in all her interactions, including with her allies. She brooks no dissent and does not bother to hide her disdain for anyone who challenges her, however slight and justifiable the challenge may be. Her combative stance with her real opponents has won her much admiration, but that same stance, taken with those on her side, has made her a number of unnecessary enemies. She has very few friends.

The way Johanna's personality impacts her subordinates and colleagues is a perfect demonstration of the title of this chapter – sometimes she is loved; sometimes she is hated – but rarely do people feel neutral about her. Her perfectionism and exacting demands can bring out the best in people who strive to find her approval and avoid her dismissive disdain. Her controlling and excessively punitive approach to any who deviate from her carefully laid plans, breed resentment and distrust. The key to dealing with Johanna seems to be high levels of respectful honesty. She is not a narcissist (see Table 4.4), she is capable of understanding another person's point of view, but she does want to dictate what that point of view should be. Careful but honest engagement that does not threaten her sense of control and ignoring her visible irritation when challenged allows me to work with Johanna in a way that is functional without undermining the positive side to her demanding and combative style.

What can anxious, fearful and rigid people contribute to the workplace?

Cluster C people can be very loyal, tenacious and can be supportive team players who do not necessarily compete with fellow team members. They can work hard for managers they believe in and feel believe in them. OCPD people are often very serious about their jobs and can pay excellent attention to detail. This is an asset in a safety-sensitive work environment requiring careful focus and able to accommodate a slower and steadier work pace. In fact there are roles in occupations such as engineering, law, medicine, accounting, architecture and construction where attention to details is essential.

Particular problems anxious, fearful and rigid people may pose to the workplace:

Although they may work hard, the productivity and success of people with Cluster C personality styles is compromised by their anxiety and their social challenges. Those who are dependent can be extremely needy and require high levels of reassurance, draining colleagues and team leaders. Those people who are consistently critical, prone to judging others and finding fault can drain the morale from a team.

All of the people with these types of personality structure are prone to anxiety and depression and substance misuse, and may struggle with loneliness and social isolation.

The perfectionism and self-doubt of Cluster C people can be a liability in a workplace that is fast moving and demands agility and quick decisions and where "perfect" can be the enemy of "good". They may be chronically unable to meet deadlines, and get caught up in details and not be able to get the bigger picture, or "see the forest for the trees".

OCPD people may become unpopular at work as they can be the stereotypical "control freak" or "know-it-all", and in a supervisory or management role can frustrate employees with their excessive micro-management, nit-picking at any small mistakes or imperfections and the unrealistically high standards they impose on others. Controlling perfectionists appear to live by the belief that, "if you want something done right ... do it yourself", so they are reluctant to delegate tasks to others. However, they will then feel burdened and resentful that they have done most of the work themselves and will be critical of staff for not having helped. This puts employees in a no-win situation. The stress of working with or for a controlling perfectionist can become overwhelming.

How best to manage anxious, fearful and rigid people in the workplace

- As with all people with difficult personalities, clear, direct and tactful communication is helpful and may help to minimise misunderstandings and misperceptions.

- As a manager, monitor the time management of this kind of employee as their anxiety and perfectionism may be an obstacle to meeting deadlines. This is a good time to encourage the principal of "perfect is the enemy of good".

- Encourage work-life balance and as a manager or team leader, model setting limits on work hours and insist on valuing family and social time.

- Engage and get to know your employee but maintain the boundaries between work and social relationships to avoid getting into positions where you become responsible for the emotional wellbeing of a dependent person.

- Do not take the criticisms and complaints personally and understand these as a strategy the person uses to cope with their own sense of imperfection or failure.

- Do not collude or enable the dysfunctional work avoidance behaviours and consistently document any performance-related concerns or problems.

- If the fear and anxiety component of these personality types is compromising work output it may assist the person to consider getting medical advice on whether treatment may assist to regulate their experience. See Chapter 3 on anxiety disorders for more information.

- Be aware that socially anxious and avoidant people tend to find large social functions and giving public presentations excruciatingly painful. They are likely to need consistent support, encouragement and practice.

- Refer to your EWP and support ongoing individual counselling and group psychotherapies.

How best to deal with a controlling perfectionistic person as a manager

When you find yourself working with or for a controlling perfectionist it is often common to feel angry and frustrated. However, feeding into their critical rigidity will exacerbate the problem and may make you feel inferior or like you can't do anything right. The strategies for dealing with a controlling perfectionistic boss are similar to those we have suggested when working for a narcissistic boss.

Here are a few mini-experiments to try:

- Do not be defensive about criticism – and similarly to managing a narcissistic manager – agree with the criticism, but then ask what your boss what like you to do differently. This conveys that you are willing to learn and that you are open to their mentoring you.

- If your goal is to keep your job, convey that you're a committed team player. Anger and frustration may overcome your willingness to work with your difficult boss or co-worker, but it's generally better not to express these frustrations in the workplace. Rather talk out your feelings with a trusted friend or therapist.

- If you feel you're right you may decide to stand your ground. Do this by simply stating your view and then move on. Try do this without criticising your boss. This is especially helpful with "know-it-all" types of controlling perfectionists. Remember, under their veneer of perfection is an insecure individual, so you don't need to go head to head to prove your point. You'll only end up losing in the end. Better to take a collegial approach and simply state the facts as you know them and move on.

- Set your own work goals and agenda. Because controlling perfectionists tend to get lost in the details, they will often lead you down several different paths. It may be more helpful to ask the them to help you prioritise the tasks they've assigned to you, or even better yet, set your own goals for what you need to achieve and what you need to do. If you can become adept at judging yourself against your own, more realistic, output measures you will be able to work on your own intrinsic sense of achievement and value yourself more authentically.

Conclusion

Dealing with personality disorders in the workplace is a challenge for all involved. The challenge is more manageable, however, when you are able to recognise that the difficult behaviour is part of a recognisable and identifiable set of 'symptoms' that can help to make it more understandable and less personal. This chapter has provided a list of such symptoms and how they may impact on the workplace and also suggested ways in which individuals with such personality disorder can be managed to both their benefit and the benefit of the organisation.

Chapter 5

Workplaces gone wild: Destructive Behaviours in Organisations

Introduction

So far in this book we have focused on the mental health vulnerabilities and conditions that are primarily related to individual psychopathology. In this chapter we look specifically at conditions and situations that present with problematic and destructive behaviours. These behaviours do not only emerge from mental illness, but often are symptomatic of toxic organisational cultures and broader social and societal ills.

Sticks and stones and words that hurt: workplace bullies

Bullying does not get left behind on the school playground once we have grown up, and it is not just children who bully or are the victims of bullying. Unfortunately, workplace bullying is a real and serious phenomenon with significant negative impacts on both the health and productivity of organisations and the psychological well-being of employees.

Defining workplace bullying or harassment

Workplace bullying or harassment is the "repetitive and systematic engagement of interpersonally abusive behaviours that negatively affect both the targeted individual as well as the work organisation. These behaviours oftentimes occur when there are actual or perceived power imbalances between the perpetrator and the victim. The behavioural repertoires of the perpetrators typically include intimidation, degradation, and humiliation of the victim".[1] Furthermore, workplace bullying is a chronic stressor

---

1   Askew, Schluter & Dick, 2013, p.186.

where an employee perceives themselves to be mistreated and abused over time and finds it difficult to defend themselves against these actions.[2]

Physical violence and direct aggression are forms of bullying that can be easier to identify and deal with than psychological harassment. Importantly workplace bullying or emotional abuse also includes acts of incivility, rudeness, condescension and disrespect as well as harassment, tyranny and injustice. These are all forms of interpersonal mistreatment. It is essential not to minimize the significant negative impact of what might mistakenly be believed to be milder forms of bullying. Seemingly minor forms of interpersonal bullying can, over time, precipitate major interpersonal conflicts and organisational harm.

Workplace bullying by a supervisor or manager may be related specifically to one's tasks and can take the form of unreasonable deadlines, meaningless tasks, or excessive monitoring of work.[3] It may seem to the bullied employee that the manager is overly focused on petty complaints or issues. Public shaming or criticism is a particularly damaging form of workplace bullying. In addition, shouting at employees, privately or publicly, singling out of employees for criticism, microaggressions, teasing, making jokes at employees' expense and excluding people inappropriately from access to information and decision making are examples of bullying.

Consequences of workplace bullying

Workplace bullying is consistently associated with reduced mental health and positively related to depression, anxiety, PTSD symptoms and stress-related psychological complaints.[4] It has also been recognized as a main source of distress that is associated with decreased well-being,[5] lowered job satisfaction and performance, reduced commitment, and higher levels of absenteeism.[6] Employees targeted by or witness to workplace bullying are more likely to have a negative mood, be cognitively distracted and feel fear.[7] Even low-level interpersonal mistreatment can engender organisational violence and damage individual psychosomatic functioning.[8]

A critical aspect of workplace bullying is that is not limited to one single event, but that it is an ongoing negative and corrosive experience. Because people spend a great deal of time at work, those feeling victimised and powerless at work are not typically able to compartmentalise this experience. So, we see a huge impact of workplace harassment on the individual's social, emotional and physical functioning. The effects

2   Nielsen & Einarsen, 2012.
3   Ortega et al., 2009.
4   Verkuil, Atasayi, & Molendijk, 2015.
5   Hoobler et al., 2010.
6   Ortega et al., 2011.
7   Barling, Dupre & Kelloway, 2009.
8   Andersson & Pearson, 1999.

of workplace bullying are not only due to actual encounters with the bully and the impact is not only observed during working hours. These experiences "are likely to be recreated over and over again in the minds of people that are being bullied. Such perseverative, intrusive thoughts have been shown to prolong the stress response beyond actual bully experiences, thereby adding to the wear and tear effects that these experiences have".[9]

The negative outcomes of ongoing and poorly managed workplace bullying tend to be longstanding and are unlikely to be resolved simply by removing the bully or the victims from the bullying situation. Staff who have been emotionally harassed over time and have not had direct and decisive support from management typically lose confidence, have persistent psychological vulnerability and are likely to become less trusting of the workplace in future.

Legal implications for workplaces in dealing with workplace bullying

In addition to adverse outcomes for those employees who are targeted by or witness to workplace bullying, there are significant direct and indirect costs to the organisation. These include the risks of litigation, constructive dismissal and incapacity claims, early retirement, absenteeism, increased staff turnover, tardiness, diminished employee morale, and reduced productivity.[10] Although bullying maybe going on without the knowledge of management, the prevention of bullying and harassment is still the organisation's responsibility.

Legislation regarding workplace bullying

According to existing labour laws in South Africa, bullying is not specifically defined. However, the following acts may be used to address this issue:

1. The Labour Relations Act (66 of 1995) - bullying is an unfair labour practice and employees who resign as a consequence of bullying would have a good claim of constructive dismissal under labour law.

2. Protected Disclosures Act (26 of 2000).

3. Protection from Harassment Act (17 of 2011) - while this could help to deal with bullying events in the workplace, it is preferable to try deal with the problem initially under labour legislation rather than this Act, as this would entail laying criminal complaints and result in criminal investigations.

---

9   Verkuil et al., 2010, p.87.

10 Bond et al., 2010.

4. As regards health and safety issues:

    • Occupational Health and Safety Act (85 of 1993)

    • Compensation for Occupational Injuries and Diseases Act (130 of 1993).

5. Promotion of Equality and Prevention of Unfair Discrimination Act (4 of 2000).

6. The Employment Equity Act (55 of 1988) in section 6 (1) does contain a prohibition against unfair discrimination, stating that "no person may unfairly discriminate, directly or indirectly, against an employee, in any employment policy or practice, on one or more grounds, including race, gender, sex, pregnancy, marital status, family responsibility, ethnic or social origin, colour, sexual orientation, age, disability, religion, HIV status, conscience, belief, political opinion, culture, language, birth or on any other arbitrary ground." Section 6(2) states that "Harassment of an employee is a form of unfair discrimination and is prohibited on anyone, or a combination of grounds of unfair discrimination listed in subsection (1)." Generally, bullying is recognised as a form of harassment, and therefore constitutes unfair discrimination.

Even if the reason for the bullying is not one of the listed grounds (e.g. race or gender) provided that the reason can be shown, a case for harassment can be made. The employer is liable for any harassment suffered by their employees during the course of their work.

Best practices when managing workplace bullying

It is very important that workplaces have a written bullying policy in place. This will not necessarily prevent bullying, but it can serve as the basis for any corrective or disciplinary measures that may need to be taken when it does occur. This policy should spell out how the company defines this behaviour, including examples, and what steps employees, and managers, can take to address instances of bullying.

• If you see someone engaging in workplace bullying, say something. If you do not, you are giving it permission to continue. This is perhaps one of the trickier tips: What if the person who is being inappropriate is your supervisor, or the president or CEO of your organisation? It is awkward; it can be uncomfortable; but telling someone, or telling the person if you are able, is helpful and necessary to prevent the behaviour from continuing

• It can be uncomfortable getting involved in interpersonal disputes, but if you do not manage these issues when they arise the cost to your business can be high.

• Even if you have a written policy and active measures to have a zero tolerance for bullying workplace, there's no way to guarantee bullying or harassment will not happen. When bullying is suspected or reported, it's essential for managers to take it seriously and act quickly, thoughtfully and carefully.

- As a start take whatever measures are possible to keep the target of the bullying safe, perhaps by moving them to a location away from the alleged bully.

- Assess the situation, while some employees may side with bullies as a form of protection, assessing everyone's perspective, while not making it seem like an interrogation, can clue you into what's really going on.

- If the facts indicate that the actions of the accused did constitute bullying or harassment, then that individual should apologize to the target and face other potential consequences (up to and including dismissal).

- Depending on the severity and extent of the bullying, it may be appropriate to provide the target with counselling, paid time off, or other support.

- Supervisors should also always look out for retribution after the fact. Just because employees may have reached a resolution does not mean that one (or both) aren't holding grudges.

Sexual harassment

Sexual harassment is a form of workplace bullying, that is subject to the same legislative codes, but needs to be highlighted as a problem in its own right. South Africa is a country plagued by excessively high levels of gender-based violence (GBV)[11] and the workplace is not immune from this. The worst excesses of GBV tend to be related to intimate partner, domestic and community settings. Sexual harassment in the workplace is a component of this broader serious societal issue, with extremely negative consequences for the mental health of the victim.

Violence-Prone Individuals in the workplace

Employees at a large retail outlet reported a co-worker who posted a photo online of his military style haircut "for when I go psycho." The same employee also told a colleague that if he failed a product knowledge test for the second time, he would kill his manager.

People who threaten violence or behave aggressively are a clear risk to the physical and psychological safety of organisations. In America the media has coined the term "going postal" to refer to becoming extremely and uncontrollably angry, often to the point of violence, and usually in a workplace environment. The expression derives

---

11 Maluleke, 2018.

from a series of incidents from 1986 onward in which United States Postal Service (USPS) workers shot and killed managers, fellow workers, and members of the police or general public in acts of mass murder. Interestingly American researchers have found that the homicide rates at postal facilities were actually lower than at other workplaces. The media depiction of an employee returning to work for revenge on his boss is not actually accurate. In fact, more than half of mass workplace shooting are by current employees, and a little under a quarter are by employees who have been at their job for less than a year.[12]

Defining workplace violence

Workplace violence is any act or threat of physical violence, harassment, intimidation, or other threatening disruptive behaviour that occurs at the workplace. It ranges from threats and verbal abuse to physical assaults and even homicide. It can affect and involve employees, clients, customers and visitors. It can involve threats made by striking workers against non-striking workers, to threats made by members of a community against company officials. Workplace harassment, racism and bullying may also be considered forms of workplace violence. Additionally, domestic violence may spill over into the workplace in the form of assaults, threats or other actions by outside parties with whom employees have relationships.

In major industries in America, the highest rate of 2.1 homicides per 100,000 workers per year was in retail.[13] In South Africa one of the workforces most affected by violence is the South African Police Services (SAPS). In 2017/18, 11 SAPS officers were killed as a result of domestic violence, seven of them by fellow SAPS officers. Similarly, three officers killed other officers during arguments in this period.[14]

The prevalence of violence (including murder-suicide events) in this sector reflects the interplay of issues around South African masculinity, violence and mental health played out in the context of policing. Exposure to high levels of violent crime, ongoing personal risk, shift work and access to weapons, mean that psychologically vulnerable people in these contexts are at risk of acting out their frustrations in very damaging ways.

Risk factors that contribute to workplace violence

Researchers in this field suggest that two factors contributed to risky, dangerous workplaces – "violence-prone individuals" and "incident-prone environments." For

---

12 Lee & McCrie, 2012.

13 (Menéndez, et.al., 2013.

14 Faull, 2018.

a discussion of the impact of, and how to identify and manage the violence prone individual see Chapter 4 (Some we love, some we hate: Personality Disorders in the workplace). While individual factors are important to deal with, threats or acts of violence are also more likely in an environment that lacks opportunities for advancement, is perceived to operate unfairly, is in a state of transition (either in a process of downsizing or rapid expansion in relatively short periods of time), avoids dealing effectively with employees' grievances and emotions, allows or encourages managerial styles characterized by aggression, dismissiveness and humiliation, tolerates or ignores workplace bullying or allows frequent disruptions and frustrations. These may include staff shortages, excess noise, insufficient privacy, demands for excess overtime or even an uncomfortable room temperature. Organisations with cultures which support fair working conditions and zero-tolerance for workplace aggression have been shown to help mitigate workplace violence.

The duty to ensure a safe workplace

There is a common law (and common decency and sense) obligation for workplaces to be safe places, both physically and psychologically. The duties of organisations are also detailed in various acts falling under the Department of Labour. In South Africa, employers have a legal duty to ensure a safe work environment. For example, Section 8 of Occupational Health and Safety Act (85 of 1993) provides that all employers have a duty to provide and maintain, as far as reasonably practicable, a safe, healthy working environment which is free of risk to their employees. According to the Employment Equity Act (55 of 1988) if a worker is alleged to have contravened a provision of the EEA by, for example, sexually harassing a colleague and the employer does not take the necessary steps to deal with the allegations of harassment, the employer is deemed also to have contravened the EEA. Section 60(3) of EEA holds an employer vicariously liable for the unlawful, discriminatory conduct of their employees.

In the face of workplace violence, each employer has to be able to answer the following questions:

- Have we implemented effective mechanisms for addressing grievances or concerns?

- Have we trained supervisors or managers to recognize truly troubled employees and provided support to those who are in need of help?

- Do we provide opportunities for job rotation or advancement?

- Do we try to manage external disruptions in the work environment, e.g., temperature too hot or too cold; poor air quality; overcrowded workspace with little privacy; excessive overtime; personnel shortages; high noise levels?

- Do we perform adequate background and reference checks when hiring people, to prevent employing those with violent pasts?

- Do we avoid promoting, rotating or ignoring problematic, less competent or emotionally charged individuals who should not be in management level positions?

- Do we try keep employees' personal lives out of the workplace?

- Do we perform regular safety and security reviews of the premises?

- Have we installed CCTV cameras, safety glass, physical barriers that protect staff, adequate lighting in parking areas etc?

- Do we have an explicit and active policy against workplace violence?

The individual characteristics of violence-prone individuals

In Chapter 7 we elaborate on the social and environmental factors that may contribute to violence in the workplace. Here we will look at the individual characteristics of the violence-prone or destructive individual and how best to manage these. Of course, these are very general characteristics, but if someone is exhibiting a number of these characteristics it is fair to assume that there is some risk of possible violence.

Table 5.1: Identifying violence-prone individuals

Violence-prone people:
<ul><li>may be extremely impatient; hypersensitive and hyper-reactive to even the smallest issues</li><li>may be unreasonably self-righteous and judgmental; have rigid standards by which everyone else will fall short</li><li>are highly suspicious (even bordering on paranoid); often having an "it's me or it's them" attitude</li><li>have a need to control everything</li><li>believe that they are above the rules and, therefore, should be immune from consequences</li><li>intimidate others through threats, extremely aggressive behaviour or by constantly ridiculing or demeaning others</li><li>have sudden and dramatic mood swings</li><li>may constantly allow themselves to be bullied and picked on by others, until they reach a breaking point</li><li>have a history of violence, substance abuse or problems dealing with authority</li><li>are preoccupied with or own a large number of weapons</li><li>may have been involved in a recent traumatic event such as a physical altercation, domestic violence, crime</li><li>may have problems at work such as negative performance appraisal, threatened disciplinary action or retrenchment, or recent or frequent disputes with supervisors or co-workers</li></ul>

Best practices for managing violence-prone people at work

Given that workplace violence is not easily predictable, strategies to deal with this must be multifaceted. By noticing and addressing "at risk" or intimidating behaviour in the early stages, the threat may be minimized or hopefully even avoided, before it becomes dangerous or even life threatening. Sadly, after the fact in many tragic instances co-workers will say they were aware something was wrong but that they didn't want to interfere or get involved. They often hoped the problem would "just go away" or assumed that someone else would deal with it. The most common myth is "it can't happen here", sadly workplace violence can happen in any organisation, irrespective of size, type or location.

- Clear and regular communication should be promoted as it can help to clarify misunderstandings and defuse tensions, thus lowering the risk of workplace violence.

- Have clear rules about what kinds of behaviours and attitudes are acceptable or not in the organisation. Workplaces that turn a blind eye to offensive language, hostile verbal interactions, and bullying situations raise the risk of violent events.

- Creating awareness amongst managers and supervisors of which types of situations and behaviours indicate a risk of future violence has been demonstrated to be helpful.

- Make it easy to report threats of violence, possibly even anonymously. Aggressors thrive on their target's silence, having effective lines of communication can make it easier for the victim to report the problem.

- Interpersonal conflicts amongst staff should be dealt with quickly so they are not allowed to fester and get worse.

- Evidence indicates that most workplace violence is planned, not spontaneous or random, and happens after a series of escalating incidents. It is thus essential to take note of concerning comments and behaviours and take any warning signs seriously.

- Do not ignore the potentially violent person, rather if possible, try understand and assess what their grievances are.

- Do not make promises you can't keep, be honest about what you may be able to do to assist the employee, and what the limits of your influence may be.

- Aggression tends to breed aggression, and timidity and fear on the part of the manager may also embolden or provoke the violence prone employee, so try maintain a calm, but decisive and assertive manner when engaging with them.

- Document your concerns and escalate to senior management.

- Involve your company EWP to consult with both concerned management and the aggressor.

- Take appropriate precautions to prevent a violent situation at or after any disciplinary meetings with the employee.

- When an employee leaves the company make sure that access passes, keys, name badges are collected.

Substance use/misuse/abuse/addiction

As with all mental illnesses and behavioural disorders, there are lots of myths, misunderstandings and a huge amount of stigma plaguing the understanding, identification, and treatment of addiction. Firstly, addiction is not primarily about what you do or use, or how much you do it or use it, or whether it is legal or illegal to do it or use it. Addiction is all about what you will do to use or do it, how that need (or craving) impacts on your behaviour, thoughts and feelings, and how you behave and feel after you have used the substance or performed the behaviour.

There is a great deal of hypocrisy with regards to addiction. Many people who are profoundly dependent on legal medications such as tranquilizers, or over the counter medications such as codeine, would be horrified to be categorized alongside methamphetamine or heroin users. But they are all addicts and even an addiction to a legal substance, like alcohol, can be devastating.

Distinctions between substance use, abuse and dependence (or addiction) are confusing and hard to make. Many people can use substances, legal or illegal, recreationally or occasionally with minimal negative impact. The obvious example is of alcohol, widely used internationally, and with most people who drink having no problems as a result. In fact, light to moderate alcohol consumption, defined as up to one drink per day for women and up to two drinks per day for men, is even considered to have some health benefits in terms of cardiovascular functioning according to some large-scale studies.[15]

Importantly, however, the same studies do point out that moderate or heavy use of alcohol raises the risk of various cancers, obesity and of course alcoholism.

---

15 Mostofsky et al., 2016.

Addictions historically have been seen as a moral failing or deviance, or personal weakness, whereas current mainstream thinking is that addiction is the result of a number of factors including genetic or biological predisposition, poor early attachments, experiences of sustained stress or trauma, interpersonal disconnection, social pressure and a sense of purposelessness or a crisis of meaning. Currently addiction is often framed as a psychiatric disorder or an illness in an attempt to remove the moral stigma associated with alcohol or drug misuse.

Behavioural addictions

Behavioural addictions (sometimes called process addictions) are another controversial area. They are a type of addiction that involves a compulsion to engage in a rewarding non-substance-related behaviour despite significant negative consequences to the person's physical, mental, social or financial well-being. There is no agreed upon definition of these but clinically these are seen as "repeated behaviour leading to significant harm or distress. The behaviour is not reduced by the person and persists over a significant period of time. The harm or distress is of a functionally impairing nature".[16]

These conditions are sometimes referred to as impulse control disorders, and the type of excessive behaviours identified as being addictive include gambling, binge eating, sex, use of pornography, use of computers, playing video games, use of the internet, exercise, and shopping. Presently the only behavioural addiction that is classified as an official psychiatric condition is gambling addiction. Internet gaming addiction is included in DSM-5 as a condition for further study.

Self-medication

Self-medication is a term used to describe the self-soothing use of substances or engagement with behaviours in order to cope with untreated or undiagnosed mental distress, mental illnesses, and/or psychosocial trauma. According to this theory the person uses drugs or alcohol in order regulate their emotions and achieve psychological stability. Substance abuse and behavioural addictions such as gambling, online gaming or sex addiction serve a compensatory function by soothing the self from unmanageable, uncomfortable or highly distressing psychological states.

"... while much has been written about how the widespread availability of addictive drugs, their pleasure producing effects, and the human proclivity for self-destruction make addiction likely, our clinical experience convincingly demonstrates that the short-term ability of addictive substances to relieve, change or make more tolerable

---

16 Kardefelt-Winther et al., 2017.

the distress associated with the problems of dysregulated emotions, self-worth, relationships, and behaviours powerfully reinforces dependence on the substance".[17]

Who is at risk for addiction?

People who struggle to cope with strong feelings are at risk. A simple everyday version of this is when a person has to have a drink before going to a party in order to feel more relaxed or has a cigarette before an important work meeting in order to calm their nerves.

The American Society for Addiction Medicine[18] provides this useful general definition "Addiction is a primary, chronic disease of brain reward, motivation, memory and related circuitry... Addiction is characterized by inability to consistently abstain, impairment in behavioural control, craving, diminished recognition of significant problems with one's behaviours and interpersonal relationships, and a dysfunctional emotional response. Like other chronic diseases, addiction often involves cycles of relapse and remission. Without treatment or engagement in recovery activities, addiction is progressive and can result in disability or premature death."

Addiction and the workplace

Contrary to popular belief, most people struggling with a substance use disorder or behavioural addiction continue to hold down a job, so addiction is a significant issue for employers. Many employees with alcohol or other drug problems can continue to remain adequately functional at work, although this does not mean they are healthy or able to sustain this status long term. In fact, according to the USA National Survey on Drug Use and Health, more than 70% of individuals with alcohol or illicit drug use continue to maintain employment. In addition, over 26% of employed adults report substance abuse or addiction in their family. Over 42% of these employees felt their productivity suffer as a result.[19]

It is difficult to get accurate figures regarding the extent and impact of substance abuse or alcoholism on the South African workplace. There are lots of over the top, untrue claims – "SA has lost the war on drugs", read a headline in a national paper, the Times, on March 27 2013, The Anti-Drug Alliance South Africa report of 2012, which was widely disseminated and quoted, describes a "nation under siege" and states that it is "now a fact that 1 in 3 adults in South Africa uses drugs on a regular basis". There's

---

17 Khantzian & Albanese, 2008, p. 13.

18 American Society of Addiction Medicine, 2011.

19 SAMSHA, 2018.

lots of fake news out there.[20] Given such unreliable statistics it is almost impossible to accurately quantify the economic impact of substance abuse on South Africa. The South African Medical Journal published a study[21] claiming that the measurable cost of alcohol use alone was R37.9 billion in 2009. This included healthcare costs, lost productivity, the cost of road traffic accidents and the costs of responding to crime related to alcohol abuse.

The only nationally representative epidemiological survey of substance abuse and psychiatric disorders in South Africa, carried out between 2002 and 2004, suggested that 13% of the population has an alcohol or drug use problem, with alcohol accounting for the vast majority of cases.[22]

Statistics from the World Health Organisation in 2018 suggest that globally alcohol causes 5.3% of all deaths or 3 million deaths annually and accounts for 5.1% of disease burden.[23] Many of these deaths are the result of health conditions or injuries caused directly or indirectly by problem drinking. Harmful use of alcohol is also linked to a range of other mental and behavioural disorders, an increase in the incidence of infectious diseases such as TB and HIV/AIDS, and significant social and economic losses to individuals, communities and workplaces.

The problem of alcohol-related injuries is particularly alarming in South Africa, where alcohol consumption is increasing, injury rates are extremely high, and appropriate public health policies have not yet been implemented.[24] Based on data from the Road Traffic Management Corporation in 2010, the WHO[25] claimed that 58% of fatal road accidents in South Africa are attributable to alcohol use. Another marker of the extent of the alcohol abuse problem in South Africa is the prevalence of Foetal Alcohol Syndrome. Tragically we are the world leaders in this condition which is the result of alcohol consumption during pregnancy. FAS is incurable, but completely preventable.[26]

Drug abuse and addiction impact negatively on South African companies as a result of lowered productivity, increased absenteeism, physical injuries and accidents at work and fatalities.

---

20 Africacheck, 2013.
21 Matzopoulos, et al., 2013.
22 Pasche, & Myers, 2012.
23 WHO, 2020.
24 Seggie, 2012.
25 WHO, 2019.
26 Olivier et al., 2016.

Some further problems related to the impact of substance addiction at work include:

- Withdrawal symptoms affecting job performance

- Impaired alertness, focus, concentration and judgement while under the influence

- Impulsive behaviours which can be a source of risk to the company and other workers

- Illegal sales of drugs to co-workers and other illicit activities

- Arrests for drunk driving not only effect an employee, but they also take a toll on the employer. One of the most immediate consequences of a drunk driving conviction is the employee dealing with a driver's license suspension or revocation. For individuals who are required to drive in a professional capacity, this situation could be career ending.

- Drinking or using drug in work contexts (including workplace social functions) raises the real risks of inappropriate interpersonal behaviour including aggression, sexual harassment or assault.

And it is not just alcoholics who can generate problems in the workplace. Research shows most alcohol related work performance problems are associated with non-dependent drinkers who may occasionally drink too much and arrive at work with a hangover or get arrested for driving under the influence of alcohol or with a raised blood alcohol level.

During a 2005 South African National HIV Prevalence Survey, cannabis was ranked second to alcohol as the most commonly taken drug, used by approximately 2% of the population. Cocaine (used by 0.3% of the population), sedatives (0.3%), amphetamines (0.2%) and inhalants, hallucinogens and opiates (0.1% each) are less commonly used. These estimates probably significantly underestimate of the true prevalence of drug use, "especially as prevalence rates for drug use among South African adolescents are much higher".[27]

Because the majority of adults who use alcohol, cannabis, over the counter, prescription and illegal drugs or have behavioural addictions are employed, addiction is a significant issue for the workplace and not simply a public health concern. Companies and organisations cannot ignore the realities and repercussions of alcohol and other drugs in the workplace.

---

27 Pasche & Myers, 2012.

How to recognise or assess substance use/misuse/abuse/ addiction in the workplace

Initially it may be hard to identify the signs of addiction. But over time, the person who is in active addiction will demonstrate some of the following:

Table 5.2: Signs of active addiction

- Unpredictable behaviour and personality change
- Irritability or irrational behaviour, temper outbursts, paranoia
- Erratic work output
- Decreased productivity
- Increased errors, deterioration in quality of work
- Unexplained absences or lateness
- Presenteeism, distractibility, deterioration in focus and concentration, forgetfulness
- Poor self-care, loss of interest in hygiene
- People who use substances excessively over weekends may often miss work on a Monday or come late to work if they use substances the night before
- Smelling of alcohol
- Bloodshot eyes, cold sweaty palms, shaky hands
- Sleepiness, lethargy, lack of coordination, lack of focus
- Slurred speech, unsteady walk, clumsiness
- Uncharacteristic talkativeness, reduced inhibition, restlessness (typically associated with stimulant abuse)
- Frequent (excessive) use of the bathrooms
- Misjudging time
- Secretiveness
- Financial difficulties

None of these signs in isolation is enough to make a diagnosis of an addiction, but if you notice clusters of these symptoms in the context of a deterioration in work performance, or social relationships then it is worth taking further action to assess and if necessary intervene.

Typical treatments of substance use/ misuse/ abuse/ addiction

If the individual is heavily addicted to substances, they will need a medically supervised detoxification programme, usually in a hospital. In this regard, alcohol is one of the most dangerous substances to withdraw from following prolonged excessive use.

If a heavy drinker simply goes "cold turkey" and stops drinking without medical supervision, they run the risk if having seizures and even dying as a result. This is also true of people who have severe tranquilizer addictions. Following physical detox or withdrawal, some addicted people need a hospital admission or inpatient rehabilitation programme. These typically last from two weeks to six weeks. After this there are secondary care programmes (or extended inpatient care programmes) that can run for up to three months to assist the recovering addict to begin a more balanced, healthier lifestyle and establish healthier coping strategies. If an admission isn't possible for financial, family or work reasons, there are intensive outpatient programmes offered. Typically treatments include individual and group psychotherapy or counselling, attendance at support groups (such as Alcoholics or Narcotics Anonymous), family therapies and medication from a psychiatrist or GP. For additional information, refer back to Chapter 3 and the sections on treatments available.

Risks and challenges of substance abuse to the workplace

"Don't be a spoilsport – come for drinks after work with us"

"If you want to get ahead in this industry you are going to have to socialise with and entertain clients, and they expect you to drink with them"

"Everyone at the industry awards is going to party hard – if you want to join them do a line of coke in the bathroom during the dinner"

The workplace is the primary space in which employed people spend much of their time of time, so it is essential to understand substance use within the context of each organisation. Whether it's drinks with clients, downtime in the pub after work, partying at work conferences or off sites, or events to celebrate the end of the work day, week, month, financial year-end, awarding of bonuses, landing the big contract or just surviving till the year end function, each workplace will have rules and/or cultural norms, both overt and unspoken, that may facilitate, encourage or inhibit substance use.

From the self-medication hypothesis perspective, a stressful workplace may cause psychosocial distress which, in turn, leads to alcohol or illicit drug use, particularly for individuals with problems regulating negative emotions.

How the employer can assist the employee with an addiction

There is a widespread social belief, emanating from the 1980's American programmes that urged people to "just say no to drugs", that workplaces should be drugfree places, and implying that people who use substances or have an addiction should be punished and excluded from the mainstream. This is not only simplistic, unrealistic and counterproductive, but represents a complete misunderstanding of the nature of addiction.

Employers can educate themselves and employees on not only identifying the signs and symptoms of alcohol and drug use, but also the necessary steps to take when one suspects that a co-worker may need help.

Conclusion

Throughout this book we have stressed that every staff member has the right to a safe working environment. Bullying, harassment, and violence can result in physical or psychological harm or threat of harm to employees and cannot be tolerated. This chapter has proposed some ways of identifying the risks associated with these dysfunctional behaviours, and finding ways to address them. Substance abuse also presents the risk of harm to self or others in the workplace and must be addressed and managed.

Chapter 6

When bad things happen: difficult life experiences and the workplace

We spend 90,000 hours at work over a lifetime, almost a quarter of our entire lives, and we bring ourselves, and our inevitably messy lives to work. Work shapes our experience of ourselves, builds or erodes our self-esteem. People are not able to perfectly compartmentalise their experiences and feelings and not allow life crises to impact on their work, or difficulties at work to impact on their personal life. In this chapter we will look at some of the most common difficult life and work experiences that impact on the mental wellbeing of employees. We will cover:

- Stress and Burnout
- Trauma
- Loss and Bereavement
- Relationship challenges
- Loneliness and alienation
- Marginalisation of difference

Stress and Burnout

Stress means different things to different people and there are numerous definitions and views of stress in the literature. These can, however, be summarised into three main approaches: Stress as a stimulus; stress as a response; and stress as an interaction between the stimulus and the response.

Stress as a stimulus refers to stress as an environmental demand that places pressure on an individual. Examples of such demands include major life events such as death of a loved one or losing one's job or daily hassles such as traffic. There are numerous theories and measures of stress based on this approach but on its own this approach does not acknowledge the subjective nature of stress and it does not take individual differences into account.

Stress as a response refers to the way in which we respond to the demands made on us by the environment. The stress response approach typically addresses the negative consequences that occur when individuals are unable to adapt to the demands placed upon them. Hans Selye,[1] widely regarded as the father of stress research, identified the General Adaptation Syndrome (GAS) as a model of the stress response. Within this model Selye argues that initially people's responses to stress are adaptive and can be positive (Selye termed this 'eustress' or good stress). However, if the demand on the person continues, the organism moves into a state of distress which results in physical and emotional exhaustion. Since Selye's ground-breaking work in this area, numerous strains or consequences of stress have been identified, including psychological strains (e.g. anxiety and depression), physical strains (e.g. musculoskeletal disorders) and behavioural strains (e.g. substance abuse). The identification of stress responses has been a key factor driving research in this area, but this approach taken on its own also fails to incorporate the full stress cycle and again omits individual differences in stress responses.

The third approach to stress views stress as an interaction between person and environment with individual variables intervening between stimulus and response. The most comprehensive model associated with this approach is Lazarus and Folkman's[2] transactional model of stress and coping. The central premise of this model is that the experience of stress is a process. "Process means that the psychological state changes over time and across diverse encounters." Lazarus[3] argues that a transaction between the person and the environment is stressful only when it is evaluated by the person as a threat to their wellbeing. The term for this evaluation is appraisal. There

---

1   Selye, 1976.
2   Lazarus & Folkman, 1984.
3   Lazarus, 1995.

are two types of appraisal: Primary appraisal involves the individual's assessment of the degree of threat the situation or demand poses to their wellbeing. Secondary appraisal involves an assessment of one's coping resources and ability to meet the demand or manage the challenge. Coping mechanisms are activated after these appraisals and the ultimate outcome of the stressful transaction depends on these appraisals and the effectiveness of coping processes. These then feed back into the stress cycle.

Thus, the transactional model of stress places the main emphasis on individual variables and the dynamic, cyclical nature of stress. Based largely on the transactional model of stress, work stress can be defined as: "a mismatch between the demands and pressures on the person, on the one hand, and their knowledge and abilities, on the other. It challenges their ability to cope with work. This includes not only situations where the pressures of work exceed the worker's ability to cope but also where the worker's knowledge and abilities are not sufficiently utilised and that is a problem for them."[4]

Understanding the above approaches to stress is important because each approach utilises different terminology in relation to stress and, most importantly, each approach suggests a different solution. It is therefore necessary to clarify and utilise consistent definitions and terminology. Based on the approaches described above, we use the following terminology:

Definitions

Stressors

Stressors are the environmental stimuli or demands that have the potential to cause stress. In other words, stressors are challenges that place real or perceived demands on a person. One of the most effective ways of managing stress in the workplace, is by tackling the stress at its source i.e. reducing or eliminating stressors. Albeit that the subjective nature of stress means not everyone views stressors in the same way, the World Health Organisation (WHO) has managed to identify an evidence-based list of workplace factors that are typically perceived as stressors (see Table 6.1). Managing stress, based on this approach, involves undertaking a risk assessment and identifying which of these factors are present and eliminating or reducing them.

---

4   Leka, Griffiths & Cox, 2004, p.4.

Table 6.1: Psycho-social risk factors at work (Stressors)[5]

Job Content	• Monotonous, under-stimulating, meaningless tasks • Lack of variety • Unpleasant tasks • Aversive tasks
Workload and Work Pace	• Having too much or too little to do • Working under time pressures
Working Hours	• Strict and inflexible working schedules • Long and unsocial hours • Unpredictable working hours • Badly designed shift systems
Participation and Control	• Lack of participation in decision making • Lack of control (for example, over work methods, work pace, working hours and the work environment
Career Development, Status and Pay	• Job insecurity • Lack of promotion prospects • Under-promotion or over-promotion • Work of 'low social value' • Piece rate payments schemes • Unclear or unfair performance evaluation systems • Being over-skilled or under-skilled for the job
Role in the Organisation	• Unclear role • Conflicting roles within the same job • Responsibility for people • Continuously dealing with other people and their problems
Interpersonal Relationships	• Inadequate, inconsiderate or unsupportive supervision • Poor relationships with co-workers • Bullying, harassment and violence • Isolated or solitary work • No agreed procedures for dealing with problems or complaints
Organisational Culture	• Poor communication • Poor leadership • Lack of clarity about organisational objectives and structure
Home-Work Interface	• Conflicting demands of work and home • Lack of support for domestic problems at work • Lack of support for work problems at home

---

5   Leka, Griffiths & Cox, 2004.

Stress

Stress refers to the individual's attempts to adapt to the demands placed upon them. Where individuals are exposed to stressors, whether the workplace psycho-social risk factors mentioned above, or stressors emanating from other areas of their lives, they will attempt to utilise their resources to adapt to these risks. The more demands placed on their resources, the more pressure the individual will feel. Most healthy functioning individuals accept the presence of pressure as a natural part of work and may find it difficult to be motivated without some sense of pressure. However, when the pressure is unrelenting or exceeds the coping and other resources of the individual, strain becomes a likely outcome.

Individual differences

These refer to factors intrinsic to the individual that may influence the relationship between stressors, stress and strain. Such factors include genetic disposition; demographic characteristics; physical health and fitness; and personality. The key to stress appraisal, as identified in the transactional model, seems to lie within the ways in which coping strategies are used. In Chapter 9 we discuss Psychological Capital (PsyCap), a modifiable set of individual characteristics, relevant to the workplace, which can also play an important role in the stressor → stress; stress → strain relationship. When resources are depleted, whether they are individual or organisational, so that the person no longer feels that they can meet the demands placed on them, strain occurs.

Strains

Strains are the negative consequences that can result from stress. As mentioned previously strains can manifest in various ways: psychological strain, including low levels of mental wellbeing, anxiety and depression; physical strain, including physical ill health; and behavioural strains, including substance abuse. While all of these strains are of concern, burnout is a specific strain, firmly anchored within the workplace, discussed in more detail below.

Burnout

Patricia stood on the sidewalk looking great from a distance. She was trim, well-groomed and elegantly dressed in a knee length skirt and tailored jacket. As I got closer though, the cracks began to show. Her face was not just thin but gaunt and there were dark circles under eyes. She was tapping one of her high heels impatiently against the pavement and when she saw me she dispensed with any greetings and immediately began complaining – excessively irritated by her daughter who was running 5 minutes late to pick her up. I tried to use the opportunity to ask about a case I had been seeing which I thought would interest her. As I started speaking I saw that she was not listening and she interrupted quickly, continuing her litany of complaints. Her daughter arrived and, tight-lipped, she got into the car which then drove away – her face pale and unhappy against the window. I later found out that the irritability, tiredness, and complete lack of interest that she was exhibiting were symptoms of a severe burnout which nearly destroyed Patricia's burgeoning career. Fortunately, she sought help and with the assistance of a psychiatrist, time off and very supportive colleagues, she was able to return to work – somewhat subdued but able to contribute productively again to a profession she loved. The burnout had taken its toll however. Patricia's clients did not receive the care they deserved while she was suffering. Patricia's colleagues, having been highly supportive at the time, found themselves with lingering resentment and mistrust of Patricia. Some felt she had taken advantage of their goodwill in passing her work on to them. Others watched her closely, concerned that she would start 'letting them down again' and many, in retrospect, found her fragility annoying. They had worked under the same conditions but had not needed 'special treatment'. She should have 'manned up', 'put on her big girl panties' and 'sucked it up'. Even though Patricia received help and recovered sufficiently to return to work, the costs for her, the team in which she worked, and the organisation were high.

There is some debate in the literature over whether there is a distinction between burnout and depression, and indeed burnout may be treated with anti-depressants, as was the case with Patricia. While these debates are academically important, what is relevant from the perspective of this book, is that burnout is a form of workplace strain akin to depression. Burnout is a risk factor for the development of depression but the major distinguishing feature clinically is that burnout can be treated by removing the stress from the person or the person from the stress. Depression cannot simply be treated by removing stress.

The term 'burnout' itself is highly evocative – conjuring the image of a cigarette butt underfoot at the end of the day – used up and discarded. It refers to the sense of depletion that occurs when an individual operates for too long in a demanding environment which consistently exceeds their ability to respond effectively. It is typically characterised by three symptoms: 1. Exhaustion – a bone-wearying tiredness which has nothing to do with the physical demands being made on one's body but which saps one of all energy and enthusiasm. 2. Reduced personal accomplishment – a depletion in confidence and self-belief which makes us doubt our ability to achieve anything of value; and 3. Depersonalisation – a sense of disconnection and lack of concern for clients, patients and customers which can manifest itself in cynicism and callousness.[6]

---

6   Leiter & Maslach, 1988.

Given the demotivation and alienation associated with burnout, it is difficult to treat without professional intervention. Medication, psychotherapy, and mindfulness are some treatment modalities that have been proposed. Unfortunately, there is still very little research available that can guide practice in this area. There are, however, some things that organisations can do to prevent burnout:

1. Encourage self-care. Employers can support and encourage employees to take care of themselves. Many organisations now have some workplace health-promotion initiatives which encourage healthy lifestyles. Supporting employees in eating well and making time for exercise is not only about physical health. There is now clear evidence that exercise in particular has a positive effect on mental health and burnout.[7]

2. Ensure that employees take their statutory leave. Rest and recreation alone are not a cure for burnout but taking time out can give people the opportunity to disengage from work in an appropriate way and replenish some of their inner resources. Within the 'always on' economy it can be difficult to completely detach from work but an institutional culture which frowns on disturbing people on vacation and that makes contingency plans for when staff are off can help.

3. Support staff in developing and maintaining meaningful interpersonal relationships. One way of doing this is by building workplace teams in which all staff feel valued and included. Fun team-building activities can assist with this and there is a very interesting stream of research on the role of fun in the workplace (e.g. Georganta[8]). Where these activities contribute to a sense of inclusion in the team and provide relief from some of the daily hassles and pressures at work, they can be a helpful preventative measure. Similarly, a focus on work-life balance can assist in reducing the risk of burnout. Social support is a strong moderator of the relationship between stress and burnout.[9] Building relationships outside of work (familial and others) is perhaps one of the strongest weapons in our arsenal against burnout. In addition to the fact that social support is successful in preventing burnout, a major stressor for many people is the role of caregiver whether it be to children, elderly parents or extended family. An effective work-life policy and programme can assist in addressing both these issues.

---

7   Gerber et al., 2013; Naczenski, 2017.
8   Georganta, 2016.
9   Etzion, 1984.

Trauma

Whether it's the talk around the kettle in the tearoom or the sharing of various warnings via Facebook and WhatsApp groups, bad news – of illness, crime and trauma – spreads rapidly through workplaces and communities. And the sharing of this creates atmospheres of imminent threat and disaster and contributes to increased anxiety, low morale, feelings of helplessness and negativity. This negativity is amplified when people have direct encounters with traumatic experiences.

It is important when considering the impact of trauma on the workplace to acknowledge that South Africa is a very violent country, struggling to address the social, psychological and economic impact of our history of colonialism and apartheid. According to Statistics South Africa[10] an estimated total of more than 1,5 million crime incidents were experienced by 1,2 million households constituting 7.5% of all households in 2017/18. Looking at individual crimes, an estimated 3.7% of the population over 16 years old have been victims of crime. It is not surprising that Statistics SA found that South Africans have been feeling increasingly unsafe, are extremely concerned about trying to make their homes and possessions more secure and that the fear of crime prevents many people from doing ordinary things like going to open spaces, allowing children to play outside and walking around their neighbourhoods. In fact, the 2018 Victims of Crime survey found only 32% of the population say they feel safe to walk alone in their neighbourhoods after dark. Even more worryingly a 20-year research project that tracked 2,000 children born in Soweto in 1990 found that 99% experienced or witnessed violence and that 40% had multiple experiences of violence in their homes, schools and communities.[11]

With this as the daily reality of the population, this is also the daily reality of the South African workforce, and something that managers and employers need to acknowledge.

The 2009 Stress and Health Survey[12] into aspects of mental health across a cross-section of South African adults found that around 75% of the population reported exposure to a traumatic event. But of even greater concern is the fact that almost half of all respondents to that survey reported that they had experienced more than one traumatic event, and some people reported as many as seven events. In addition, traumatic events happening at work are not uncommon in South Africa. These include hijacking of company vehicles, cash in transit heists, robberies of offices, retail outlets and banks, mining accidents, assaults, sexual violence, homicides and suicides at work.

---

10 Statistics South Africa, 2018a.

11 Richter et al., 2018.

12 Herman et al., 2009.

South African trauma expert, Professor Gillian Eagle, comments that "if one considers indirect exposure in the sense of witnessing violent or traumatic events and hearing these recounted by work colleagues, friends, family, and members of close social networks, exposure to accounts of direct victimisation is very high, contributing to widespread awareness of potential threat in a range of environments".[13]

Trauma refers to extreme events that are life threatening, or potentially life threatening. These may be crime, accident or health related. They may have happened directly to the individual or to someone close to them. According to the DSM-5[14], traumas are experiences that expose the survivor to actual or threatened death, serious injury or sexual violence. The exposure can be direct, witnessed, or indirect (by hearing of a relative or close friend who has experienced an accidental or violent death.). Examples of traumas include:

- Criminal acts of violence or terrorism: being hijacked on the way home from work, being the victim of an armed robbery, sexual assault, domestic violence.

- Accidents: these may be at work or at home and include witnessing a colleague getting injured or killed while on the job, being involved in a car or taxi accident.

- Natural disasters such as flooding or earthquakes.

- A personal history of severe childhood neglect and/or physical, sexual and emotional abuse is often described by psychologists as complex or developmental trauma.

An event is more likely to be experienced as trauma when a person perceives the incident to be unexpected, outside of their control, something they were unprepared for, unpreventable and the result of intentional cruelty.

Professionals (such as first responders, emergency health workers, police, firefighters, soldiers, social workers, medical professionals) who experience repeated or extreme indirect exposure to traumatic events during the course of their work, may become traumatised in a "second hand" kind of way – this is called vicarious or secondary traumatisation.

The response to being involved in a trauma depends on many factors such as the severity and meaning of the event, and the pre-existing psychological health and resilience of the people involved in a trauma. Because by definition traumas are extreme events, the majority of people involved in traumatic situations will not simply be able to walk away without being affected in some way. Following traumas, people often have to manage

---

13 Eagle, 2015.
14 American Psychiatric Association, 2013.

a range of practical, physical and psychological consequences of the event. These may include significant amounts of bureaucratic administration, medical and legal issues, and the ongoing impact of any physical injuries, chronic pain or disability, and adjustment to significant life changes. Trauma survivors need time to cope with possible lifestyle modifications, adapt to their new realities and mourn their losses.

It is important to be aware that people who hold positions of authority and status in the workplace may find the sense of powerlessness related to a traumatic incident difficult to process and deal with. Some people, especially successful, action- and achievement-oriented individuals, may struggle to express (or even allow themselves to feel) feelings of distress and vulnerability. Be careful of assuming that just because a person has "got on with it" that they are coping psychologically. Denial and minimisation of difficulties are a real possibility.

Employers can play an important role in facilitating the physical and emotional recovery of employees, whether the traumatic event occurs in the workplace, at home or in the community. For an employee, recovery from a traumatic event and a return to work fitness is compromised if the trauma is in any way connected to their job.

Post-Traumatic Stress Disorder (PTSD) is a possible consequence of being exposed to trauma, but it is, in fact, fairly uncommon and does constitute a serious psychiatric condition that requires treatment by mental health professionals.

To diagnose PTSD the person must have been exposed to a life-threating or serious trauma. While experiencing a bereavement, losing a job or getting divorced may feel traumatic to most people, these are not the kind of traumas considered for the purpose of diagnosing PTSD. For a diagnosis to be made the individual must have been symptomatic for at least a month, and be impaired at work and at home. These are the clusters of symptoms to look out for:

1. Ongoing re-experiencing or intrusion in the form of intrusive thoughts, memories, nightmares about the event, flashbacks (feeling or acting as if the event is happening again) and emotional or physical reactions to reminders of the event.

2. Avoidance of memories, thoughts, feelings, people or situations connected to the trauma. For example, refusing to drive on a highway after being in a serious car accident.

3. Negative changes in the person's mood or thoughts including negative thoughts or beliefs about one's self or the world, a distorted sense of self-blame related to the event, a stuckness in severe emotions related to the trauma (e.g. horror, shame, sadness), significantly reduced interest in pre-trauma activities, and ongoing feelings of detachment, isolation or disconnection from other people.

4. Increased arousal behaviours including difficulty concentrating, sleep problems, irritability, more irritability or anger, hypervigilance (scanning the environment for any possible threats) and being easily startled. This set of symptoms is related to the ways that the traumatised brain remains "on edge," wary and watchful for future threats.

5. Dissociation – feeling disconnected from yourself (depersonalisation) or a sense that your surroundings are not real (derealisation).

Trauma may also cause generalised anxiety, depression, panic and even substance abuse. Often, however, the impact of trauma is more insidious. People who have been through a trauma may start withdrawing from social relationships, limit their usual activities, have less energy or hope, feel less confident, and become suspicious and untrusting. These more subtle consequences of trauma are damaging to society and workplaces.

PTSD, or any other psychological or social problem that results from exposure to a traumatic event in the workplace, is considered an injury at work. Employers are required by law to take all reasonable steps to protect employees from exposure to traumatic events. When such protection fails, an employer is obliged to ensure that the employee is given all the help necessary for a full recovery (see Appendix 3 for a comprehensive overview of aspects of South African labour law with specific reference to mental health by C. Gilliomee).

Helpful workplace responses to traumatised employees:

The best way to assist is to plan ahead. Companies should have emergency response plans in place in the event of trauma at work and protocols for response to traumas happening to employees outside of work too. With regard to the workplace, get staff involved in drawing up emergency plans in conjunction with company safety/security staff and employee wellbeing best practice advice. Consider the following types of possible risk events in workplace:

*   Fire, poisonous chemicals, dangerous machinery
*   Crime or terrorism
*   Clients who may pose a risk to employees
*   Staff working alone, in isolated areas or at night, or staff using public transport late at night or very early in the morning (especially shift workers).

Prepare and teach staff how to access emergency resources in line with your emergency response plan. Ensure staff know where emergency equipment is stored such as fire extinguishers, First Aid and CPR supplies. All staff should know who they can contact in an emergency and where they can find up-to-date contact details for fire brigade, ambulance and police services as well as the details of nearby medical facilities.

If a traumatic event happens in the workplace, these are some things you can do in the aftermath:

1. Stay calm and act rationally

2. Find out what is happening/has happened

3. Assess if there is any ongoing danger and ensure the immediate physical and psychological safety of all employees

4. Protect employees from shocking or gory scenes.

5. Communicate according to the lines of communication you have decided on in your emergency plan. Keep staff informed in concise, clear and transparent messages about what is happening.

6. If a dangerous situation is ongoing, communicate this directly and clearly to staff and keep updating information regularly. Frequent and honest communication reduces confusion, anxiety and minimises panic. Even if there is not much practical information to share, simply having management communicate regularly is reassuring to staff.

7. Empower managers and team leaders to assist their team members. Employee Wellbeing programmes can be a valuable resource for managers who want to increase their effectiveness in managing staff who have been exposed to a traumatic event.

8. If there has been a serious incident at work, call staff together and provide basic information and as much reassurance as is authentic and helpful. Validate their reactions to the event, and listen attentively to those who want to share their feelings about what has happened. Share your own reactions to the event but avoid clichés and empty promises such as "everything happens for a reason" or "it will be fine". If staff members are experiencing strong emotional reactions after the trauma such as severe anxiety, fear, shock or show signs of confusion, ask colleagues to help by sitting with them. Shock is an adaptive, protective mechanism which prevents individuals from being overwhelmed by the acute reactions they are experiencing as a result of the event. Remember that people usually recover within a short period of time. Allow staff to console and comfort one another, and to call family members or, if necessary and possible, to go home early.

9. Consult with HR or your EWP provider about counselling and support services available to assist employees after a trauma. In addition local resources may be found in Appendix 2.

What about trauma debriefing?

Voluntary counselling or trauma debriefing sessions for staff who have been affected by a trauma at work can be of benefit, but this is not usually something that should be done on the same day as the traumatic event. Immediately after a trauma what people need is practical support, information and psychological containment. This is sometimes referred to as emotional first aid and is an important way that management can show support to staff. The goal of emotional first aid is to give people permission to express their emotions during a time of acute distress and is the freely giving of support without becoming intrusive or demanding results or resolution. When administering emotional first aid, do not push the contact with the traumatised person. Take "no" for an answer. If you are concerned about the well-being of the individual, stay nearby, find them something to drink, or make some gesture of caring for their well-being. Formal group or individual debriefings are recommended, according to best practice research, after 48 to 72 hours.[15]

Returning to duty after a trauma in the workplace

The workplace may be the best place for employees to return to following a traumatic event as it provides co-workers with an opportunity to be in a familiar place with colleagues and talk about what happened with people they know who shared the experience and are trying to make sense of what happened.[16] This assists in re-establishing some sense of safety and predictability which may have been shattered by the trauma. Colleagues are a source of consolation, comfort and reassurance. It can feel uncomfortable to engage with a traumatised person on their return to work, but it is important for all concerned that the event is acknowledged, and that space is made to talk about what has happened.

- Arrange meetings if possible and wanted, with an EWP counsellor in order to start the grieving and healing process.

- Plan a workplace memorial ceremony if appropriate

- Arrange to visit injured/bereaved co-workers and meet with their families

- Arrange to attend colleagues' funerals

- With the permission of the family, perhaps prepare a statement or eulogy

---

15 Kaminer & Eagle, 2010.

16 Rick, Young & Guppy, 1999.

- Set up a relief fund for the families of those killed or injured.

- If some uninjured employees have not returned to work and the workplace is safe and operational, contact them to provide any new information, see how they are doing and advise them to return to work.[17] Should they require further emotional support, encourage them to contact your company's EWP or one of the resources listed in Appendix 2.

Bereavement

A person may experience loss as a result of retrenchment, financial crisis, physical illness or bereavement. All of these losses constitute a challenge to the sense of self of the person and are often experienced as traumatic. Unlike the traumas listed above, these do not meet the diagnostic criteria for clinical purposes, but their impact can be significant. Bereavement is the most common form of "normal" but difficult loss and can take the form of the death of an employee, which impacts on teams and leaves colleagues bereaved and possibly traumatised. More commonly this involves the death of an employee's loved one.

Bereavement is particularly significant in the workplace as bereaved staff members have to manage practical, cultural and religious obligations as well as dealing with sadness and grief. When grief and loss are not dealt with in healthy ways, these can create relational tensions in teams – feelings of resentment and awkwardness. Poorly processed bereavement can precipitate mental illness (such as complicated bereavement, depression and adjustment disorders.)

Bereavement is an intensely personal experience that has an impact on the employee's psychological, social, physical and spiritual functioning. Some people want to spend time with family or friends after a death while others welcome the distraction of being at work. Some people want to talk to colleagues about the deceased person while others prefer not to. It is helpful for managers and colleagues to take their cue from the employee. This means you will have to ask directly and respect the wishes and needs of the bereaved person.

Managers need to have a respectful, flexible and compassionate response in order to minimise the impact on the workplace and optimise healing for the bereaved in the period immediately after the death and in the longer term. Bereavement, like trauma, presents a special challenge to organisations as these cannot be planned for. They often happen unexpectedly and require that an employee takes time off to complete religious and cultural rituals, and deal with family responsibilities.

---

17 Ferguson & Towhey, 2001.

To be an effective manager in the South African context, you need to develop cross-cultural competencies and know (or be prepared to find out) the religious rituals and cultural taboos associated with death in your staff member's community. It can be damaging and offensive to make assumptions about what is "normal" and appropriate before educating yourself. Given South Africa's racially divided past, where ignorance of other's cultures was a given, this is a particularly sensitive area in the workspace.

Because of a societal anxiety around facing grief (our own and that of others) and talking about loss, colleagues and managers of the bereaved person often struggle to know how to offer appropriate support. Insisting employees return to work immediately after a significant bereavement and expecting them to resume full responsibilities prematurely, promotes "stifled grief" which may lead to longer-term psychological and work dysfunctionality.[18] Conversely, research in the UK suggests that thoughtful approaches by companies to bereaved staff members shows that the organisation values its employees, helps build commitment, reduces sickness absence, and assists in employee retention. Addressing loss and bereavement actively and compassionately builds trust between the bereaved person and their workplace and goes some way to developing a culture of caring and a stigma-free environment.[19]

Workplaces should have compassionate leave policies that allow employees who have recently experienced a bereavement to be given reasonable time to grieve and to begin to process the loss. These need to be in line with the minimum legal requirements. According to Section 27 of the Basic Conditions of Employment Act (BCEA) 1997, any employee who has worked for longer than four months with the same employer, and who is employed on more than four days per week with the same employer, qualifies for three days of family responsibility leave during each leave cycle. This is the type of leave that was called "special leave", or "paternity leave" or "compassionate leave" in the past. This covers birth, illness of a child and the death of the employee's spouse or life partner, parent, adopted parent, grandchild, grandparent, or brother or sister. The death of any other relative is not covered. According to the BCEA this absence can be treated as annual leave. But employers or companies can make exceptions and grant special leave or unpaid leave or annual leave as necessary. Employers are entitled to ask for reasonable proof of the death. 'Reasonable' is not defined but may include an obituary notice or copy of a death certificate. This can feel intrusive and unnecessarily bureaucratic. Asking a bereaved employee for proof of the death should be done with sensitivity and discretion.

---

18 Eyetsemitan, 1998.
19 Hall, Shucksmith & Russell, 2013.

Each organisation should develop its own specific bereavement protocol. This could cover who liaises and communicates with the bereaved employee, what information is shared with other staff members (this should definitely take into account the bereaved person/family's wishes), what form of condolence messages are sent to the family, who can or should attend funerals or memorial services and make bereavement visits.

Guidelines for helping the employee who is grieving

Many people feel uncomfortable and at a loss for words in the face of bereavement. We are not sure what to do or say. The best thing to do is to do something. Pretending nothing has happened or ignoring the bereaved person is the worst strategy to adopt. A simple acknowledgement of the loss and your sympathy is the best way to start. "I am sorry for your loss", "my condolences to you and your family". Keeping in touch with the bereaved employee and indicating that you are thinking of them while they are on family responsibility or compassionate leave is helpful. Make it clear that, as management, you will deal with, reallocate and manage their work responsibilities while they are away. If possible and appropriate, arrange for colleagues and representatives of the organisation to attend the funeral or visit the person at the house of mourning. If this is not possible consider sending a card, flowers, a donation or other culturally meaningful offering to the bereaved employee and their immediate family. Once the employee has returned to work, suggest that they find a supportive person to approach should they be having a difficult day or time, and encourage them to care for themselves. Remember, during the initial stages of the grief process, the bereaved person's emotions may shift quickly and alternate between the depths of sadness, outbursts of anger, and periods of seeming and acting absolutely ordinarily. While people grieve in different ways, and there are no rules for what constitutes "normal", there are some problematic expressions of loss, including those which are potentially harmful to the person or others. These include prolonged isolation, extended periods of poor self-care, self-harming and a turning to self-destructive behaviours such as substance misuse.

Mary's husband died suddenly of a stroke early in the morning. She was scheduled to be at a meeting to present a pitch to new clients on that same day. She called her manager who assured her that she didn't need to worry about work and asked her what she would like her colleagues to know regarding her husband's death. Over the course of the next few days, her line manager spoke with Mary telephonically and reassured her that her workload would be dealt with by other members of the team. The manager arranged for flowers and a condolence card on behalf of the organisation and agreed to speak with Mary after the funeral to discuss how she was doing and whether there was anything the company could do to offer support and make the return to work easier. Mary felt that her loss had been acknowledged and that she had been supported.

Relationship difficulties and family breakdown

"It's the quality of our relationships that determines the quality of our lives"[20]

With more than 50% of South African marriages ending in divorce within 14 years[21] and in line with international rates – in the USA, 43 - 46% of every marriage is likely to end in divorce,[22] – it is no surprise that a great number of employees are struggling with conflict and transition in their personal lives. Reasons for relationship difficulties are varied, but infidelity, domestic abuse and addictions all place relationships under strain. Couples are also vulnerable to conflicts over money, extended family (and it's not always the mom-in-law's fault), conflicting attitudes to religion or cultural practices. Social media has certainly complicated the relationship space, with increasing numbers of people having online affairs, sexting, and flirting or hooking up over social networks. While infidelity has existed since marriage was invented, in the era of social media, according to relationship guru Esther Perel, "it's never been easier to cheat, and it's never been more difficult to keep a secret."[23]

Perel also points out that intimate relationships in the modern era are made more intense and complex because of the expectation today that marriages (and other long-term committed relationships) are not simply economic arrangements:

"We have a romantic ideal in which we turn to one person to fulfil an endless list of needs: to be my greatest lover, my best friend, the best parent, my trusted confidant, my emotional companion, my intellectual equal. And I am it: I'm chosen, I'm unique, I'm indispensable, I'm irreplaceable, I'm the one. And infidelity tells me I'm not. It is the ultimate betrayal. Infidelity shatters the grand ambition of love. But if throughout history, infidelity has always been painful, today it is often traumatic, because it threatens our sense of self."[24]

Interpersonal stresses and relationship problems do not stay at home. They leak into the workplace. Because relationship crises and especially breakups often play out over extended periods of time, there is a consequent prolonged impact on all aspects of the individual's life. Whether it's because the employee is feeling unhappy, angry or anxious (or a mix of difficult emotions), relationship conflicts lead to increased distractibility, poor concentration and presenteeism, as well as late-coming and increased absences from work and consequent reduction in productivity, poorer decision making and an increase in physical illness and mental health problems.

---

20 Perel, 2018.
21 Statistics SA, 2018b.
22 Amato, 2010.
23 Perel, 2015, TED talk.
24 Ibid.

Distressed employees often require ongoing support, validation and advice from colleagues; this potentially decreases the productivity of those around them. In some cases, highly distressed employees may have a "breakdown" or an acute crisis which can be extremely disruptive (see Chapter 7 for more on acute mental health crises in the workplace.)

Unhappily married couples were almost four times more likely to have a partner abusing alcohol than in happily married couples. Those with alcohol problems skip or miss work 30% more than those without such problems.[25]

An employee who is separating from, or divorcing, their partner, is likely to need additional emotional and practical support from their environment. At the best of times divorce is complex, but if the proceedings involve conflict around access to children or financial settlements, the stress is enormously increased. Psychologists understand that divorce has the same impact on the individual's functioning as grief and trauma.

An extremely complex area to address is the cases in which employees are experiencing abuse in their relationships. This may take the form of physical, emotional, sexual or financial abuse. Broadly these behaviours fall into the category of intimate partner violence (IPV), a form of domestic abuse. While we have located this issue in a chapter about "normal" life difficulties, in no ways can abuse ever be considered normal. Tragically, IPV is a significant and common problem in South Africa. The Department of Social Development reported that between 2014 and May 2019 they received over 300 000 calls to their Gender-Based Violence call centre.[26] While the abuse of men is definitely underreported,[27] the majority of victims of IPV are women.

It is naïve to believe that domestic violence (IPV) is simply a private issue. It is a business issue and a significant public health issue. According to American estimates, domestic violence costs their economy $8 billion a year in lost productivity and healthcare costs alone.[28] Perpetrators of IPV and abuse have been known to try to block their victims from getting to work, make their victims late and constantly harass their victims during work hours, hounding them with calls, emails or texts or threatening to arrive at the victim's workplace. This creates high levels of stress and distraction in the workplace, compromising the victim's work performance. If the victim of IPV loses their job, they become increasingly vulnerable to the abuse as adequately reimbursed employment is a source of independence and freedom.

---

25 U.S. Department of Health and Human Services, 2004.

26 Vodacom, 2019.

27 Gass et al, 2011.

28 Presidential Memorandum, 2012.

According to the Employers against Domestic Violence project, a quarter of women between the ages of 18 – 65 have experienced some form of domestic violence. What is critical for workplaces is that 74% of employed battered women were harassed by their partner while at work. 71% of EAP providers surveyed have dealt with an employee being stalked at work by a current or former partner, and 83% have assisted an employee with a protection order. This resulted in notable tardiness and missed workdays.[29] These statistics do not capture the additional productivity costs likely to be associated with the psychological impact of dealing with trauma and abuse.

Alice de Jonge[30] points out that "(d)omestic violence is a serious issue, and the costs for business of failing to address the impacts of domestic violence in the workplace are high. New technologies and economic shifts towards services sector industries are fast dissolving the boundaries between the workplace and the home in many national labor markets." She argues that organisations are expected to meet higher standards of behaviour in fulfilling their responsibilities to employees and wider society. It is clear that IPV in South Africa is widespread and constitutes a social crisis.[31] There is a duty on all South Africans, and especially employers, to acknowledge the impact of this, and all forms of Gender Based Violence, including sexual harassment (which we address in Chapter 5) and be conscious of their responsibility in this regard.

In response to the high incidence of domestic violence in South Africa and its impact on the work-life of those affected, in March 2019, Vodacom announced a new policy to facilitate support of victims of gender-based violence or abuse. This includes an allowance for 10 days fully paid leave, access to the company's Employee Assistance Programme, and to a 24-hr Gender-Based Violence victim support and counselling call centre. The company said that they would be providing staff training and awareness on the issue and would be offering measures to those people who were concerned about their safety such as location or schedule changes and changing of work contact details (such as email addresses). This measure is one that can protect employees whose abusive partners may be stalking and threatening to harm them.

Guidelines for helping the employee who is having a relationship crisis

It is worth encouraging employees going through relationship crises to let their immediate managers or team leaders know. This does not mean that all the details or drama of the breakup need to be disclosed, but as this is a significant transition, and typically extremely disruptive and stressful, it makes sense to share this with the necessary people in the workplace. The key, as someone going through a breakup, is to communicate the practicalities to your manager: *"I am getting divorced/separated, I*

---

29 Olivier, 2014.

30 de Jonge, 2018.

31 Gass et al. 2011.

am committed to meeting my responsibilities as usual, but I may need some flexibility to go to lawyers' appointments etc."

If as a manager or colleague you are aware that someone is struggling with a relationship breakup, it is vital to offer support:

- Talk to them directly about what they are dealing with and what help they might need. A simple "how are you doing?" is a good opening line.

- Help them generate solutions that will assist in maintaining their productivity and keep up with their workload.

- Discourage office gossip.

- Be accommodating of the employee's changed circumstances. They may need some time off to attend legal appointments or counselling sessions and may need some flexibility while they juggle with changed child-care arrangements.

While EWP counselling services may assist with immediate stress and short-term crises, the individual who is dealing with the dissolution of a long-term relationship often needs ongoing longer-term support. In this regard individual psychotherapy and support groups through religious or community organisations are a valuable resource.

Loneliness and the workplace

The workplace: dozens or even hundreds of employees can work side by side for hours, spending more time with each other than with anyone else, yet they can feel lonely and disconnected from each other. Loneliness isn't just damaging to mental health; it can also lower job performance.

We have all read that sitting is the new smoking and sugar and/or fat/ and/or sleep deprivation will do us harm. But what many of us may not know is that loneliness has been identified as a major long-term health risk. Loneliness, which the classic poet Emily Dickinson (1861-1865, in *Complete Poems*, 1976)[32] described as "the Horror not to be surveyed", is being widely reported in the media as an epidemic. In January 2018 Britain appointed its first "minister for loneliness," who is charged with tackling what ex British Prime Minister Theresa May (in Walker[33]) called the "sad reality of modern life". It is also something more: a serious public health issue deserving of public funds and national attention. The global lockdowns and physical distancing mandated to try contain the spread of Covid-19 in 2020, and the rapid move to remote working, have exacerbated problems of social isolation and loneliness.[34]

---

32 Dickinson, 1976.

33 Walker, 2018.

34 Groarke et.al, 2020.

Loneliness can be understood as an unwanted experience of feeling socially disconnected and isolated. Loneliness is a subjective feeling, and the word "subjective" is critical here, meaning it is how I feel about it, whether my emotional or social needs are being met, and feeling unhappy when they're not met. The reason "subjective" is so important is that you could have the same two employees in exactly the same environment, but if they have different levels of need for closeness, then one could be lonely and the other may not.

Loneliness is not the same as aloneness or solitude or social isolation. Solitude can be positive, and some degree of solitude is healthy, allowing time and space for reflection, renewal, processing of difficult or challenging experiences, and development of independent thought and creativity.

Social isolation implies few social connections or interactions, whereas loneliness involves a discrepancy between one's desired and actual level of social connection. People can be socially isolated and not feel lonely; they simply prefer a more hermit-like existence. Likewise, people can feel lonely even when surrounded by lots of people, especially if those relationships are not emotionally rewarding.

Some of the most lonely individuals are married, live with others and are not clinically depressed. While being unmarried is a significant risk for loneliness, not all marriages are happy ones. It is essential to look at the quality of relationships, not simply their existence or quantity, when understanding loneliness.

Social media connections only appear to bring people closer, but in fact reported rates of loneliness in the USA have doubled since the 1980s. According to a 2010 survey by Wilson and Moulton, 40% of adults reported feeling lonely. Within work settings the number of people who feel they have a close confidante has dropped and 50% of CEOs surveyed stated that they felt lonely in their roles.

Loneliness has its roots in factors such as increased urbanisation and geographical mobility leading to people leaving their families and communities and moving to bigger towns and cities for work opportunities. Societies throughout the world have embraced a culture of individualism, and more people are living alone, and aging alone, than ever.

The gig economy means that workers are often vulnerable free agents, and when jobs disappear, things fall apart fast. Trade unions, civic associations, neighbourhood organisations, religious groups and other traditional sources of social solidarity are in steady decline. Increasingly, we all feel that we are on our own.

Impact of Loneliness

Loneliness is an aversive signal much like thirst, hunger or pain[35] and denying you feel lonely makes no more sense than denying you feel hunger. Yet the very word "lonely" carries negative connotations, signalling social weakness, or an inability to stand on one's own. Anxiety about loneliness is a common feature of modern societies. Freud[36] observed that "the first situation phobias of children are darkness and solitude". In many preliterate cultures, solitude was thought to be practically intolerable.

A series of studies published in the journal *Science* in 2014 found that many participants preferred to administer an electric shock to themselves rather than be left alone with their own thoughts for fifteen minutes. Wilson et.al.,[37] showed that people had difficulties in sitting alone in a room and concentrating on their thoughts. When the participants were given a button that administered an electric shock, scientists found that 67% of men and 25% of women couldn't stand loneliness and preferred to shock themselves so they could feel something at least.

Zhong and Leonardelli[38], showed that lonely people perceive things differently. Feeling lonely might make you feel colder and gravitate towards warmer food or drinks. As with everything else, these links are believed to be formed in us during infancy, when babies get to associate warmth with social interaction. Similarly, researchers found the brains of lonely people do not react when shown pictures of other people enjoying themselves.

Loneliness left untreated is not just psychically painful; it can also have serious medical consequences. It is only in the past several years that loneliness has been examined through a medical, rather than psychological or sociological, lens. Loneliness has been associated with a reduction in life span equivalent to smoking 15 cigarettes a day and is a greater health risk than obesity.[39] Epidemiological studies by Cacioppo et.al.[40] have linked loneliness and social isolation to raising levels of stress hormones and inflammation, which in turn can increase the risk of heart disease, cancer, depression, arthritis, Type 2 diabetes, dementia and even suicide attempts.

This research has shown that loneliness affects several key bodily functions, at least in part through overstimulation of the body's stress response. Chronic loneliness is

---

35 Cacioppo & Patrick, 2008.
36 Freud, 1920.
37 Wilson et al., 2014.
38 Zhong & Leonardelli, 2008.
39 Holt-Lunstad, Smith & Layton, 2010.
40 Cacioppo et.al., 2014.

associated with increased levels of cortisol, a major stress hormone, as well as higher vascular resistance, which can raise blood pressure and decrease blood flow to vital organs. This research has also shown that the danger signals activated in the brain by loneliness affect the production of white blood cells, thus impairing the immune system's ability to fight infections.

Impact of loneliness on the workplace

The impact of loneliness and weak social connections on the workplace may not be immediately apparent to employers. The phenomenon may be dismissed as an issue about the employee's personal life and therefore not relevant to an employer. Ozcelik and Barsade[41] in their 2012 study of work loneliness and employee performance found that lonely employees have reduced task performance, limited creativity and less efficient reasoning, decision making and poorer overall executive brain functioning. In addition, workplace loneliness is linked to an increased risk of clinical illnesses including heart disease and dementia, burnout, depression and anxiety. As such it poses a risk to the employee and employer and has significant human and economic costs. The mental and physical impacts of social isolation lead to higher costs for sick leave, medical aid claims and incapacity processes.

The former American Surgeon General Dr Vivek Murthy[42] comments that while workplaces and governments have invested time and money in antismoking and obesity reduction programmes, very little has been done to develop strategies around strengthening social connections. Margaret Heffernan[43] in her work on social capital highlights the positive value for organisations of building social connections at work. Positive social relationships minimise staff turnover and influence productivity positively (for an extension of our thinking on the importance of belonging and social interaction in a healthy organisation, see Chapter 8). Heffernan explains that making staff compete does not foster more productivity and innovation and that "if people are forced to compete, evidence shows they won't help each other, they won't share information and they won't share ideas that accelerate innovation... Highly creative, highly resilient organisations are characterised by helpfulness, by very tight social bonds and by the norms of social capital by which I mean generosity, reciprocity and trust. This creates an environment where it is safe to ask tough questions, safe to propose crazy ideas, safe to share insights and information. This is the sort of gold standard toward which today's most innovative and resilient organisations are headed."[44]

---

41 Ozcelik & Barsade, 2018.
42 Murthy, 2017.
43 Heffernan, 2015.
44 Heffernan, interviewed by Keogh, 2016.

Heffernan examines specific ways that companies encourage social connectedness and get teams to work together and bond. For example, some companies discourage eating meals or drinking coffee at desks. Instead, staff are encouraged to go to a common room, take a break, and talk to fellow employees while having their drink or snack. When Alex Pentland[45] studied the communication patterns at a call centre, he recommended that coffee breaks be rescheduled so that everyone in a team took a break at the same time. On the face of it, this didn't sound efficient, but providing that one opportunity to build social capital yielded the company $15 million in productivity gains, while employee satisfaction increased by up to 10 percent.[46]

Positive, collaborative relationships are crucial to our survival as a species as these are the mechanisms for human progress. One of the longest studies of adult life in history, the Harvard Study of Adult Development,[47] has tracked hundreds of people for over eighty years, and the findings are consistently that good relationships with family, friends, colleagues, and people in our communities, make for happy, healthy lives.

While a great deal needs to be done to strengthen social cohesion in a broader community and national sense, there is a need for the institutions where people spend much of their time to engage with this issue. This means that schools, families, social organisations and workplaces need to play their roles.

Companies have a great deal of leverage to effect change and build social connections that can resonate and impact positively at both the organisational and societal level. In the interests of nation building (a necessity for us all according to the preamble to the South African Constitution) companies that are able to facilitate healthy interpersonal and group functioning between employees, clients and strategic partners are in a position to inspire others and build hope for the future.

While there are no quick fixes to address the issues of social disconnection and loneliness, there are some strategies organisations can use to start tackling these problems:

- Evaluate what workplace rules and policies may be preventing meaningful connections in the first place. These may range from systems that encourage staff to compete with each other for salaries or bonuses to establishing rigid and unnatural privacy through the use of thick cubicle dividers that promote isolation.

---

45 Pentland, 2014.

46 Waber et al., 2010.

47 Waldinger, 2017.

- Employees without close or supportive relationships at work are more likely to feel disconnected from their jobs so it is worth considering the value of keeping work teams consistent over time, setting up workplace buddy systems, allowing social time over lunch, encouraging shared coffee breaks, promoting small company projects such as pavement vegetable gardens where people can go and pick weeds or water plants when they need a break.

- Some companies offer massage sessions or yoga classes to employees. This kind of activity can be positive for physical health and give people something to look forward to. In one of our large client companies, the monthly head or foot massage that can be booked through the wellness programme is a highlight for many employees. It feels like a treat, offers a sanctioned time out and it also offers, for lonely people, the physical touch that humans require in a manner appropriate for the office.

- In general actions are more meaningful than words. Instead of asking a co-worker if they want a coffee or tea, on occasion just bring them their favourite drink. Let them know if you thought of them while reading an interesting article or saw a project similar to something they have been working on. Introduce them to initiatives in the organisation that they may be interested in joining. Silent gestures are a very powerful way to communicate to someone that they matter.

- Be careful not to confuse introversion, or a preference for solitude for social isolation. If you are aware of a colleague who may be lonely tread carefully. It is not your role to interrogate them about their personal problems or to force them into group activities. Rather invite them to join you at the canteen table when you are eating lunch, or suggest they come along with you when a co-worker is throwing a celebration

- Making sure everyone feels included is a good way to boost positivity and initiate the process of bonding as a team. However one-off or once a year splashy team-building events are not typically the best way to establish or enhance social connectedness at work. Typically, once a year off-site events like ten-pin bowling, or drumming workshops or rock climbing, or even charity-based endeavours involving staff in building or renovating projects or even more elaborate set ups such as cooking competitions or hiring an orchestra to spend time with a management team to extend the metaphor of team work and harmony, are at best fun or interesting, and at worst patronising or embarrassing. In general, however, they are a fairly costly undertaking that yield little in the way of sustained social connection or enhanced performance.[48] True team building is an ongoing, daily process of small gestures and thoughtful attitudes.

---

48 Valdes-Dapena, 2018.

Mental health and marginalisation in the workplace

(contributed by Pierre Brouard, Clinical Psychologist)

What does it feel like for an employee to have a 'marginal' identity in a workplace? By marginal we mean being one of a few members of your particular group – for example, being black, a woman, gay or lesbian, transgender, working class, or living with a disability – in a working context which is dominated by people who have privilege because their identity is taken as the standard of 'acceptable', 'trustworthy' and 'competent'.

A brief review of the literature[49] suggests not only that inequality is still real in South Africa, and especially in corporate workplaces, but that marginalised individuals, often bringing with them histories of hurt and exclusion, struggle to feel welcome and quickly get the message that they need to assimilate into the dominant workplace culture to survive.

According to Naidoo,[50] an institution's culture develops throughout the history of the institution; it has its own way of conceptualising and doing things. Institutional culture, say Kuh & Whitt (in Naidoo[51]), is defined as "the collective, mutual shaping patterns of norms, values, practices, beliefs and assumptions that guide the behaviour of individuals and groups and provide a frame of reference within which to interpret the meaning of events and actions". This definition emphasises the intricacy of institutional culture and reveals the way that members of an institution "perceive and interpret the surrounding world, as well as the way they behave in it"[52] According to Nussbaum and Chang[53] "there are a set of unwritten rules that dictate what is considered to be the acceptable way; group members convey social expectations by how they act."

From this we can infer that the dominant workplace culture into which marginalised employees are expected to assimilate does not evolve with them but sets out (often hidden and subtle) rules and norms to which they must adjust. In addition, those who are 'other' in some way, or lack social power, often feel they are not trusted, need to go out of their way to prove themselves, or are treated in ways which are demeaning or patronising.

---

49 Steyn, 2013.
50 Naidoo, 2017.
51 Ibid.
52 Schein 2004, 36 in Naidoo, 2017.
53 Naidoo, 2017

Examples of this may include the following:

- Having one's qualifications and experience mistrusted and second guessed.

- Feeling a need to constantly prove oneself and work harder than others in the same job category.

- Being judged on the basis of one's identity rather than performance.

- Feeling that errors are attributed to one's identity characteristic or social category rather than a genuine mistake.

- Feeling that there is extra vigilance and scrutiny about one's performance.

- Being seen as representing every member of that social category, rather than as an individual with a complex personal history and story.

- Having the historical and current harms directed towards one's social category being trivialised or minimised.

- Not being paid the same as others in the same job category.

- Being, in some instances, seen as an 'affirmative' or 'equity' appointment and thus not naturally and normally able to perform according to the requirements of the job, by being 'artificially' promoted into the position. One experiences being a 'token'.

- Feeling that one has to adapt aspects of the self to assimilate into the dominant culture – this could include the way one dresses, speaks, eats, and manages personal challenges or even handles how one's name is pronounced or used.

- Having one's suggestions and proposals second guessed – or requiring that they are 'approved' by someone with a higher organisational status.

- Being told that one is 'over sensitive' when difficulties or experiences of being marginalised are raised.

- Being positioned as 'difficult' when one raises experiences of discrimination – and thus confirming bias about those of one's social category.

- Having important aspects of one's identity erased, commented on constantly, or repeatedly 'forgotten'.

- Not experiencing recognition for aspects of difference which challenge the default of gender and sexual norms – how partners, and relationship and family arrangements and responsibilities are recognised and understood.

- Assumptions being made around one's class position and therefore ability to engage in activities which require access to money, transport, smart phones and data.

- Where two persons share a marginal status, for example, both are black men, the heterosexual male (especially if he is married with children) will achieve greater acceptance and promotion than his gay counterpart.

- Many women will experience repeated and demeaning forms of sexual harassment which are not taken seriously or ineffectively handled.

- Finally, it is important to note that many of these fall into the category of 'microaggressions'. Microaggression is the term used for brief and commonplace daily verbal, behavioural, or environmental indignities, whether intentional or unintentional, that communicate hostile, derogatory, or negative prejudicial slights and insults toward any group.[54]

These experiences – and one individual can experience combinations of them – can have a significant effect on the mental wellbeing of an employee. They can lead to depression and anxiety, feelings of loneliness and isolation, and can also arouse hurt and anger. One can experience the minimisation of one's feelings and experiences as a form of "gas-lighting", where one begins to doubt one's own reality, leading to lowered self-esteem and feelings of resignation and helplessness.

Where one feels a need to compensate for a 'second-class' identity a person can be driven to working long hours and taking on too much, which are detrimental to physical and mental health over time. And then in some instances, where resources are limited, those with a marginal identity can compete with or even turn on each other, leading to feelings of shame and/or superiority, depending on who 'wins'.

What can be done to address marginalisation in the workplace?[55]

An organisation should commit to formal diversity and transformation work. Organisations would benefit from exploring the power of dominant identities, unpacking institutional culture, and developing interventions (including workshops) and policies which build awareness of privilege and prejudice and actively value diversity. This allows for new and more equitable and inclusive institutional cultures to evolve. In sum, the starting point is for there to be systemic and structural change, not just work at the person-to-person level.

Nevertheless, the nature of leadership is critical, and leaders need to have done their own 'work' on their biases and privilege.

---

54 Sue, 2010, p.xvi.

55 Some ideas are drawn from https://www.w24.co.za/Work/Jobs/ashwin-willemse-and-microaggressions-in-the-workplace-how-do-you-deal-with-it-20180521

It is important to think of ways in which a more diversity-friendly and inclusive workplace culture can be developed. This does not mean tinkering with the existing culture in a superficial way, but rather finding ways for a new culture to emerge which is the result of all contributions. This means compromise and some discomfort will have to be tolerated.

What can you do as an individual?

If an employee is in a situation where they are the target of ongoing microaggressions, and they cannot escalate the issue to HR or higher management, they may be forced to address the issue themselves. One way to do this without causing further problems is to call on the support of colleagues who are willing to stand up to the perpetrator. Another is to address the perpetrator directly, asking them 'Why do you think that?' Or asking them to explain what they are saying. This can lead to unconscious bias being exposed and addressed in a direct but non-threatening way. Individual employees can also, in some instances, seek alliances with other colleagues who may share the same 'lowered' identity status, forming associations or networks which allow for meetings to share experiences and to strategise and advocate for change.

What is the role of the manager or HR practitioner in working with these issues?

- Recognise your own biases, socialisation and prejudices about the 'other' and do your own work on this so that you offer a more open-minded service to the employee who consults you.

- Adopt an 'intersectionalities' approach to these issues: intersectionality theory argues that discrimination is often based on multiple, interacting, factors and can have a compound effect.[56] So marginalisation on the basis of race *and* gender, or sexuality *and* class, or disability *and* age, can be worse than on the basis of one factor alone. This allows you to focus not just on one obvious form of discrimination but allows you to see how discriminations interact.

- Where possible, work with groups *and* individuals. Prejudice is socially constructed and reinforced and the 'system' must change, not just individuals. Where you can have an impact on policy, so much the better. The development of codes of conduct, an examination of how holidays, and cultural and religious commitments are honoured, and input into hiring and firing systems are all recommended strategies.

- Workshops on diversity which go beyond the superficial essentialism of cultural 'differences and habits' can be useful.

---

56 Crenshaw, 1990.

- At the individual level, the marginalised employee needs affirmation, support and recognition for their story and experience, and victim blaming is unhelpful. Assertiveness and confidence training is useful, as well as encouraging the employee to seek out like-minded individuals in order to feel less alone. It may be helpful to offer mediation, or even a restorative justice option, to allow the harmed and harming persons to find healing and resolution.

- Linking employees with marginal identities to others in their same social category who are more senior, as a form of informal mentorship, can be useful, noting that just because two people share the same category does not mean they will have the same life experience or aspirations.

Conclusion

In this chapter we have highlighted some of the ordinarily occurring but extraordinarily difficult life situations that frequently impact employee mental health. Since our work lives extend throughout different life phases and stages, it is inevitable that some of the difficulties, losses and traumas we will all inevitably face by virtue of our humanness, will confront us in the workplace. It's difficult for others to know how to deal with each challenge sensitively and supportively and finding a balance between intrusiveness and a failure to acknowledge distress is complex. During the course of this chapter we have identified some strategic approaches to dealing with these issues. An informed and thoughtful workplace is well situated to be a source of support in the face of the challenges of modern living.

Chapter 7

Walking the High Wire: Strategies for managing a mental health crisis

Introduction

It is the stuff of nightmares. An employee weeping uncontrollably in your office. Or maybe even more frighteningly, raging at you, throwing things, threatening harm to you, or others, or themselves. While these situations are not everyday occurrences, they do present a significant enough risk factor in any workplace for managers, HR practitioners and Occupational Health and Safety workers to need to have some plans in place. Psychological "breakdowns" or "melt downs" can be frightening, even bizarre at times, and this means that they may be dismissed or ignored or not taken seriously. This chapter empowers managers to take meaningful and immediate action when faced with a crisis.

Managing a mental health crisis is like walking the high wire with no guarantee of a safety net below. The stakes are high, and it can feel like a single misstep can plunge you into disaster.

This chapter aims to provide that safety net. We focus on the options available to managers, Human Resources departments and wellbeing practitioners for intervening most effectively when having to deal with an employee with mental health issues. We suggest practical interventions for acute incidents, as well as strategies for longer-term mental health problems. These include how to talk to a psychotic employee; and a psychological first aid guide for helping people in the early stages of mental illness or in a mental health crisis. The legal issues and ethical implications of dealing

127

with mental health issues in the workplace will be addressed and resources related to workplace accommodations and further referrals will be provided.

This chapter will define what an acute mental health crisis is and the likely and less common presentations in the workplace. It is this chapter that gives the title to our book – *Beyond Tea and Tissues*. It is our experience that typically, managers and HR practitioners believe they have little else to offer people in crisis in the workplace beyond some basic comfort. While "tea and tissues" have their place, this is not enough. We will suggest strategies for intervention and suggest what NOT to do when someone is in crisis.

One step at a time: Acknowledge, Alert and Address

The first step is to **acknowledge** that this can happen in any workplace, to any level employee – from CEO to temporary cleaner. Acknowledging that mental illness or a crisis can happen to anyone, at any level, is difficult because it entails an acknowledgement of our own vulnerability. This can evoke shame and denial. For an excellent discussion of this issue see Brene Brown's book *Daring Greatly: How the Courage to Be Vulnerable Transforms the Way We Live, Love, Parent, and Lead.* [1] Many modern workplaces expect employees to cope, no matter the stressors. This contributes to a culture of denial and minimisation of difficulties. This is even more true when dealing with psychological difficulties because of ignorance about, and the stigmatisation of, mental illness.

Acknowledgement of a mental health crisis at work means that employers are unable to bury their heads in the sand and hope that the issue will somehow resolve itself without intervention. Acknowledgement means that organisations and the people working within them are **alerted** to deal with the issue directly. There are, of course, legal, financial and practical implications once management "knows" that an employee has psychological difficulties. While this need to **address** the issue is often daunting (and even inconvenient, or costly) it is an essential component of effective management.

Addressing a mental health crisis thoughtfully and compassionately contributes to developing both a healthy organisation and a healthier society. Chapter 8 looks directly at how psychologically healthy organisations function.

The way we deal with the most compromised, vulnerable and often difficult employees sends a potent message about our values and humanity to the rest of the workplace,

---

1   Brown, 2012.

and society at large. By acknowledging the reality that this can happen to anyone and that management can and will help when it does, we shift the focus from individual pathology to communal healing, and from individual problem to communal problem solving. This also assists with the important task of destigmatising mental illness or crisis.

Stigma, with its resultant feelings of shame and isolation, causes "needless suffering, potentially causing a person to deny symptoms, delay treatment and refrain from daily activities. ... Thus, stigma can interfere with prevention efforts, and examining and combating stigma is a public health priority".[2]

Acknowledgement of the complex interplay of individual susceptibility and environmental impact requires a nuanced and mature approach to mental health crises. Acknowledgment of physical illness or disability is generally easier. Physical health emergencies, with their attendant blood, physical distress and bodily manifestation are often clearer and less strange to the bystander. Instances of mental health crises, particularly of panic or anxiety, may be confused with physical emergencies such as heart attacks. Researchers in a large Canadian study found that about 25% of patients presenting with chest pains at a hospital emergency room in fact had panic disorder. They note that panic disorder "is a significantly distressful condition highly prevalent in ED chest pain patients that is rarely recognised by physicians. Nonrecognition may lead to mismanagement of a significant group of distressed patients."[3] If it is difficult for trained medical professionals to sometimes distinguish between a physical health emergency and a mental health crisis, it is of course even more difficult for untrained people to do so. In addition, many mental health crises present initially in subtle and confusing ways.

What is a mental health crisis?

A crisis is defined as a state of emotional turmoil. Emotional crises have four characteristics:

1. They are (or seem) sudden.

2. The "normal" method the individual has of coping with stress has failed.

3. They usually last from twenty-four to thirty-six hours and rarely for longer than six weeks.

---

2   Manderscheid et al., 2010, p.620.
3   Fleet, et al., 1996, p.375.

4. They have the potential to produce dangerous, self-destructive, or socially unacceptable behaviour.

A mental health crisis is typically an incident that starts abruptly or suddenly (although often there has been evidence of the person concerned showing symptoms or having difficulties for some time before) and has the potential to progress rapidly and requires urgent and immediate action. In everyday language it is a term for a situation in which a person is behaving unpredictably, or even bizarrely, showing emotional distress or anger, having mood swings (what professionals call a labile mood). There may be threats of self-harm, suicide or harm to others. Professionals may explain that the person is decompensating or regressing.

An acute mental crisis is considered an emergency that requires immediate attention.

Most events that look like an "out of the blue" crisis are in fact the final point of a long process of deteriorating psychological functioning. There are, however, occasions when an incident appears to happen suddenly and without warning. Most truly acute or sudden onset mental health crises are related to trauma, use or abuse of substances, loss and threats of loss.

A mental health crisis may be triggered by traumatic events

Triggering traumatic events may be related to crime, accidents or health. They may have happened directly to the individual or to someone close to them and are experiences that expose the survivor to actual or threatened death, serious injury or sexual violence. The exposure can be direct, witnessed, or indirect. An indirect exposure could be hearing of a relative or close friend who has experienced an accidental or violent death or repeated or extreme indirect exposure to qualifying events (also called vicarious trauma). There is a wide range of workers vulnerable to vicarious trauma including first responders, healthcare workers, and even call centre employees. The recent Covid19 pandemic has highlighted the impact of all direct and vicarious trauma on the range of people working across the frontline of the healthcare sector.[4]

A mental health crisis may be triggered by losses – real or threatened

The experience or threat of loss of some sort, whether at work or at home, is a common precipitator of acute crises. The conservation of resources theory[5] explains how and why a potential or real loss can be traumatic. The theory suggests that we each have a store of resources that contribute to our wellbeing in that they determine our ability

---

4   Muller, Stensland & van de Velde, 2020.

5   Hobfoll, Shirom, & Golembiewski, 2000.

to attain goals. When these resources are under threat, the individual experiences extreme levels of stress which may contribute to a mental health crisis.

Depending on the employee this may be a result of spillover of personal or relationship losses into the workplace or be a response to threats within the workplace. This is common in the face of disciplinary procedures, retrenchments, restructurings and the realities or fears of a loss of status, job, career opportunities or income.

A mental health crisis may be substance induced

Substance-induced crises may be the result of using illegal drugs such as crystal meth (tik), marijuana, and even steroids used for bodybuilding. They are also often a consequence of overuse or misuse of legal substances such as alcohol, prescription and over-the-counter pain killers containing codeine, tranquillisers (benzodiazepines such as Xanor or Urbanol, and sleeping tables such as Stilnox or Dormicum), and even stimulant medications. Less commonly, a person may have a negative psychological response to antihistamines, or the stimulant components (such as pseudoephedrine) in weight-loss and cold and flu medications. This may result in a transient psychosis and the person behaving bizarrely.[6]

These mental health emergencies may happen in otherwise healthy and well-functioning people. The diathesis–stress model attempts to explain a disorder as the result of an interaction between a predispositional vulnerability and a stress caused by life experiences. The model explores how biological or genetic traits (diatheses – from the Greek word for vulnerability or predisposition) interact with environmental influences (stressors) to produce psychiatric disorders such as depression, anxiety, or schizophrenia.[7]

We tend to expect that only people with pre-existing issues will respond in an extreme way to psychological threats, but this is a myth. All of us are vulnerable, depending on our personal histories and experiences, to a failure of coping. There are some people who are so vulnerable to trauma or loss that experiences that the majority of people can cope with, may trigger a collapse; and there are some traumas or stressors that are so severe (such as being kidnapped or raped) that most people would be expected to have a trauma response.

---

6   Caton, Samet & Hasin, 2000.
7   Ingram & Luxton, 2005.

What an acute serious mental health crisis looks like

A "quick and dirty" way of categorising mental health crises is into three clusters: mood/anxiety/stress-related problems (or being SAD), being out of touch with reality or psychotic (what nonmedical people may think of as MAD) and aggression, criminality or volatility (what we all recognise as BAD.)

SAD

We often hear and use the term *nervous breakdown* to describe someone who has stopped functioning due to mental distress. While this is not an official term, it does capture the experience of falling apart and not coping that is a feature of severe depression and anxiety.

Vishnu, a polite and quiet, and historically reliable employee was absent from work and had not let his team leader know. He had recently been taking sick leave, with increasing complaints of fatigue and headaches. Nobody could reach him and he did not answer his phone. His concerned manager contacted his family, who found that he was at home and had not left his bed for days. He was unkempt, weeping and threatening suicide as he felt his personal problems were insurmountable. The psychiatrist who treated him diagnosed depression and with treatment and support from his colleagues, he was able to return to work.

Someone who is struggling with a mood or anxiety disorder and has reached a particularly low point in their illness, severe burnout or has just experienced a trauma or received shocking news may present in one of the following ways:

1. They may faint or physically collapse, be unable stand, or move or shake uncontrollably.

2. They may be extremely tearful, weep or sob inconsolably or seem numbed and almost paralysed or frozen.

3. People having panic attacks often feel that there is something physically wrong with them. They feel faint, dizzy, have chest pains, and cannot breathe.

4. It is likely the person is unable to think clearly, they are easily distracted or exclusively focused on their internal distress or concerns. It can be difficult to communicate with someone who is in a state of psychological crisis.

5. Suicidality and a desire to harm oneself are worrying features of a low or hopeless mood.

MAD

The feeling of being out of control in response to a very difficult experience or extreme trauma, as part of the process of a severe psychiatric illness or as the result of a medical condition or acute drug or alcohol intoxication may manifest in disorganised or "crazy" seeming behaviour. Someone in this state may appear out of control, their speech may be fast, their ideas bizarre or jumbled or paranoid and their behaviour erratic or unpredictable. This may be because they are out of touch with reality (psychotic), paranoid, and suffering from delusions or hallucinations.

Brad, a senior accountant with an important role in client relationships, abruptly fled from the board room as he was being introduced to new clients. His colleague followed him out and found him crouched underneath the reception desk, rocking in a foetal position. Wide-eyed and gasping, Brad insisted that there was no way he was going to shake hands with someone whose fingers were snakes. Brad's real terror was hard to witness and nobody was able to reason with him or calm him down. His colleagues called an ambulance, and he was hospitalised. It emerged that he had a benign brain tumour and once this was treated, his psychosis disappeared.

BAD

In this state people behave in aggressive, threatening, malicious or destructive ways. More frequently bad (or antisocial) behaviour does not present as a crisis but is part of a longer standing pattern of personality style or even a personality disorder (see Chapters 5 and 6). But under severe stress someone who has difficulty controlling their angry and destructive impulses may be extremely frightening to those around them, and in fact may pose a significant threat to the safety of others and the workplace. The out-of-control angry person may be ranting, threatening others with harm or violence, or physically lashing out. "I'll get you," "I'm going to kill you," "You'll be sorry," or "You'd better watch out" are all threats and should be taken seriously. Behaviours can also include throwing things around, destruction of property, shaking fists, rude gestures or shoving other people. The anger and hostility may be a result of something difficult happening at home, or at work. Typically, these incidents are related to impending, feared or actual job loss, feelings of humiliation (such as after a disciplinary process or negative performance appraisal), or as the result of substance intoxication or withdrawal.

Nobody expects to get involved in a violent event at work, but knowing how to respond if a violent incident happens is an essential survival skill. This is especially important since most critical incidents end before security or emergency personnel can get there. This means that employees must be able to assume some responsibility for their own safety. The first step towards survival during a life-threatening incident begins with the ability to manage fears and emotions. Panic and fear can result in the inability to think clearly and respond appropriately during a time of unmanageable stress. While violent explosions don't happen very often in the workplace, these low-frequency tragedies are high consequence events that need to be taken seriously.

We have mentioned that although mental health crises may seem unexpected and appear to have developed out of the blue, they often are the endpoint of a long and gradual process of struggle, distress, irritability and deteriorating function. It is often only in retrospect that we can see that there has been evidence accumulating of the individual building up to a crisis. It is essential that management and colleagues stay **alert** to signs of crisis or impending mental health problem.

Early warning signs that may alert you that a person is having mental health difficulties

Increased absences, slipping standards with regard to output, conflicts with colleagues, increased complaints and deteriorating self-care are all warning signs that the individual is experiencing mental health difficulties. This insidious onset of difficulties makes mental illness harder to detect than you may think. What an employer needs to be aware of is a process of change. To know if there has been a change, a manager needs to be aware of the employee's usual behaviour or output or relational style. This highlights the importance of a consistent, emotionally present, vigilant management and the value of meaningful relationship building between staff, and between staff and management.

Specific examples of warning signs include a persistent change in attitude, energy level, output, work or personal habits. Concerns should be raised when employees become accident prone, start making uncharacteristic mistakes and have inexplicable trouble meeting performance targets. It is often noticed that individuals have become more emotional, are easily upset, have outbursts, and that relationship or home issues are starting to become apparent during work hours. This might take the form of excessive phone calls or texting that are clearly not work related, that may seem to cause distress and may disturb colleagues. Increased absences, late coming and repeated physical illness may all indicate deteriorating psychological health.

Obstacles to immediate action

When someone is showing signs of distress or deterioration, and even by the time someone is in crisis, we often fail to act decisively and helpfully. This is not because we are uncaring or incompetent, but for a number of intersecting reasons:

1. We do not know what to do.

2. We are afraid of making a situation worse. We want to do the right thing, but we are not sure what this would be.

3. We are afraid of the legal and corporate consequences of acting.

4. Our own issues and anxieties are triggered.

5. We do not want to get involved with the messiness or stress of dealing with a person in crisis.

6. We do not want to acknowledge the problem, so we may minimise the situation in our own minds and delay taking action. We hope that the person will get better on their own or that the situation will resolve itself magically. This denial is always unhelpful as experience and evidence show us over and over again that mental health problems unaddressed will likely get worse.

7. Tea and tissues approach: sometimes offering simplistic and superficial solutions is all we can think of or all we feel equipped to do. If we do not tackle mental health crises actively and cannot acknowledge and address the legal, psychological, and interpersonal complexity of these situations, we are in fact increasing the risk to the employee, the workplace and even society at large.

What to do if you think something is wrong

Address the issues early on:

If you have been alert and noticed changes in a staff member's behaviour or psychological functioning (or if another employee has raised this with you), you have the opportunity to raise the issue proactively and possibly pre-empt a crisis. This is a wonderful chance to prevent harm, and do good by acknowledging the problem, alerting the employee and the organisation to this, and **addressing** the issue actively and promptly.

Even if this appears to be a noncritical incident such as habitual late coming, or a manager's awareness that a worker is frequently off sick or has become less productive, or staff have complained that a colleague is creating difficulties in a team, it is important not to delay intervening.

1. Prepare

The first step is to gather basic information about the nature and extent of the concerns. Consult discreetly with any people who may have raised concerns. Be careful not to be seen to be gossiping behind anyone's back. This may increase the anxiety or paranoia of a depressed or psychiatrically ill person.

2. Engage

2.1. If you are concerned about someone, approach the person in a caring and non-judgmental manner to discuss your concerns. The person you are trying to help might not trust you or might be afraid of being perceived as "different", and therefore may not be open with you. You should approach the person privately about their experiences in a place that is free of distractions.

2.2. Set up meetings as soon as practical with the individual at risk and be prepared to spend some time with the staff member involved.

2.3. Be as direct and truthful as possible about the concerns that have been raised.

2.4. Clarify the reason for the meeting and what you hope to get from the meeting.

2.5. Explain that the meeting is voluntary and is not related to the employee being in trouble, or being disciplined, but that you hope that the meeting will allow you (and the company) to understand and assist the employee who appears to be having some difficulties.

If you are able to keep the engagement with the employee as open and non-threatening and non-punitive as possible this will assist the individual to start to trust that you have their best interests at heart and are not simply concerned about punishing them and protecting the company's bottom line.

3. Explore

It is important to establish the nature and extent of the difficulties that the individual is dealing with. While diagnosis is certainly something best left to professionals, it will help with effective interventions if you can start to get a sense of how serious the situation is.

Basic listening and questioning skills can be invaluable in this regard.

3.1. Adopt an approach that is respectful, boundaried, compassionate and interested and do not make assumptions about the person or the problem. Refrain from judgmental comments or the use of clichés such as "calm down" to reassure or pacify the person. Also refrain from catastrophising or over-dramatising the issues.

3.2. You should state the specific behaviours you are concerned about and should not speculate about the person's diagnosis.

3.3. Ask open-ended questions such as "what do you think would help you feel better?" Ask the person if they have felt this way before and if so, what they have done in the past that has been helpful. Try to find out what type of assistance they believe will help them.

3.4. Always ask for clarification when something is unclear: "You said that this keeps happening to you. What do you mean by that?"

3.5. After you have asked a question, listen without interrupting and wait for a natural break in the conversation before resuming the conversation. However, do not leave long silences as these can increase the anxiety of the employee.

3.6. Explore alternative understandings of the problem. Do not dismiss the employee's explanation, even if it you feel it is defensive, evasive, or inaccurate. Also do not minimise their feelings, even if you feel they are overreacting or being over dramatic. It is not helpful to take a judgmental stance at this point. Rather acknowledge what they have said and try to offer your alternate explanation as another possible view. It is not important at this stage to get perfect agreement in order to move forward.

3.7. Explore options for moving forward and evaluate the feasibility and practicality of these. Suggest possible strategies for moving forward but keep checking in with the employee as to what they believe is possible and what they feel may assist them.

3.8. Do not promise things to the employee unless you can deliver. Broken promises and unfulfilled reassurances can increase a distressed employee's sense of helplessness, hopelessness, resentment or cynicism and is likely to result in a worsening of the working relationships between the employee and the organisation.

4.   Address – Do Something

In order to move forward it is important to encourage the person to search for a satisfactory course of action. It is always helpful to be able to provide realistic, practical information on the relevant professional and community support available. Your HR, employee wellbeing or occupational health partners can be a great resource, as can Google! Appendix 2 has a list of some current sources of support in South Africa.

Discuss the immediate steps the employee is prepared to take to get help and clarify what you are able to do as well. This means looking at what they can do straight after the meeting: *"when you get back to your desk, you will call your GP to make an appointment to see her as soon as possible"*; *"I will email you the contact details for our Employee Wellbeing partner right away so you can call to speak to a counsellor"*; *"I will inform your team leader that you will need some time off this afternoon to go and see your doctor/psychologist."* If the person decides to seek professional help, you should make sure they are supported both emotionally and practically in accessing services.

Try to determine whether the person has a supportive social network and if they do, encourage them to utilise these supports.

What if the person does not want help?

The employee may refuse to seek help even if they realise they are unwell. Their confusion and fear about what is happening to them may lead them to deny anything is wrong. In this case you should encourage them to talk to someone they trust. It is also possible a person may refuse to seek help because they lack insight into their illness. They might actively resist your attempts to encourage them to seek help. In either case, your course of action should depend on the type and severity of the person's symptoms.

Under South African law a person with a mental illness cannot be forced into treatment, unless they meet the criteria for involuntary committal procedures (for more information on involuntary committal see SA Department of Health policy guidelines on 72-hour assessment of involuntary mental health care users, 2011). If they are not at risk of harming themselves or others, you should remain patient, as people experiencing psychological or psychiatric disturbances often need time to develop insight regarding their illness. Never threaten the person with forced hospitalisation or involuntary treatment. Instead, remain friendly and open to the possibility that they may want your help in the future.

5.   **Document and follow up**

    5.1. Document the meeting and decisions made.

    5.2. Let the individual know you will follow up with them at an agreed upon time and seek agreement from them on this.

    5.3. Make sure you do follow up (here a reminder or calendar App can be a good friend to the busy manager.)

Hopefully, by following the above steps, you can prevent any exacerbation of the problem and a consequent mental health crisis or breakdown.

The individual's psychological functioning may still deteriorate despite your best efforts. While it is frustrating to know that a breakdown is not always preventable, this is a useful and humbling reminder that we are not omnipotent and that human beings are complex and challenging to deal with.

What to do in an EMERGENCY SITUATION

Joy is an HR manager and has just had an intense meeting about a high-pressure project with her team. She walks out of the room last and hears sobbing coming from the corridor. She sees a junior member of her team weeping uncontrollably while talking on her cell phone. Joy stayed a discreet distance away until the call was over and then approached James and asked if he's ok. Joy was apprehensive about asking this as she felt unsure what to do if he said he wasn't OK. When he replied, "I can't do this anymore, I can't go on", Joy's heart sank. She was extremely worried about James's mental state and did not know what to do next.

We have developed the Acronym **AS IF** as a reminder of what to do if you are ever in an equivalent situation:

    A = Attend to
    S = Safety
    I = Inform (alert)
    F = Follow up

Attend

It's important in a crisis to attend to the problem as soon as possible. That does not mean acting without thinking but initiating some kind of intervention as soon as possible. This is where it is important that as an organisation, more is offered than simply tea and tissues.

Attending means asking for as much information about the employee and the triggering event as is *immediately* available. See yourself as providing emotional first aid – the freely giving of support without becoming invasive. The first stage of emotional first aid is through making a connection with the employee in crisis. When administering emotional first aid, do not push the conversation with the person. Take "no" for an answer. If you are concerned about the well-being of the person or others, stay nearby, find them something to drink, or make some practical gesture of caring for their well-being.

Try to keep things private in order to maintain the dignity and confidentiality of the employee. Ask the person to come with you to a private space, or if the person is too distressed to move, ask fellow workers who may be in the vicinity to give you some privacy while you address the immediate crisis behaviour. Use a calm, even tone of voice and keep your body language open and unthreatening and limit your movements. Do not touch the person without their permission. If someone is highly emotional, it is useful to speak slightly slower and with a lower tone of voice than usual. Speaking really fast, loud or in a high-pitched way is associated with feelings of panic and drama and will not help defuse the situation.

Keep your language clear and your comments brief. For example, *"It must really hurt"*; *"You must feel very bad."* Ask clear, simple questions like *"Can I help?"* and provide basic and easily manageable suggestions: *"Let's have a glass of water while we sort this out"*; *"It's okay to go and see the nurse"; "I know that our EWP service will be able to help you."*

After you say something, be patient and allow plenty of time for the person to process the information and respond. Tailor your approach and interaction to the way the person is behaving. For example if the person is suspicious and is avoiding eye contact, be sensitive to this and give them the space they need. Importantly, be honest when interacting with the person and never make any promises you cannot keep.

Skills that will assist you in engaging with a tearful, anxious, depressed or hopeless employee:

Make sure you are meeting in a private, comfortable space that feels safe. It is often more helpful to sit alongside or near the distressed person, rather than sitting with a desk between you. Keep your non-verbal communication (body language) open, relaxed and non-threatening and make eye contact with the person.

Do not panic if it seems that the person is unable to stop crying or sobbing hysterically. Be patient with the person, the sobbing will stop when the person is exhausted. Make the person as comfortable as possible and consider covering them with a blanket.

In rare instances, the distressed individual may become self-destructive by running around the room and crashing into objects. You may have to encourage the person to use words rather than actions. Try to distract them in order to contain the physical expression of distress. Try restraining them without harming or trapping them. Do not leave the person alone but get additional help as quickly as possible.

Skills that will assist you in engaging with a psychotic, paranoid or confused person:

In these situations, your focus should be on containing the person and encouraging them to get help from professionals rather than on problem solving or performance managing. Avoid confronting the person and do not criticise or blame them. Understand that these are symptoms of an illness and do not take them personally.

Treat the person with respect. You should try to empathise with how the person feels about their beliefs and experiences without stating any judgments about the content of those beliefs and experiences. The person may be behaving and talking differently due to psychotic symptoms. They may also find it difficult to distinguish between what is real and what is not. It is important to understand that the delusions and hallucinations are very real to the person having them. You should not dismiss, minimise or argue with the person about their delusions or hallucinations. Similarly, do not act alarmed, horrified or embarrassed by the person's delusions or hallucinations. Never laugh at what the individual is saying or doing.

The psychotic person may be frightened by their own thoughts and feelings, so be very sensitive so as not to escalate their anxiety and do not encourage or inflame the person's paranoia. Do not make patronising, dismissive statements such as *"don't be so silly"* or use sarcasm: *"of course you are so important that's why the CIA are bugging your phone".*

People experiencing symptoms of psychosis are often unable to think clearly. Respond to disorganised speech by communicating in an uncomplicated and direct way, and repeat things if necessary. If the person is showing a limited range of feelings, you should be aware that it does not mean that the person is not feeling anything. Likewise, you should not assume the person cannot understand what you are saying, even if their response is limited.

If the person is unwilling to speak with you, do not try to force them to talk about their experiences. Rather, let them know you will be available if they would like to talk in the future. Ask the person about what will help them to feel safe and in control and reassure them you are there to help and support them, and you want to keep them safe.

If possible, offer the person choices of how you can help them so they feel they have some control. Convey a message of hope by assuring them help is available and things can get better.

Safety

It is imperative to consider the immediate safety of all people involved in the situation – the distressed employee, colleagues, yourself, as well as the longer-term safety of all involved. Where possible stay with the staff member until the crisis resolves or ask a colleague to stay with them even if you only have to leave for a short time.

Skills that will assist you in engaging with an angry, aggressive or threatening employee:

Consider how likely it is that the threatening person will follow through on their words and how immediate the threat is. There is a huge difference between a threatening email and a man standing in the office waving a knife.

If the threat is immediate, quickly and calmly look for potential safe spaces and escape routes. If the threat is more undefined and abstract, then try to get a clearer picture of what exactly is going on. Make sure that you understand what the actual risk is.

Seating arrangements: If the employee is very angry and aggressive make sure that you are seated nearer the door and have unencumbered access to the door. If you are at all unsure of your own safety, keep the door open and ask for someone (perhaps security) to be aware of your meeting and to station themselves outside the door.

Body Language: keep your tone calm, confident and steady. Do not raise your voice to match the raised voice of the threatening person.

If there is any risk of violence however, it is important to stay in a public space or at least be in a space that you are able to leave unimpeded. Make sure that your colleagues or security are informed as to where you are and what you are doing. It is essential to ensure your own safety. If necessary, ask security to wait outside the meeting space, or have a trusted colleague join you in the meeting.

Focus on shifting the person in crisis from a state of high negative emotional arousal (fear, anger, distress, helplessness) to a more emotionally regulated state where they are then able to think, communicate and plan ahead more clearly and more rationally. Use your attending skills to help the person be more contained and calmer, both physically and emotionally, and work on building psychological safety and relational trust with the person.

If someone is threatening suicide or violence, do not simply send them home from work alone, however tempting it may feel to "get rid" of the problem. It is sometimes a good idea to call your security company or the police if the individual is presenting an immediate danger to themself or others. A mental health crisis response team (paramedics or emergency medical services) may be able to provide a less threatening form of intervention if no significant danger of violence to others exists. See Appendix 2 for a list of local resources.

Inform

Tell your own colleagues or manager as soon as possible of the situation and what you plan to do. If possible, and appropriate, inform family or significant others of the person in crisis about the situation so they can assist – possibly fetch the person from work, follow up with healthcare providers or at least know what they might expect when the person comes home from work.

Keep senior management and Human Resources in the loop about what has happened. Document the event and what you have recommended and how you intervened and share this information with the necessary channels.

As a manager or HR practitioner please keep in mind the ethical and legal obligation to maintain confidentiality regarding the individual. South African law guarantees everyone, within reason, the right to privacy. This means that if an employee or colleague discloses information about their mental health, this needs to be kept confidential. Those who unlawfully violate this constitutional right can be held liable for any damages.[8]

In all these situations it is helpful if you have access to a professional Employee Wellbeing/Assistance Programme. These structures have significant experience and access to resources to assist with mental health crises. It is helpful to understand the benefits of such a programme,[9] as well as be realistic that there are no magic solutions that can insulate all workplaces from all consequences of mental health crises.

Follow up

If the individual's manager is not already aware of the issue, make sure they are informed as they are responsible for the continuing management and support of their staff in the workplace. Remind them to maintain confidentiality and discretion.

---

8   Blom & Vale, 2018.
9   Martins & Ledimo, 2018.

If you have been actively involved in dealing with the crisis take some time to check in with yourself. Involvement in either a critical or non-critical mental health incident may leave you feeling distressed, worried, frustrated and depleted. Taking care of your own psychological wellbeing is an essential part of your role as a supervisor, manager or HR professional. You may benefit from counselling or debriefing, as might any other staff that were involved in the incident.

Remember to follow up with the employee, making sure to implement any actions agreed upon. Check in with the employee's support systems and find out how things are going and what might be necessary in future. Finally, follow up with any service providers you have involved. Show concern and interest in a boundaried and professional way.

Be prepared

Each organisation should have context-specific protocols for dealing with a mental health crisis similar to those that exist for dealing with fire or any other safety risks. This would include creating and updating a response resource list (see Appendix 2 for some local resources) with contacts and resources such as crisis support lines, for specific critical situations such as violence and suicide. Include all phone numbers, e-mail addresses and work schedules (opening hours, days off, and specific contact person, if any).

Provide mental illness awareness training to appropriate individuals within the organisation to allow them to recognise common warning signs of mental illness in order to intervene timeously.

Helpful leadership responses to crises

If there is a crisis, especially one involving violence, trauma or loss, the response of the organisation's leadership directly impacts on how employees cope, how the incident will be perceived and interpreted by the broader community and how the organisation will emerge from the crisis.

During a crisis it is essential that managers inform the leadership of the organisation as soon as possible. If the crisis is of a large or significant scale (such as a hostage situation or if it involves a death or traumatic criminal incident) leaders should ensure that they are present and seen to be dealing with the issue. Leaders need to stay calm and measured and focus on minimising harm, getting as fully informed as possible, accessing the best resources to assist without placing themselves at risk.

As a crisis situation unfolds, or in the aftermath, leaders should be transparent in communications, without breaching confidentiality or creating unnecessary fear. Keeping staff regularly updated about the situation and what is being doing to assist, can alleviate the worst fears and anxieties of a workforce.

Some principles to hold in mind:

- These are sensitive and complex matters. Importantly, there is no quick fix or one-size-fits-all solution.

- Focus on building psychological safety and trust for employees, their families and for the staff of the organisation more generally in order to foster resilience.

- Expect and tolerate the emotions that may emerge after a trauma. These could range from anger, resentment, fear and anxiety to relief and even the use of humour to cope.

- The leadership of the company needs to be seen to be present, open, authentically concerned, engaged and thoughtful.

Warnings: Things NOT to do:

Do not ignore, deny or minimise the problem, but also refrain from excessive interrogation or unnecessary probing. While acknowledging the problem is important, having a catastrophic or overly dramatic, negativistic approach is unhelpful and likely to exacerbate the problem. It is not your role (or in your competencies) to diagnose mental illness. Do not make promises you cannot keep or give assurances that are not honest. You do not need to be a hero or rescuer, just doing your job ordinarily is good enough. Attempts at heroism may simply exhaust you and end up enabling learned helplessness or colluding with problematic behaviours.

After a mental health crisis

In the aftermath of a mental health crisis, help employees to take care of themselves, arrange for supportive counselling/debriefing sessions (individual and group) and be sure to offer support to management as well. You may want to offer time off for recuperation for individuals who have been significantly involved but ask each person if this would be helpful and how long they would need. Prolonged time off after a trauma may not be helpful as this allows for the development of maladaptive avoidance strategies and hampers return to normal life. Strategies for self-care include regular physical exercise, medical checkups and monitoring of sleep patterns and substance use. Relaxation, mindfulness and leisure activities should be encouraged. Human Resources practitioners or line managers should check in with affected employees on a regular basis for the few months after a crisis event.

Reasonable accommodations

Once aware that an employee has mental health problems, management needs to be proactive. South African labour law, in alignment with our Constitution and Bill of Rights, provides guidelines to employers.

The Constitution of the Republic of SA (1996) guarantees the rights of people with disabilities to be treated equally and to enjoy the same rights as all other citizens. The Employment Equity Act (1998) seeks to outlaw discrimination and promote equal opportunities for designated groups in the workplace. The Promotion of Equality and Prevention of Unfair Discrimination Act (2000) regards the failure to provide reasonable accommodation measures to people with disabilities as discrimination.

South African legislation requires that all workplaces take reasonable steps to accommodate employees with disabilities, including mental health problems.

Some reasonable accommodations may include:

- Providing of assistive devices such as noise-cancelling headsets.
- Time off to attend medical appointments and access clinic hours for medication and checkups (this is particularly relevant in the South African context for those employees who need to make use of state medical services).
- Regular time off on a weekly basis to attend psychotherapy or counselling sessions or group interventions.
- Job restructuring.
- Modified work hours where possible and necessary.
- Flexible workdays.
- Work from home opportunities.
- Access to private workspaces.

For further details on aspects of South African labour law relating to mental illness, that will greatly assist in understanding the legal obligations of employers, Appendix 3 should be consulted.

Conclusion

If you have walked the highwire and managed to step back onto firmer ground, take the time to reflect on what happened and why, and what helped and what hindered. This is an opportunity to learn from the crisis and understand more about the strengths and vulnerabilities of your people and your organisation.

The shift to remote working as a result of Covid has made it more difficult to identify those at risk of a mental health crisis. The physical distance may also make managers and colleagues feel even more disempowered about their ability to help. But the guidelines suggested in this chapter will be helpful, even in a remote working context. The key is to maintain individualised contact with each staff member. Even if the contact is not face to face, the principles of Acknowledge, Alert and Address provide a framework and guide to assist anyone attempting to help in the event of a mental health crisis to walk that tightrope safely, even if they are physically distant.

We have a legal, moral and ethical imperative to support the most vulnerable in our workplaces. We have more resources available to us than simply our sympathy and good wishes, our tea and our tissues, to assist those in crisis. This chapter has provided guidelines and practical strategies when we are called upon to deal with mental health crises at work. Those who are struggling cannot be left to find their footing alone.

> *"The darkness around us is deep. But our great calling, opportunity, and power as professionals is to shed light in dark places. In a world that needs new professionals – true professionals – in every institution, let us resist the temptation to respond with a fearful "no" or an elusive "maybe" and allow our lives to speak a clear and heart-felt "yes."* Parker Palmer[10]

---

10 Palmer, 2017, p.214.

Chapter 8

The Healthy Organisation

Work is about a search for daily meaning as well as daily bread, for recognition as well as cash, astonishment rather than torpor, in short, for a sort of life rather than a Monday through Friday sort of dying.[1]

The environment in which individuals work has a profound influence on their mental health. There has been a substantial amount of research which has identified the psycho-social workplace conditions that create or exacerbate poor mental health. It is important to identify the psycho-social factors that are hazardous to employee wellbeing so that we can, wherever possible, eliminate them at their source. In the same way that organisations strive to protect worker health by identifying and addressing physical hazards, we need to identify and strive to reduce the psycho-social hazards to which employees are exposed. At the same time, we need to identify the workplace factors that can contribute to a psychologically healthy organisation. A healthy workplace creates opportunities for all its members to maximise their potential, work performance, and psychological and physical health.

Our focus here is on the responsibility of workplaces, rather than simply on the responsibility of individual workers to manage their own mental health. We believe that workplaces have an ethical and moral obligation to take this stance. This is a responsibility we as a society share, to do good, and above all do no harm. These principles, of beneficence and non-maleficence, are part of our constitutional obligation to participate in nation building and ensure health and prosperity for all.[2]

If we emphasise the individual, with their strengths and weaknesses, as the primary site of intervention, we miss an opportunity to make a broader impact on our wider

---

1 Terkel, 1974, p.9
2 Constitution of the Republic of South Africa, 1996.

society. The risk of focusing in on the individual is that it can lead to blaming the "victim" for their difficulties. This traps organisations in a cycle of individual crisis management, without generating the impetus to leverage change and improvement on a systemic basis.

There is extensive and rigorous research evidence (see[3]) that has identified the key factors that need to be in place for an organisation to be considered a psychologically safe and healthy place in which to work. Drawing on this research, we present a series of questions designed to help managers think more deeply about what organisational factors they can focus on to design a healthier work environment. These questions, and the underlying healthy organisational construct they reflect, are presented in Figure 8.1.

Psycho-social Conditions associated with Healthy Organisations

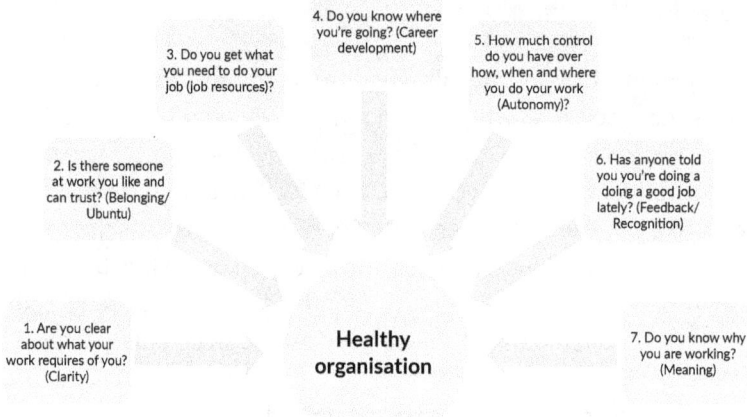

4. Do you know where you're going? (Career development)

5. How much control do you have over how, when and where you do your work (Autonomy)?

3. Do you get what you need to do your job (job resources)?

2. Is there someone at work you like and can trust? (Belonging/ Ubuntu)

6. Has anyone told you you're doing a doing a good job lately? (Feedback/ Recognition)

1. Are you clear about what your work requires of you? (Clarity)

Healthy organisation

7. Do you know why you are working? (Meaning)

Figure 8.1: Questions to help identify healthy organisational psycho-social conditions

Questions to help identify healthy organisational psycho-social conditions

8.1. Clarity: "Are you clear about what your work requires of you?"

This question talks to the clarity of goals and clarity of expectations that are crucial for a highly productive, low-stress work environment. The importance of clarity at work is by no means new: Kahn et al.'s classic *Organisational stress: Studies in role conflict and ambiguity*[4] identified the risks associated with low levels of clarity which result in

---

3   Harter, Schmidt, & Keyes, 2003; Kelloway & Day, 2005a, 2005b; Warr, 1999.
4   Kahn et al., 1964.

role conflict and role ambiguity. Depression, dissatisfaction, and low productivity are just some of the outcomes of lack of clarity that have been established in over four decades of research.[5]

However, clarity is often a difficult issue to raise with management as it seems so obvious – you cannot achieve your goals at work unless you know what they are, how they fit into the bigger organisational picture and how you need to go about achieving them. Managers will point to employees' job descriptions, their Key Performance Areas (KPAs) and annual goal setting and performance appraisal meetings to illustrate how work expectations are communicated to employees. These are crucial for communicating expectations, yet in an increasingly complex and ambiguous 21st Century organisational context, they are not always enough. There are very few organisations today that can provide a stable, unambiguous, perfectly structured set of instructions to employees that are valid at all times, with all stakeholders and under all conditions.

Palesa was confused, she had been told that her role in customer care involved following written company protocols regarding complaints and her KPAs included "speedy resolution of client complaints with minimal escalation". But now she had been called in to her manager's office because she had not immediately agreed to reimburse a client for a query on their monthly subscription. Although the complaint itself was individual, the complainant was the PA to the CEO of a major corporate who was now threatening to cancel their corporate service agreement. The manager screamed at Palesa, suggesting her work was deficient as she should have known to use her judgement in this case. Palesa couldn't sleep that night, stressed and distressed, anxious that she didn't understand what was expected of her in such situations. The only thing she felt sure of was that she would be disciplined if she made the same call again and would be disciplined if she didn't follow written protocols.

Different stakeholders within and outside the organisation make different and often conflicting demands on employees' time and capabilities and most employees have more than a single role to play both within and beyond the organisational context. Individuals need to have more than a list of job tasks and goals to know how to process what is required and translate the demands into manageable actions. In the last interview before his death, the father of Total Quality Management (TQM), W. Edwards Deming, spoke to Tim Stevens about quality, management and innovation. He identified clarity as key to all of these things:

> *"People must understand what their jobs are, how their work fits in, how they could contribute. Why am I doing this? Who can I depend on? Who depends on me? Very few people have the privilege to understand these things. Management does not tell them. ...When people*

---

5   Bedeian & Armenakis, 1981; Schmidt et al., 2014.

understand what their jobs are, they can make joy in their work. Otherwise, I think they cannot".[6]

A strong organisational culture, driven by a clear and compelling vision communicated and consistently reinforced by committed leadership, serves as an organising framework around which clarity can be attained.

8.2. Belonging/Ubuntu: "Is there someone at work you like and can trust?"

This seems like an odd question to ask in relation to the workplace and often managers will look strangely at anyone posing this question. That is because most of us are not comfortable with using such a 'touchy feely' term in the work environment. In fact, there are some workplaces which actively discourage the formation of close workplace friendships.[7] Highly pressurised contexts, such as manufacturing assembly lines and more recently call centres tend to apply a strictly Taylor's approach[8] to job design, reducing the worker to little more than a pair of 'hands', placing them under extremely close surveillance, and providing no control over the pace at which they are expected to work. There is no room for friendships in such places, where workers are dehumanised and expected to operate as automatons with no needs or feelings.

Fortunately, this approach has lost currency recently as there is increasing recognition that negative effects of such work design are both harmful to the individual employees' wellbeing and inappropriate for the requirements of the modern world of work. We address the high cost of loneliness on individuals, organisations and society in Chapter 6. Social support is now recognised as a crucial buffer against the negative effects of work stress[9] and organisations are starting to recognise the value of social capital – *"the stock of active connections among people, the trust, mutual understanding and shared values and behaviors that bind the members of human networks and communities and make cooperative action possible."*[10]

The value of social networks is vividly illustrated in a series of experiments undertaken by Alex Pentland and colleagues. In one study, they used electronic badges to monitor the social signalling and conversational patterns of employees in an IT Department. The badges were fitted with various sensors and recorders. Based on the data sent from these sensors and recorders, the researchers were able to track the extent of social cohesion in the work groups they were monitoring. When the researchers

6   Stevens, 1994 Part 1.
7   Milner, Russell & Siemers, 2010.
8   Taylor, 1911/1967.
9   Boren, 2014; Heaney, Price & Rafferty, 1995.
10 Cohen & Prusak, 2001 p.3.

analysed these levels of social cohesion in relation to work group productivity, they established that groups who fell in the top third of scores on peer cohesion were more than 10 percent more productive than the average.[11] "This result underscores the extent to which we are social animals and that our connection with our peers at a local level is vitally important".[12]

The sense of connectedness that makes social support and social capital such powerful forces taps into a deep-seated need for belongingness that is as relevant to the workplace as it is to any other area of human endeavour. South Africa has an advantage over other countries when it comes to developing connectedness at work in that the philosophy of Ubuntu captures this value in a uniquely African way. "An organizing concept of ubuntu is human inter- dependence. The driving norms are reciprocity, suppression of self-interest, and the virtue of symbiosis".[13] The phrase *umntu ngumntu ngabanye* [a person is a person through others] is the defining characteristic of Ubuntu – reflecting the core idea that a person becomes a person only by virtue of their relationship with, and recognition by, others.[14]

8.3. Job Resources: "Do you get what you need to do your job?"

Again, this seems to be a deceptively simple question. Yet, Bakker and Demerouti[15] have shown that job resources are a key weapon in our fight against a ubiquitous and devastating form of poor mental health at work – burnout. Every job has a specific set of demands that it makes on individual employees, physical, cognitive and emotional. When these demands become excessive and we feel that we are unable to meet them in a consistent sustainable way, burnout ensues (for a more comprehensive explanation of burnout and how it manifests in the workplace, see Chapter 6). Job resources counter the negative effect of these demands. They "refer to those physical, psychological, social or organisational aspects of the job that (a) are functional in achieving work goals, (b) reduce job demands and the associated physiological and psychological costs, or (c) stimulate personal growth and development".[16]

To fully understand the impact of job resources on wellbeing at work, we need to consider two types of resources. The first are physical resources – the actual tools, equipment, and other physical materials that are needed in our work environments. At the most basic level these impact our wellbeing directly through their effects on

---

11 Pentland, 2011.
12 Pentland, 2011, p. 26.
13 Mangaliso, 1992, as cited in Mangaliso & Damane, 2001, p.24.
14 Mangaliso & Damane, 2001.
15 Bakker & Demerouti, 2007.
16 Bakker, Demerouti & Euwema, 2005, p. 170.

our physical health and safety. Indeed, safety at work is an area which can tolerate no compromise. You need to ensure that employees are issued with the requisite safety equipment, are properly trained on the proper use of such equipment and that safety procedures are enforced.

Research coming out of the Covid-19 pandemic and its effect on frontline healthcare workers has highlighted the harmful impact of a lack of adequate provision of Personal Protective Equipment (PPE) on their psychological health and resilience.[17]

In South Africa, it is also necessary (and part of labour legislation) to go beyond the bounds of the actual workplace when thinking of employee safety (Basic Conditions of Employment Act, 1997). Given the very high levels of road accidents and road deaths in South Africa, as well as the prevalence of violent crimes and Gender Based Violence, some of the issues that employers should consider include:

- Can you assist employees with finding safe transport to and from work?

- If employees work shifts or work at night, is there a safe, well-lit place for them to wait for transport?

- Can the route that they walk to access transport be made safer through, for example, collaboration with a Community Policing Forum; liaison with local police; cross-company initiatives with regard to private security and lobbying local councils to ensure that streets in the area are well lit.

Care for employees' safety is even more important when the work that they do places them directly in harm's way as a result of the high levels of crime and violence in our society. Some of you reading this may remember the spate of violent, armed bank robberies that took place in South Africa in the 1990s and early 2000s. The banks did not ignore them or characterise them as an unavoidable traumatic consequence of doing business in South Africa. They sought to ameliorate the negative effects introducing specialist trauma interventions specifically targeted at the types of work and trauma that their employees experienced.[18]

The design of the physical environment can also be construed as a job resource. Google pioneered the notion of creating an office environment that reflects and encourages a fun innovative organisational culture to enhance employee satisfaction, motivation and engagement. In a series of studies in South Africa, Thatcher and Milner[19] explored the impact of green office design on employee wellbeing. Through

---

17 Arnetz, et.al., 2020; Xia, et.al., 2020.
18 Ortlepp & Friedman, 2001, 2002.
19 Thatcher & Milner, 2012, 2014.

carefully constructed research designs they were able to compare employees working in conventional buildings with those in star-rated green buildings on a series of metrics ranging from perceptions of indoor air quality to physical and psychological wellbeing and productivity. While some of their results were inconclusive, at least one study found that employees in a 'green' building had significantly increased self-reported productivity and physical wellbeing compared to those in a traditional building.[20]

These types of physical resources impact psychological health in the workplace in two ways. First, through their direct impact on physical health (musculoskeletal disorders and chronic health conditions) which are intimately tied to psychological health. Second, through the message they convey to employees about their worth and value to the organisation. As managers, we often despair about the so-called 'toilet and tea' debates in staff meetings – the endless complaints about seemingly petty concerns. This can be annoying to management who see them as a distraction from important issues that need to be dealt with. These complaints may differ in nature according to whether people are working in a resource-rich or resource-strapped environment, yet they are ubiquitous. This is because such issues are a lightning rod for the expression of dissatisfaction and lack of recognition and they serve to amplify employee negativity. As such, they fall into the category of what Hertzberg et al.[21] called "hygiene factors". These are factors that have nothing to do with the work itself or any of the intrinsically motivating facets of the workplace. Their presence in the workplace cannot, in and of themselves, engender motivation or job satisfaction but their absence is a source of much frustration and unhappiness.

So how do we address these "nuisance problems", especially in resource-strapped environments? First, when addressing resource problems it is important to recognise that the issue is not really about their absolute, material value. Rather, they are signifiers of hierarchy, value and care. Allow your employees some time to vent about the tea and toilet issues, listen and address where you can and where you cannot, demonstrate congruency and sincerity in showing that you have done the best you can. In an environment where care and concern for employees is paramount, they will soon stop sweating the small stuff.

8.4. Career development: "Do you know where you're going?"

One of the most vexing problems in today's organisations is that of career development. It is so key to employee engagement that the Gallup workplace audit[22] devoted three of their 12 questions on what makes a great workplace to this topic:

---

20 Thatcher & Milner 2014.
21 Hertzberg et al., 1959.
22 Harter, Schmidt & Keyes, 2003.

- "There is someone at work who encourages my development"

- "In the last 6 months, someone at work has talked to me about my progress"

- "This last year, I have had opportunities at work to learn and grow"

Flatter organisational hierarchies coupled with increased emphasis on, and access to, higher education have combined to raise expectations around career development while tightening the bottlenecks that limit opportunities. Younger employees have recognised this conundrum quicker than employers and older employees and have begun to reject the traditional career development paths which assume a linear career trajectory in a single organisation. Job security and the promise of a 20-year career with incremental advances and a gold watch at the end, are no longer viable, nor perhaps desirable, goals. Employees are now focusing on opportunities for life-long learning which prepare them for a constantly evolving career landscape.[23]

This does not absolve organisations of their responsibilities with regard to career development. On the contrary, meeting the desire of employees to learn and grow remains fundamental to a psychologically healthy and effective workplace but the emphasis needs to change. Skills development, lifelong learning and job crafting are all ways to address employee growth and development in the context of the 21st Century fluid and dynamic career environment.

8.5. Autonomy: "How much control do you have over how, when, and where you do your work?"

The seminal stress research undertaken by Karasek[24] and his colleagues has comprehensively established the role of job control in worker health. Karasek's job demand/control model looks at the interaction between the demands the job makes on employees and the level of control that the position provides (See Figure 8.2). Depending on the nature of the interaction, different levels of strain emerge. Under conditions of low demand and low control, employees experience 'passive jobs'; under conditions of high demand together with high control, employees experience 'active' jobs; high control together with low demand results in 'low strain' jobs; while high demands combined with low control culminates in 'high strain'.[25]

---

23 De Vos, Akkermans & Van Der Heijden, 2019, p. 128-142.

24 Karasek, 1979.

25 Karasek, 1979.

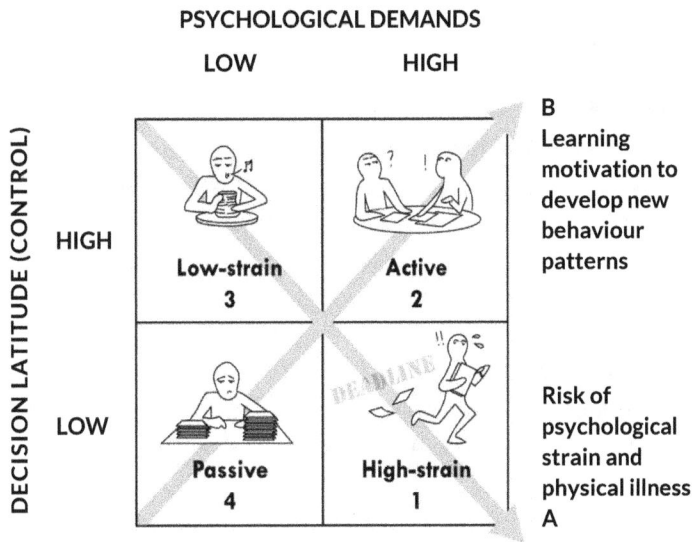

Figure 8.2: Karasek's Job Demand Control model[26]

An enormous body of research has been devoted to assessing this model,[27] which has resulted in minor changes, specifically the inclusion of social support as a further variable to consider, but also has established the negative consequences of high-strain jobs. Sanne et al.[28] established that high-strain jobs are risk factors for anxiety and depression, especially among women; and various reviews of the research has concluded that job strain is a cardio-vascular disease risk factor.[29]

The Whitehall studies in the UK have also established the primacy of job control/ autonomy in worker health, to the extent that employees in low-status jobs, with associated low levels of control have poorer health outcomes as well as lower life expectancy than those employees higher in the organisational hierarchy.[30] South African research confirms that these results are relevant to this country as well. Bowen, Edgars and Lingard[31] found that architects in South Africa experienced the lowest levels of control but highest levels of stress compared with other construction professionals, specifically civil engineers, quantity surveyors, and project and construction managers. In 2008, Jorgensen and Rothman[32] found control to be a

26 Karasek, 1979.
27 Karasek & Theorell, 1990.
28 Sanne et al., 2005.
29 Belkic, Landsbergis, Schnall, & Baker, 2004; Schnall, Landsbergis, & Baker, 1994.
30 Stansfeld et al.,1991.
31 Bowen, Edgars & Lingard, 2005.
32 Jorgensen & Rothman, 2008.

statistically significant predictor of physical and psychological ill-health in the South African Police Services (SAPS).

Given the overwhelming evidence of the role of job control in worker health, it is puzzling why increasing empowerment and scope of decision making is not used more often as a way of reducing work stress and increasing satisfaction. Organisations which seem willing to spend large sums of money to improve worker health through interventions such as expensive consultants and million rand gyms can be resistant, and sometimes openly hostile, to simple job design interventions to increase worker autonomy. In a fascinating TED talk on autonomy at work, Dan Pink[33] attributes this to a 'huge mismatch between what science knows and what business does'. This compounds the reluctance traditional managers seem to have to relinquish control. Pink describes a project done at Atlassian, an Australian software company as an example of 'radical amounts of autonomy':

Atlassian is an Australian software company who periodically allow their engineers to spend twenty-four hours working on any project they want, provided it's not part of their regular job. "The engineers use this time to come up with a cool patch for code, come up with an elegant hack. Then they present all of the stuff that they've developed to their teammates, to the rest of the company, in this wild and woolly all-hands meeting at the end of the day. It's worked so well that Atlassian has taken it to the next level with 20% time -- done, famously, at Google -- where engineers can spend 20% of their time working on anything they want. They have autonomy over their time, their task, their team, their technique. Radical amounts of autonomy."

Providing employees with opportunities to participate in decision-making, making small job changes to empower them to take greater responsibility and creating the space for people at all hierarchical and skill levels to undertake an autonomous project (as illustrated above) are different ways to incorporate greater levels of job control into employees' work lives. A final word of caution on job control is needed here. Warr[34] talks about a curvilinear relationship between job control and worker health, where increases in job control are associated with improvements in worker health to a point. Employees with excess levels of responsibility tend to experience negative health consequences.

---

33 Pink, 2009.
34 Warr, 1987.

8.6. Feedback/Recognition: "Has anyone told you you're doing a doing a good job lately?"

Let me start off by saying: "Well done for having read so far. You have shown yourself to be conscientious, dedicated and committed to employee well-being!" That didn't feel so hard, yet the number one gripe of employees in South Africa is lack of recognition[35]. Employees feel undervalued, they experience feedback as occurring only when things go wrong and often complain about a lack of fairness or justice when it comes to material forms of recognition such as performance evaluations, selection and promotion decisions.

When we talk about recognition, we are not only talking about monetary rewards. However, a central premise of this book is that people need to do decent work for decent pay and that inadequate compensation carries with it tremendous risks in the form of financial strain which is associated with a host of negative physical and mental health outcomes.[36] Many other forms of recognition do exist, and globally organisations invest substantial amounts in different employee recognition programmes which tend to have varying and often disappointing results.[37] What employees are actually looking for when it comes to recognition is thoughtful, genuine and personal acknowledgment that shows true appreciation for a job well done.[38]

Where recognition is tied to a reward, financial or otherwise, the FAIRNESS of that reward becomes a critical issue to consider in terms of its effect on mental health. There is an entire body of literature in Industrial/Organisational Psychology devoted to understanding how fairness should be understood in organisations as well as its causes, correlates and consequences. This broad literature alerts us to different types of justice that underpin employee perceptions of all allocation decisions in organisations.[39] The initial consideration is whether the recognition or reward was fairly allocated. Did the amount of reward allocated match the amount of effort put in? Did others who put in less effort get the same or more reward?! Do we have a sneaking suspicion that actually we were over-rewarded? The answers to all those questions will have an impact on motivation and wellbeing. People often feel deep upset and even rage at being unfairly treated. It is also such a natural response that rage and distress against unfair treatment is not limited to humans. Chimpanzees faced with inequitable rewards for doing the same task get angry and refuse to repeat

---

35 Based on unpublished data from DMSA's database on organisational effectiveness/organisational climate surveys across large medium and small companies in South Africa

36 Dijkstra-Kersten et al., 2015; Kahn & Pearlin, 2006; Myer et al., 2008.

37 Nelson, 2004.

38 Ibid.

39 Folger & Cropanzano,1998; Laundon, Cathcart & McDonald 2019.

the task.[40] It is impossible in a written text to do justice to the chimps' expressions and behaviour which need to be seen for their full serious and comedic impact, so we recommend you take a break from reading this book now and watch this excerpt from Frans de Waal's 2011 TED talk at https://www.youtube.com/watch?v=meiU6TxysCg (Two Monkeys Were Paid Unequally).[41]

It is also important to mention that there are other issues besides just the fairness of the actual allocation of rewards that concern humans. We also consider HOW the allocation was made. Were the processes used in making the decision around the reward fair? Did we get a say in it? Were they consistent and how were we treated when those decisions were made? Were we treated with dignity and respect? The answer to all these questions will help us decide whether we have been fairly treated, and if not, the implications for our health are severe. Kivimaki et al.[42] asked 6 000 men five questions about fairness, feedback and recognition:

- "Do you ever get criticised unfairly?"

- "Do you get consistent information from your supervisor?"

- "Do you get sufficient feedback from your supervisor?"

- "How often is your supervisor willing to listen to your work problems?"

- "Do you ever get praised for your work?"

After controlling for all known biological risk factors, they found that perceptions of unfairness predicted new instances of Coronary Heart Disease five to eight years later.

8.7. Meaning/task significance: "Do you know why you are working?"

This is the pinnacle of what we are trying to achieve in developing healthy organisations. All the other psycho-social workplace characteristics discussed previously are important in and of themselves but also because they help to create an environment imbued with meaning.

Viktor Frankl[43] spoke of the "Will to Meaning" – that people are not content to live meaningless lives; people are inherently inclined to search for values and ideals outside of themselves. This is not necessarily organised religion, but a desire for connectedness to something outside of the self. Without the above goals, the individual is spiritually

---

40 Brosnan, 2013.

41 De Waal, 2011.

42 Kivimaki et al., 2005.

43 Frankl, 1985.

unfulfilled and deprived of a genuine motivation to live. Frankl[44] believed that the central psychological issue is not the struggle to survive, but the struggle to find a meaning in survival.

Frankl's own life story provides a perfect illustration of his theories. In his late 30s he spent 3 years as prisoner number 119,104 in concentration camps including Dachau and Auschwitz. He felt his theories were confirmed by his experiences in the camps. Frankl lost his wife, parents and brother and his life's work. He describes his story in his book *Man's Search for Ultimate Meaning*.[45] On April 27, 1945, Frankl was liberated by the Americans. Among his immediate relatives, the only survivor was his sister, who had escaped by emigrating to Australia. In the camps, Frankl noted the significant role of values in people's lives. Having something to live for was what enabled prisoners to hold onto the will to live in circumstances that made death feel like a solution.

The role of meaning in life is starkly illustrated in Frankl's work. His work as a therapist together with his own experience of immense, inconceivable suffering led him to conclude that our will to find meaning is our main motivator in life; that much modern psychological suffering is a result of people experiencing their lives as meaningless, and that we can find meaning in life under all circumstances, regardless of how terrible those circumstances may be.[46]

While Frankl conceived his philosophy under the most extreme adversity, his profound insights have relevance to the mundane everyday work and life environments in which the majority of us operate. Psychologists writing today, in circumstances far different from those that Frankl lived through, continue to place meaning at the forefront of their thinking on wellbeing and positive mental health. Management consultants McKinsey talk of the Meaning Quotient (MQ) and define meaning as "a feeling that what's happening really matters, that what's being done has not been done before or that it will make a difference to others".[47] One of the strategies that they suggest for increasing MQ at work is for managers to tell five stories at work:

1. Stories of company turnaround: Employees can find meaning in the excitement and challenge of changing a company's fortunes or pushing its performance to its peak but the meaning associated with this story is limited in its depth and scope.

2. Stories of customer happiness: Meaning derived from customer service/customer need satisfaction can also provide a source of meaning at work. A junior manager

---

44 Ibid.
45 Frankl, 1985.
46 Marshall & Marshall, 2012.
47 Cranston & Keller, 2013, p.5.

in a company that sells biscuits once told me of the enormous sense of pride he feels every Christmas as he watches people waiting for taxis to go home for the holidays with the tins of his biscuit brand amongst their packages. He believed that these biscuits represented homecoming, family and celebration to his customers and as a result he was really concerned about and committed to quality control. He was convinced of his role in making his customers' experience a really positive one – not for the company's sake but 'for the customers'.

3.   Stories of community building; the idea that one is working for a cause that is bigger than oneself is one of the most potent sources of meaning in a person's life. For some organisations these are easy stories to tell as their work directly links to some form of social good. Others need to go beyond their core mission in order to have a positive social/community impact. Business is increasingly focusing on the triple bottom line in company objectives and reporting. The triple bottom line refers to measures of entity performance based on financial as well as environmental and social impact. In sharing stories of social impact and linking them directly or indirectly to the work performed by every employee, their sense of the meaningfulness of their work can be enhanced.

4.   Stories of team support and belonging: The sense of comradeship and community derived from group identity and team cohesion talk as much to the construction of meaning at work as they do to the importance of social capital. "Taking one for the team": feeling like your team "has your back" and celebrating team victories provide a great sense of affirmation for the individual in the team. The individual's role in, and contribution to, the team provides a sense of meaning to the work they are doing.

5.   Stories of personal contribution and value. For many South African workers, the simple fact of having a job in a context in which over a quarter of the population is unemployed provides an important sense of purpose and meaning in people's lives. The ability to put bread on the table and support one's family is not something that is taken for granted in most South African households. The importance of paying staff a living wage so they can do this with dignity needs to be seen as a precursor to any individual stories of personal value and contribution at work. Treating employees with dignity and respect and acknowledging the value they add, regardless of role or position in the organisation, is fundamental to creating a sense of meaning amongst all employees. Too many people in organisations labour under the impression that the work they do is not acknowledged or even noticed by those higher up the organisational hierarchy. It is difficult to see the significance of your work if no one seems to notice it (unless you have done something wrong in which case everyone notices the slightest error).

Cranston and Keller[48] talk about the importance of using small gestures to convey value, thereby building meaning. They list the following as examples of such gestures:

- At ANZ Bank, John McFarlane gave all employees a bottle of champagne for Christmas, with a card thanking them for their work on a major change program.

- The CEO of Wells Fargo, John Stumpf, marked the first anniversary of its change program by sending out personal thank-you notes to all the employees who had been involved, with specific messages related to the impact of their individual work.

- Indra Nooyi, CEO of PepsiCo, sends the spouses of her top team handwritten thank-you letters. After seeing the impact of her own success on her mother during a visit to India, she began sending letters to the parents of her top team, too.[49]

Conclusion

It is possible to build a healthy and productive organisational climate, rather than having to focus on "fixing" or curing "stressed" workers. It is not necessary to address all of the healthy organisation factors at the same time. The research evidence is quite clear – small changes can have a big impact. What is important is that changes are introduced based on context-relevant conditions and need. The most effective interventions involve matching and creating synergy with other elements of the organisational system and focusing on small changes that can be sustained.[50]

---

48 Cranston & Keller, 2013.
49 Cranston & Keller, 2013, p. 11.
50 Barling, 2016, presentation at Wits University.

Conclusion

Chapter 9

Thriving

Thrive – to grow vigorously, to flourish; to prosper; to progress towards or realise a goal despite of or because of circumstances.[1]

We have called this chapter 'thriving' because the above definition encapsulates exactly what we are trying to promote – a strong, positive state of being, characterised by growth and development, enabled and nurtured by the environment.

In this chapter we move away from a disease and dysfunction paradigm of mental health towards an emphasis on human strengths and positive institutions. We focus on the benefits of promoting positive mental health in the workplace. Since this is a relatively new area of study and practice, we will introduce the work of some of the pioneering scholars in this field, both internationally and in South Africa. We begin with the work of Martin Seligman who started the positive psychology movement and then move on to the key international positive organisational scholars, including Fred Luthans (Psychological Capital), Tim Harter (Employee Engagement), Schaufelli, Bakker and Demerouti (Employee Engagement and the Job-Demands-Resources Model) and in South Africa, Deon Strumpfer (Salutogenesis). The focus here is on identifying and bolstering those factors that make individuals and organisations thrive. We also look at the evidence for positive psychology interventions and, based on this research, we propose practical ways of enhancing positive mental health in the workplace.

---

1   Merriam-Webster, (n.d.).

Pioneers of positivity

One of the core aims of Psychology has been the pursuit of human wellbeing and mental health. As a discipline, however, we have typically focused on identifying and understanding ill-health and distress as the primary means of achieving this aim. We have used a deficit model of human experience, concentrating on studying the 4 Ds – disease, dysfunction, disability and distress – and identifying their causes and consequences in order to eliminate or ameliorate them. This deficit model has been challenged with calls made to focus on 'positive psychology' – the "science of positive subjective experience, positive individual traits and positive institutions".[2] South African academic Deon Strumpfer[3] was an important early contributor to this field. His work focused on Salutogenesis, a term developed by the medical sociologist Anton Antonovsky. Salutogenesis looks at the origins (genesis) of good health (Salus) as opposed to pathogenesis, the origins of ill-health (pathology).

Instead of focusing on what is wrong, what is broken and what is deteriorating, positive psychology looks at what is right, what works and what is improving.[4] The proponents of positive psychology argue that if we genuinely want to make people happier, then we should study those who are happy; if we want to make people good, we should nurture that which is best within them; and if we want to make people stronger, we should concentrate on their strengths. In the last few years we have seen tremendous growth in this field, particularly amongst researchers and practitioners seeking positive interventions to enhance wellbeing.

Building on the work that the positive psychology movement initiated, a number of organisational theorists and researchers have begun applying this approach in the workplace, and the Positive Organisational Behaviour (POB) discipline was born. The POB scholars looked at a range of positive psychology topics within the work context including forgiveness (e.g. Fehr & Gelfand[5]), courage (e.g. Tkachenko et. al.[6]) and humour (e.g. Huber[7]) at work. The most substantial and rigorous work done from a positive perspective in organisations is the work done on employee engagement. The initial notion of employee engagement stressed the importance of employees being able to bring their full, true and authentic selves to all the roles they play in organisations.[8] Building on this work, a new generation of organisational theorists

---

2   Csikszentmihalyi & Seligman, 2000, p. 5.
3   Strumpfer, 1990.
4   Sheldon & King, 2001.
5   Fehr & Gelfand, 2012.
6   Tkachenko, et. al., 2018.
7   Huber, 2019.
8   Kahn, 1990.

emerged who marked a major transition in organisational theorising from burnout to engagement. Harter and his colleagues at the Gallup Institute were largely responsible for popularising the notion of employee engagement amongst practitioners, HR professionals, consultants and even policy makers through their research evidence on the substantial financial impact that engaged employees can make to organisations. They identified the 12 features of an engaged workplace (Gallup 12) which were covered in Chapter 8.[9]

Dutch psychologist Wilmar Schaufeli[10] looked at engagement from the employees' side, providing a clear description of what an engaged employee looks like, as well as a tool for measuring the extent to which employees feel engaged. According to Schaufeli, engaged employees have energy (vigour); they are highly committed to their jobs (dedication) and experience a sense of flow at work (absorption). By providing a means for assessing these different levels of engagement, Schaufeli enabled the development of testable models that could establish the determinants of engagement. This also allows us to unpack the way in which engagement may be seen as both the converse of burnout as well as an independent construct in its own right. This brings us to the next set of pioneers of positivity – Bakker and Demerouti – and their job demands resources model.[11]

Bakker and Demerouti[12] argue that all jobs can be classified according to the extent of the demands the job makes on employees and all the resources available to meet these demands. For example, the CEO of a large listed company may have very high job demands in the form of a complex, challenging and dynamic work environment, and significant levels of responsibility but is also likely to have a range of resources at her disposal to meet those demands. In contrast, a social worker in the state services also has high levels of work demands in the form of a heavy workload, and emotionally demanding work with low levels of resources in terms of things like administrative, material and emotional support. Bakker and Demerouti's model posits that job demands and resources interact with one another and impact employees through a dual process – a health-impairment process and a motivational process. In contexts where job demands are high and resources are low, health impairment – typically burnout – ensues. But in situations in which job demands are high and job resources are high as well, motivational processes are activated and positive states, typically engagement, ensue.

---

9   Harter, Schmidt & Hayes, 2002.

10 Schaufeli, 2013.

11 Bakker & Demerouti, 2007.

12 Ibid.

By including burnout AND engagement as outcomes of the job demands resources model Bakker and Demerouti[13] fundamentally changed the negative focus that had been characteristic of theorising and research of this nature. Rather than just seeing the opposite of burnout as being no burnout, this model extends the continuum to identify "engagement" as a state to which employees can aspire. The typical characteristics of burnout identified in Chapter 6 – exhaustion, cynicism and inefficacy[14] – find their positive counterparts in Schaufeli's model vigour, dedication and absorption, respectively. The job demands resources has been painstakingly conceptualised and rigorously researched, but its basic premises are straightforward and general enough to be easily applied. Numerous tools exist for identifying the demands and resources of any job and organisational environment. Work can be made healthier and more engaging by introducing and strengthening job resources.

Psychological Capital

While strengthening job resources is key to engagement, much of this falls under the category of job design, addressed comprehensively in Chapter 8. Fred Luthans and his colleagues[15] have identified a set of personal resources (individual competencies) that can be learnt by employees to enhance wellbeing and performance at work. Luthans, Youssef and Avolio,[16] undertook a series of studies which looked for individual characteristics that were positive, teachable and impactful. Through some careful empirical research they whittled an array of potential variables down to just four – Hope, Efficacy, Resilience and Optimism (HERO). Drawing on analogies with financial capital (monetary resources available to an organisation), human capital (the qualifications, skills and competencies that employees bring to the job) and social capital (networks of useful connections) they termed these characteristics Psychological Capital (PsyCap). PsyCap refers to a set of psychological resources that an individual can invest in and enhance so that they are available to be drawn upon when needed.

It is worth looking a little more carefully at these characteristics to avoid the assumption that a superficial reading of terms like 'hope' and 'optimism' sometimes create. What Luthans and colleagues are talking about is not a boundless fantasy of an inexhaustible supply of fairy dust and rainbows – that if you just think positively, look on the bright side, adjust your attitude and see the glass as half full – the real challenges and constraints that exist in the complex and imperfect world of work will magically dissolve. Rather, we understand PsyCap to be referring to a set of resources

---

13 Bakker and Demerouti, 2007.

14 Maslach & Leiter, 2016.

15 Luthans, Youssef & Avolio, 2007, 2015.

16 Ibid.

derived from a rich theoretical and empirical base that are individual in nature but developed through organisational interventions and practices, and that operate in concrete ways to effect positive outcomes. Each characteristic will be discussed in more detail in the following pages.

Hope

Hope refers to a way of thinking that enables people to believe they are capable of achieving their goals. Perhaps more importantly, hope enables us to think about different pathways to follow in order to achieve those goals.[17] In his work on hope, Snyder uses the old expression 'where there's a will there's a way' to make the idea of hope concrete. He locates the notion of hope firmly within the pursuit of goals. Jerome Groopman,[18] an oncologist and haematologist, writes about hope in the face of a terminal illness diagnosis. He defines hope as "the elevating feeling we experience when we see – in the mind's eye – a path to a better future". People without hope are unable to envision a better future and therefore are unable to formulate any meaningful goals. Snyder refers to this element of hope as *Will Power* – an individual's will to shape their own future by formulating and pursuing their goals. Groopman however warns that "Hope acknowledges the significant obstacles and deep pitfalls along that path. True hope has no room for delusion." For Snyder, this aspect of hope is *Way Power* – the ability to envision different paths/different ways to achieve these goals. It includes being flexible around goals and moderating them when appropriate.

Chris, a final year student at university, comes into his lecturer's office. He is devastated. His final marks have been poor, and he is unlikely to get a place in the postgraduate course he had dreamed of since high school. It feels to him as if the harsh and demanding world of academia has destroyed his hopes and crushed his spirit. After acknowledging his distress, encouraging him to breathe slowly and mindfully, and allowing him to collect himself, his lecturer uses Snyder's ideas to help navigate this crisis.

First they work on Way Power: Is there another way to achieve this goal? Could Chris retake the course perhaps and get better marks and reapply the following year or could he apply to a similar course at a different institution perhaps? Chris has to establish which options are possible and realistic, and he will need to stay motivated to pursue them in the face of his disappointment.

It becomes clear to Chris and his lecturer that for financial reasons, none of these alternatives will work. Chris's student grant will not cover an additional year of undergraduate study, and the only alternate postgraduate course is in another province, and Chris does not have

---

17 Snyder, 2002.

18 Groopman, 2004.

the resources to move. He and the lecturer start to work on Will Power, adapting his goal to something that is still desirable but more achievable. What was it about the original goal that was so meaningful for him? Can he achieve this meaning through a different route? Is he devastated because he felt shamed by not achieving this goal and what can he do to make himself feel proud and confident again? How can he use his experiences of having overcome difficulties in the past to even get to this point, to help him in finding and working towards a new goal? Make no mistake, this was a difficult and painful conversation to have and did not entirely dissolve the hurt. But the alternative – a crushed spirit or a false hope – would have been worse for Chris. Chris established that his goal of being a psychologist was not immediately realizable, but his underlying desire to help people could be achieved in the short term by volunteering at a local helpline. His career aspirations could be advanced by doing a diploma in community development that allowed him to work meaningfully in the field of human development.

Luthans and Jensen[19] suggest the following practical steps for building hope:

1. Clarify and form organisational and personal goals. Inclusion of concrete metrics such as target dates or percentage improvements, will help in goal specificity, and setting difficult (not impossible) stretch goals will help make these objectives challenging.

2. Use what Snyder[20] called a "stepping method" to break the goals down into manageable sub-steps that will mark progress and enable small wins and success.

3. Develop at least one (preferably more) alternative pathway(s) to the goal with an accompanying action plan. Put as much thinking and effort into developing pathways and action plans for the goal as went into setting the goal.

4. Acknowledge the enjoyment in the process of working toward goals, and do not focus solely on the final result.

5. Be prepared and willing to persist when obstacles and problems are encountered. Obstacles will occur, so proactively formulating alternate pathways will enable greater persistence.

6. Be prepared and skilful in knowing when and which alternative pathways to choose when the original route to goal accomplishment is no longer feasible nor productive. "What if" and scenario planning and training can help to build such skills.

---

19 Luthans & Jensen, 2002, p. 315.

20 Snyder, 2002.

7. Be prepared and skilled in knowing when and how to "regoal" to avoid the trap of false hope. We must know when persistence toward a goal is not feasible, regardless of the chosen pathways.

There are going to be obstacles and blockages on the path to goal achievement. Helping employees recognise this and find ways of negotiating, overcoming, going around and, if necessary, embarking on new paths to goal achievement is a way of building the PsyCap element of hope.

Efficacy

Efficacy is the second positive personal component that comprises PsyCap. Based on the work of Albert Bandura,[21] efficacy refers to an individual's belief that they are personally capable of attaining their goals. So if hope is about setting goals and finding different ways to achieve them, efficacy is about developing the belief that they can be achieved. Over thirty years of research has shown that there are effective ways of developing people's self-efficacy. The most direct way is to set people increasingly challenging tasks and goals. As they attain these goals and tasks, they start to experience a sense of mastery and their belief in their ability to attain their goals is developed i.e. they develop a sense of efficacy.

Where it is not possible to allow people to practice tasks in a way that would slowly develop their confidence, Bandura proposes the concept of vicarious learning. People watch role models who are similar to themselves and who can explain and show how the task can be achieved. The watcher can both learn how to do the task and develop confidence that they are capable of doing so. In a multicultural environment such as South Africa, seeing someone whom the person can identify with achieve the task, whether it be because of their race, or gender or age, can strengthen this process considerably. The notion of visibility of minorities or previously disadvantaged communities has a key role to play here. If you have never seen someone who 'looks like you' (in terms of basic identity markers such as race, gender and sexual orientation) achieve in a particular field, it is that much harder to imagine that you can achieve in that field, resulting in reduced self-efficacy in that domain. The importance of showcasing the achievements of a diversity of people is therefore critical. This is not mere political correctness at work, but a fundamental mechanism of role modelling and vicarious learning.

Bandura[22] suggests one final way of developing self-efficacy – 'verbal persuasion'. This refers to the use of encouraging and motivational speech in convincing others

---

21 Bandura, 1982, 1997.
22 Bandura, 1982.

that they are capable of achieving their goals. Picture the fitness coach exhorting their client to do one more lap "because I know you can do it" or the sales manager explaining that "with just one big push you can absolutely achieve your quota this quarter". Verbal persuasion has to be more than just flattery. It must resonate with its target in a way that is believable and convincing. Verbal persuasion is not the strongest source of self-efficacy, but sincere and honest encouragement can go a long way towards addressing people's self-doubts and insecurities. Many people have a highly critical inner voice with a deeply undermining and repetitive refrain, comprising variations on the theme of "not being good enough" for whatever it is that they are trying to achieve. They need an encouraging external voice to actively counter that negative narrative.

Resilience

The third component of PsyCap is resilience. This is a very topical concept at the moment as we are increasingly recognising that few people make it through life unscathed by difficult and occasionally traumatic life events as well as difficult and occasionally traumatic career events. Since dealing with such adversity is now recognised as the norm rather than the exception, the importance of resilience, of being able to adapt to, recover and even grow from adversity, is evident. One characteristic of a resilient organisation is one which accrues and manages assets to mitigate its risks. Similarly, organisations can help individuals to accrue assets to minimise risks. Training individuals to manage change and assisting them in developing flexible career attitudes, skills and tools are powerful ways to shore up employees' career assets and build their resilience for hard organisational times.

Frederikson[23] argues that positive emotions broaden people's response repertoires to threats and challenges. This also builds their capacity for meeting such threats and challenges in the future (this is resilience). This is where the intentional practice of helping employees find joy in the workplace by celebrating positive events such as birthdays, allowing the informal sharing of appropriate jokes and memes, and building into the work calendar opportunities for shared pleasure such as treats on offer and enjoyable team outings.

At a more reactive level, enhancing positive emotions during difficult periods can also be useful in building resilience. The Covid19 lockdowns provided excellent examples of this practice. The Jerusalema dance challenge sparked joy for many during this crisis. This was particularly popular amongst frontline healthcare workers in clinics and hospitals, who took up the challenge enthusiastically, building resilience while they demonstrated collegiality and commitment in a pleasurable way.

---

23 Frederikson, 2013.

When positive emotions are triggered, they broaden people's perspectives and increase their considerations of potential actions. This sets up a virtuous cycle where the recognition of increased possibilities allows for a broader base of problem solving the next time adversity is encountered.

Optimism

The final component of PsyCap is optimism. This is not the innate personality characteristic of seeing the glass as half full or half empty, but rather is the acquired characteristic that talks about how we understand our successes and failures – who and what do we think are responsible for them? This explanation is based on the individual's attributional style. An optimistic attributional style allows us to explain our successes as deserved, a consequence of our personal efforts, and failures as short-lived and opportunities for learning.

When we see our successes as short-lived, arbitrary and unearned and our failures as personally blameworthy, pervasive and permanent, we construct an unhealthily pessimistic attribution style. Think about an employee whose self-talk runs along these lines: "Why can I never do anything right?" This is a pessimistic style indicating a pervasive, personally blameworthy permanent attribution, versus an employee who thinks: "Oops, I made a mistake – better make sure I don't do that again." The first example of self-talk denies the possibility of a more positive outcome in future, which is the essence of pessimism, while the second example assumes the likelihood of a better future outcome, the essence of optimism.

Optimism is a fundamental resource for thriving in organisations because it is the source of our ability and willingness to persevere in attaining goals. Optimism, understood here as the opposite of self-defeating attributions, feeds into efficacy beliefs, allows resilience to emerge and is a fundamental source of hope. Its core principles are tolerance and leniency for past failures and mistakes, an appreciation and acknowledgement of what the present allows, and a capacity to imagine and seek opportunities for the future.[24]

Optimism is not necessarily a built-in trait but rather a constant work in progress. It requires ongoing, conscious thought to move from a pessimistic to an optimistic attribution style. To do this, Seligman[25] proposes the ABCDE method. A refers to the identification of Adversity; B to the recognition of self-defeating Beliefs; C to realising the Consequences of such beliefs; D to the Disputation of self-defeating

---

24 Schneider, 2001.

25 Seligman, 2002.

'irrational beliefs'; and E to the Energy that is released when the despondency of self-defeating beliefs is countered.

For those interested in using the ABCDE approach for yourself or for coaching others, there are many online resources available. One such resource may be found here: https://booksite.elsevier.com/9780123745170/Chapter%204/Chapter_4_Worksheet_4.13.pdf

Interventions to facilitate thriving

The section above addressed the pioneers of positivity in the workplace and touched on some positive interventions that can build the resources (work related and personal) that employees need in order to thrive. In this section, we focus more closely on interventions, specifically those that are practical, relevant to the workplace and have been shown to work. We look at mindfulness interventions, gratitude interventions, and strengths-based interventions, explaining what they are; what the research says about them; and how they may be implemented in an organisational setting.

Mindfulness

Mindfulness refers to the practice of being fully engaged in the present moment. It is based on two quite different schools of thought – Kabat-Zinn's work[26] which views mindfulness through an Eastern meditation-based approach and Langer's work[27] which views mindfulness as an attention-based cognitive approach. Langer sees mindfulness as a way of thinking where individuals consciously pay attention to the people and things around them, while making the effort to remain focused on the present and all that is occurring in the moment.

One of the best ways to understand Langer's conceptualisation of mindfulness is to understand its opposite – mindlessness. This is the state of autopilot that so many of us fall into – allowing days to merge into weeks and into years without paying close enough attention to ourselves, our loved ones or the world around us. Langer defines mindfulness as "the process of actively noticing new things. When you do that, it puts you in the present. It makes you more sensitive to context and perspective. It's the essence of engagement. And it's energy-begetting, not energy-consuming".[28] In particular, Langer urges people to look for something different, novel or unusual in their interactions with others and their surroundings.

---

26 Kabat-Zinn, Lipworth, & Burney, 1985, Kabat-Zinn, 2003a, 2003b.
27 Langer, 1989; Langer & Moldoveanu, 2000.
28 Langer, 2014, p.17.

In one of her studies, Langer uses professional symphony musicians to test her theory. These are employees who would seem to have very high levels of work engagement, but who were actually bored with repetitive playing. She divided the musicians into two groups: one was told to replicate a previous performance of a piece of music (i.e. to play mindlessly); the other was told to play the piece in a way that was subtly different, making small individual changes to the way it was played (to play mindfully). When recordings of the two groups' performances were played to an audience who knew nothing about the study, they preferred the mindful playing, indicating that this basic mindfulness practice improved performance.[29]

This is not a difficult mindful practice to implement in any workplace and in any type of work. As work tasks start feeling repetitive and monotonous, look for, and encourage others to look for small details that can be done differently. This requires the opposite of the way we typically engage with repetitive tasks. Instead of paying little attention and doing them by rote, focus carefully on the task, be fully present while doing it and discover little ways of changing it up.

In contrast to Langer's conceptualisation of mindfulness, Kabat-Zinn draws on Eastern philosophy, specifically meditation, as a path to mindfulness. He defines mindfulness as "paying attention in a particular way: On purpose; in the present moment and non-judgmentally."[30]

To assist people to use mindfulness to help with chronic pain, anxiety and depression, Kabat Zinn developed the Mindfulness Based Stress Reduction (MBSR) programme. This is an eight-week course comprising formal and informal mindfulness practices. Formal mindfulness practices include various types of meditation (body scan meditation, hatha yoga, and walking meditation). Informal mindfulness practices include awareness of pleasant and unpleasant events, routine events, interpersonal communication, repetitive thoughts and feelings and their connection to bodily sensations, and habitual behaviour.[31]

The success that the MBSR programme prompted an outpouring of interest and research into this programme and the results, particularly in relation to health benefits and stress reduction, have been largely positive.[32]

---

29 Langer, 2009.
30 Kabat-Zinn, 2012, p.1.
31 Santorelli, 2014.
32 Grossman et al., 2004.

Counting your blessings? Gratitude interventions

Reflect on your present blessings, of which every man has many, not on your past misfortunes, of which all men have some. C. Dickens[33]

Every society, culture and religion has ways of giving thanks for the positive acts that others have done for them and acknowledging good fortune. All religions have rituals that involve some form of thanksgiving; and simply saying 'thank you', 'ngiyabonga', 'dankie' are basic forms of civility that denote gratitude. Going beyond the norm of reciprocity, however, it appears that gratitude may have some particular benefit to provide to those who are grateful rather than to those to whom we are grateful. "A grateful response to life circumstances may be an adaptive psychological strategy and an important process by which people positively interpret everyday experiences. The ability to "notice, appreciate, and savour the elements of one's life has been viewed as a crucial determinant of well-being".[34] In this sense, gratitude can be seen as a form of mindfulness in which we note and pay attention to that which is good in our lives.

Against this background, gratitude interventions are a set of interventions that have gained some traction in recent years in both popular psychology and more recently in the workplace. One of the earliest control group trial of a gratitude intervention was undertaken by Eamons and McCullough[35] who asked college students to "think back over the past week and write down on the lines below up to five things in your life that you are grateful or thankful for" (Examples of things for which the students were grateful ranged from God, to their parent, to the Rolling Stones). A matched group of students were asked about "hassles" that had occurred in their lives and a further matched group was just asked about general events in their lives. The researchers found that respondents in the gratitude group were more positive and optimistic compared to the hassles and general events conditions. In contrast, Sheldon and Lyubomirsky[36] did not find significant differences in subjective wellbeing between a gratitude and control group in their experimental study. A study by Seligman et al.,[37] which asked participants to actually write and deliver a gratitude letter to someone who had been kind to them but whom they had never acknowledged, found that the differences between the gratitude and placebo group were significant but the results were not long lasting. Finally, in a workplace gratitude intervention, Winslow et al.[38] asked participants to think about and note twice weekly two things about

---

33 Dickens, 1846.

34 Eamons, McCullough, & Tsang, 2003, p. 378.

35 Eamons & McCullough, 2003.

36 Sheldon & Lyubomirsky, 2006.

37 Seligman et al., 2005.

38 Winslow et al., 2017.

their jobs/work for which they were grateful and compared their responses to a non-intervention group. Unfortunately, no significant differences between the groups were found.

As can be seen from the research cited above, the evidence for gratitude interventions is mixed. This may be due to the limited and short-term nature of the interventions that were introduced. It seems as though lists of blessings may not be the most effective way to improve wellbeing and enhance thriving. This does not mean that gratitude itself is not important. As indicated in the introduction to this section, gratitude is one of the fundamental values underpinning our society. What it does suggest however, is that perhaps more extensive interventions are required to be impactful and that more research is needed in this area before such interventions can be fully endorsed.

Strengths-based interventions

When most people think about changing themselves for the better, they think about addressing their weaknesses. But positive psychology suggests the opposite. Those looking for a better life should consider focusing on their strengths, not their weaknesses. Strengths are simply defined as "the things we are good at and give us energy while we are using them".[39] Lynley and Dovey identify three core elements of any strength: performance – how good we are when we use our strengths; energy – does using our strengths deplete or generate energy; and use – does this strength come into play regularly in our lives/work?[40] They developed a dictionary of strengths as well as an online tool to help people identify their strengths. They also grouped the strengths into five clusters. These are: strengths of motivating, strengths of relating, strengths of thinking, strengths of communicating and strengths of being.

Another strengths model was developed by Peterson and Seligman[41] who searched for common virtues across religions and cultures. They identified six character strengths that cut across religions and cultures, namely, wisdom and knowledge, courage, humanity, justice, temperance and transcendence.

Using the character strengths model, Proctor et al.[42] developed a Strengths Gym for two high schools in Britain. The aim of the Strengths Gym was to provide exercises and challenges to identify, build on, and enhance the students' character strengths. The findings of the study provided support for the strengths-based intervention. Adolescents who participated in the Strengths Gym had better life satisfaction as

---

39 Lynley & Dovey, 2015 p.4.

40 Lynley & Dovey, 2015.

41 Peterson & Seligman, 2004.

42 Proctor et al., 2011.

well as slightly higher self-esteem than those who did not participate. Similarly, in a placebo-controlled study, Seligman et al.[43] assigned a group of participants to a strength-based intervention or a placebo group. The intervention group were instructed "to use one of their top strengths in a new and different way every day for one week".[44] The control group were asked to write down early memories. They found that the intervention group exhibited greater levels of happiness at various intervals up to six months after the completion of the intervention. Similarly, the intervention group had lower levels of depression up to six months after the intervention.

Some evidence also exists within workplace research into strength-based interventions. Hodges and Clifton[45] used data from 65 companies to compare organisations who had implemented strengths-based intervention with those who had not. Four of the organisations in their database had implemented strengths-based interventions and they were compared to the other 61 organisations on various metrics. The four companies that had implemented strengths-based interventions had higher levels of employee engagement across a two-year period and according to Hodges and Clifton[46] "yielded an increase in annual per employee productivity of more than $1,000. This equates to more than $1million for an organisation of 1,000 employees, and more than $5.4 million for the average sized company in the study".

Aguinis, Gottfredson and Joo[47] looked at using a strengths-based approach to performance review rather than the more typical focus on weakness. "Under the strengths-based approach to feedback, managers identify their employees' strengths in terms of their exceptional job performance, knowledge, skills, and talents; provide positive feedback on what the employees are doing to succeed based on such strengths; and, finally, ask them to maintain or improve their behaviours or results by making continued or more intensive use of their strengths".[48] They provide a review of the research evidence which suggests that a strengths-based approach to performance review is superior to traditional performance review processes and they also provide a set of recommendations for providing performance feedback based on a strengths-based perspective (see Table 9.1).

---

43 Seligman et al., 2005.
44 Seligman et al., 2005, p. 416.
45 Hodges & Clifton, 2004.
46 Hodges & Clifton, 2004, p.13.
47 Aguinis, Gottfredson & Joo, 2012.
48 Ibid, p. 107.

Table 9.1: Recommendations for providing performance feedback based on a strengths-based perspective

---

1. Adopt the strengths-based approach as the primary means of providing feedback:

    - Identify employees' strengths.
    - Provide positive feedback on how employees are using their strengths to exhibit desirable behaviours and achieve beneficial results.
    - Ask employees to maintain or improve their behaviours or results by making continued or more intensive use of their strengths.

2. Closely link any negative, weaknesses-based feedback to employees' knowledge and skills (which are more changeable) rather than personality (which are more difficult to acquire).

3. Create a support system that will compensate for any talent weakness:

    Help employees improve in their areas of difficulty while remaining realistic about the extent of possible change

    - Encourage employees to see how their strongest talents can compensate for their talent weaknesses.
    - Make it easier for employees to work with partners who possess the talents that they lack.
    - Re-design jobs for employees who are deficient in certain talents, and give other employees the responsibilities that require talents that certain employees lack.

4. Deliver feedback in a considerate manner:

    - Start the feedback session by asking the employee what is working.
    - Try to provide more positive than negative feedback.

5. Provide feedback that is specific and accurate:

    - Avoid making general statements such as "Good job!"
    - Evaluate and give feedback closely based on concrete evidence.

6. Tie feedback to important consequences at various levels throughout the workplace:

    - Explain that the behaviours exhibited and results achieved by the employee have an important impact not only on the employee in terms of rewards or disciplinary measures, but also on the team, unit, or even organisation.

7. Follow up:

    - Provide specific directions by including a development plan and checking up on any progress that is made after a certain period of time.

Adapted from Aguines, Gottfredson & Joo[49]

---

[49] Aguines, Gottfredson & Joo, 2012, p. 108.

Critique of Positive Organisational Behaviour

Positive organisational behaviour has generated an enormous amount of interest, as well as a fair amount of criticism in its relatively short history. The criticisms stem from the fact that many of the positive psychology interventions do not have a strong empirical support base. This was evident in the sample of research studies cited in this chapter. Critics of positive psychology, and by implication, positive organisational behaviour, also regard positive interventions as too focussed on changing individuals rather than changing the material circumstances that are affecting their wellbeing. This is a particularly challenging criticism in South Africa, where structural inequalities based on race, class and gender are prominent. Individualised responses to such challenges can be seen as a form of victim blaming. Examples of singular people overcoming tremendous adversity through a combination of grit, a positive attitude and hard work are often presented as an inspiration to those experiencing adverse life circumstances. This suggests that by emulating these positive attributes, everyone should be able to lift themselves out of the depths of overwhelmingly difficult socio-economic, physical or psychological circumstances. This ignores the role of luck, the realities of social circumstances and the significant challenges of physical and psychological disability. The important role that collective action, by political parties, organs of state such as the Public Protector's office, civic society and trade unions, can and has played in addressing such issues – for whole communities rather than individual actors within them – is ignored and potentially undermined by such perspectives.

Conclusion

The early chapters of this book highlighted the complexity and challenges associated with the distress of mental illness. In this final chapter we shifted the focus to how organisations and the individuals inside them can thrive. The interaction between individual role-players and institutional practices can either compromise psychological functioning and exacerbate mental illness or can create conditions that support and bolster mental health and lead to individuals, organisations and societies that thrive.

Appendix 1

Psychiatric medications commonly used in South Africa

CLASS OF MEDICATION	Chemical Name (brand names)	Used for
Selective serotonin reuptake inhibitors (SSRIs)	Citalopram (Cipramil) Escitalopram (Cipralex) Fluoxetine (Prozac, Lorien, Nuzak, Lily-Fluoxetine) Paroxetine (Aropax) Sertraline (Zoloft, Serlife) Fluvoxamine (Luvox) Vortioxetine (Brintellix)	Depression Anxiety OCD Panic disorder Eating Disorders
Serotonin and norepinephrine reuptake inhibitors (SNRIs)	Desvenlafaxine (Exsira) Duloxetine (Cymbalta) Venlafaxine (Effexor, Venlor)	Depression Anxiety Somatic /pain disorders
Norepinephrine–Dopamine Reuptake Inhibitors (NDRI)	Bupropion (Wellbutrin)	Depression Anxiety Smoking cessation
Tricyclic Antidepressants	Amitriptyline (Elavil, Endep) Clomipramine (Anafranil) Desipramine (Norpramin, Pertofrane) Dosulepin (Prothiaden) Imipramine (Tofranil) Trimipramine (Surmontil)	Depression Anxiety
Tetracyclic Antidepressants	Mianserin (Lantanon) Mirtazapine (Remeron)	Depression Anxiety
Monoamine Oxidase Inhibitors (MAOIs)	Phenelzine (Nardil) Tranylcypromine (Parnate) Moclobemide (Aurorix)	Depression Anxiety
Atypical antidepressants	Molipaxin (Trazodone) Agomelatine (Valdoxan)	Depression Anxiety Insomnia

CLASS OF MEDICATION	Chemical Name (brand names)	Used for
Mood Stabilizers: Mineral	Lithium (Camcolit, Quilonum)	To prevent recurrence of mania in Bipolar 1
Mood Stabilizers: Anticonvulsants	Carbamazepine (Tegretol) Oxcarbazepine (Trileptil) Valproate/valproic acid (Epilim, Convulex) Topiramate (Topamax) Lamotrigine (Epitec, Lamictin) Gabapentin (Neurontin)	Mood swings/stabilizing Epilepsy To promote antidepressant effect Treat anxiety
Atypical Antipsychotics (Second generation antipsychotics) – also used as mood stabilizers	Amisulpride (Solian) Aripiprazole (Abilify) Olanzapine (Zyprexa) Quetiapine (Seroquel) Risperidone (Risperdal)[1] Clozapine (Clozaril) Ziprazidone (Geodon) Paliperidone (Invega)	To manage psychosis Mood swings Severe anxiety Schizophrenia To promote antidepressant effect
Antipsychotic medications: (Some of them also come in a depot injection as well as tablets.)	Haloperidol (Serenace) Chlorpromazine (Largactil) Flupenthixol (Fluanxol[2]) Zuclopenthixol (Clopixol) Pimozide (Orap) Sulpiride (Eglonyl[3])	Schizophrenia Reduce the manic phase of Bipolar 1 illness
Sedatives : Benzodiazepines	Alprazolam (Xanor, Alzam, Azor) Clonazepam (Rivotril) Diazepam (Valium) Lorazepam (Ativan) Oxazepam (Serepax) Chlordiazepoxide (Librium) Bromazepam (Lexotan) Flunitrazepam (Hypnor, Rohypnol) Midazolam (Dormicum)	Short-term anxiety or for acute anxiety/. Panic episodes. They are not typically used long-term due to concerns about tolerance, dependence and abuse. Muscle relaxants

---

1   Also used for conduct and disruptive behaviour disorders in children 5–12 years of age
2   Also used for depression and anxiety
3   In low dosages used to treat anxiety and mild depression.

CLASS OF MEDICATION	Chemical Name (brand names)	Used for
Sedatives : Others	Zolpidem (Ambien) Zopiclone (Imovane, Zopimed, Zopivane)	Sleeping tablets
Sedatives : antihistamines	Promethazine (Phenergan) Diphenhydramine (Benadryl) Trimeprazine (Vallergan Forte)	Sleeping tablets
Stimulant Medication	Methylphenidate Ritalin short acting or LA – long acting) Concerta/ Contramyl/ Neucon sustained release	For treatment of child and adult Attention Deficit Disorders (also used for treatment of narcolepsy and fatigue in conditions like MS)
Non-stimulant treatment of ADHD	Atomoxetine (Straterra)	ADHD
Beta-Blockers	Atenolol (Tenormin) Propranolol (Inderal, Purbloka)	Situational/performance anxiety

Appendix 2

Resource list: South Africa

In a medical emergency: call your local hospital emergency unit or 10111

> **Ambulance** 10177 or 112 from a cell phone

Private ambulance services:

> Ambulance Netcare 082911
>
> ER24 084124
>
> Lifemed911 0861 086 911

Akeso Psychiatric Intervention Unit 24 Hour 0861 435 787 AKESO Psychiatric Intervention

Psychiatric and psychological treatment: State services

For emergencies please call an ambulance or visit the Casualty Department of the nearest State Hospital.

For outpatient treatment call the psychiatry department of the local state hospital or check with the provincial department of health or your municipality for community psychiatric clinics or primary mental health care services in your area

Free telephonic counselling and psychological crisis services

- **SADAG Mental Health Line** 011 234 4837
- **SADAG 24 hour Suicide Crisis Line** 0800 567 567
- **LifeLine** National Counselling Line: 0861 322 322 www.lifelinesa.co.za
- **ChaiFM Helpline** 24-hour helpline for people facing emotional distress and personal difficulties throughout South Africa *Tel:* 0800 24 24 36
- **Adcock Ingram Depression and Anxiety Helpline** 0800 70 80 90
- **Dr Reddy's Help Line** 0800212223
- **Cipla 24hr Mental Health Helpline** 0800 456 789 **Cipla Whatsapp Chat Line** 076 882 2775

Specialised services

Rape/sexual abuse/Gender Based violence:

- **Tears Foundation** 24 hr free SMS service to anyone who is a victim of rape and sexual abuse in South Africa. Tel: *134*7355# / 010 590 5920 info@tears.co.za

- **Gender-Based Violence Command Centre (GBVCC)** 24hr/7days-a-week : **0800 428 428**. This "please call me" facility: ***120*7867#**. An SMS Based Line 31531 for persons with disabilities (SMS 'help' to 31531)

ChildLine: Enables children to discuss difficulties that would be far too risky in face to face contacts 24 hours a day. Tel: 0800 055 555

Substance and Alcohol Abuse

- Department of Social Development Substance Abuse Line 24hr helpline
  080 012 1314
  SMS 32312

- Ithemba Drug Toll-Free number +27 (0) 80 022 3217

- Alcoholics Anonymous +27 (0) 86 143 5722

- Narcotics Anonymous +27 (0) 83 900 6962

ADHD Helpline 0800 55 44 33

National AIDS helpline +27 (0) 80 001 2322

Autism South Africa www.aut2know.co.za

Compassionate Friends self-help organisation for bereaved parents and siblings. www.compassionatefriends.co.za/2020/south-african-tcf-chapters/

LGBTQI issues

- OUT 012 430 3272 www.out.org.za

- Gender Dynamix www.genderdynamix.org.za 27(0)21 447 4797

Psychotherapy and Counselling services

- FAMSA – Families South Africa – relationship, parenting and family counselling services, including divorce mediation www.famsa.org.za

- Find mental health resources (private and non-profit) in South Africa www. therapyroute.com

Information, Training and Advice

- South African Forum for Mental Health - information about mental health services +27 (0) 76 078 8722, +27 (0) 11 718 1852 www.safmh.org

- Legal Aid advice line (toll free) +27 (0) 80 011 0100

Appendix 3

Aspects of South African Labour Law with Specific Reference to Mental Health

Contributed by C.L. Giliomee, B. Comm; LLM, Practising attorney of the High Court of South Africa

Introduction

The South African Constitution[1] protects, amongst others, rights to human dignity[2], equality[3] and fair labour practices.[4] The right to human dignity is a central value in the system created by the Constitution and forms the foundation of many of the other protected basic human rights. The right to human dignity is not, however, directly mentioned in South African labour law legislation.[5] The right to equality is of specific importance to the present enquiry, since it includes the prohibition that no person may unfairly discriminate directly or indirectly against any person who suffers from a disability.[6] As in the case of the right to fair labour practices[7], the right to equality finds application in all three of the primary pieces of national labour legislation mentioned hereunder.

The aforesaid basic human rights form the basis of the statutory labour protection afforded to employees in South Africa and all South African Labour law should be interpreted with these core values in mind. The main sources of South African labour law are: The Labour Relations Act (LRA), the Basic Conditions of Employment Act (BCEA)[8]

---

1   Constitution of the Republic of South Africa, 108 of 1996, hereafter referred to as "the Constitution"

2   S10

3   S9

4   S23

5   The South African Constitution is founded on the values of human dignity, the achievement of equality and the advancement of human rights and freedoms. Recognising a right to dignity is an acknowledgement of the intrinsic worth of human beings. Human beings are entitled to be treated as worthy of respect and concern. The right to human dignity is the foundation of many of the other basic human rights protected by the South African Constitution. See in general on this basic human right: The core meaning of human dignity, R Steinmann, The Potchefstroom Electronic Law Journal, 2016 vol.19 n.1 and the authorities referred to therein

6   S9(4) as read with S9(3)

7   The Labour Relations Act, 66 of 1995, (hereafter referred to as the "LRA") is the pivotal piece of legislation giving effect to this constitutional right. It provides, amongst others, that every employee has the right not to be unfairly dismissed and not to be subjected to unfair labour practices. It sets out a comprehensive mechanism through which an alleged unfair dismissal or unfair labour practice may be remedied.

8   Act 75 of 1997, hereafter referred to as the "BCEA"

and the Employment Equity Act (EEA).[9] The BCEA entitles incapacitated employees to paid sick leave amongst other benefits.[10] The EEA protects employees and job applicants from unfair discrimination on the grounds of illness or disability and the LRA prohibits employers from dismissing employees because they are disabled, unless the employer can prove that the employee's disability has rendered the employee unable to fulfil their work function and the employer has first followed the statutory incapacity procedure and has been unable to find an alternative to dismissal. So- called "codes of good practice" are also published from time to time under the authority of the LRA. When interpreting the LRA, account must be taken of these codes.[11]

In what follows, these protections will be discussed with the view to form a practical guideline, from a legal perspective, on how to deal with cases of mental disability in the workplace. However, please note that this article is aimed at highlighting the most crucial aspects of South African labour law pertaining to the mental health of employees. It is not an exhaustive enquiry into this topic, and does not deal in any detail with most of the more general South African labour law aspects. In this regard, the reader is encouraged to consult the extensive body of legal writing available about South African labour law.

Mental Disability defined

A mental illness is defined in the Mental Health Care Act[12] to mean *a positive diagnosis of a mental health related illness in terms of accepted diagnostic criteria made by a mental health care practitioner authorised to make such diagnosis.*[13] A "health care practitioner" is in turn defined as *a psychiatrist or registered medical practitioner or nurse, occupational therapist, psychologist or social worker who has been trained to provide prescribed medical health care, treatment or rehabilitation services.*[14] The BCEA determines that a medical certificate (commonly referred to as a "sick note") must be signed by a medical practitioner or other person who is certified to diagnose and treat patients and who is registered with a professional council established by an Act of Parliament.[15]

---

9   Act 55 of 1998, hereafter referred to as the "EEA"

10 S22 of the BCEA: during every cycle of three years (as from the date of commencement of employment), an employee is entitled to paid sick leave equal to the number of normal working days during every period of 36 days in this cycle. This roughly translates to one day's paid leave for every 26 days worked during each three-year cycle. S23 of the BCEA: Employees do not, in order to be paid, have to bring a medical certificate if they are off ill for less than for three days unless such absence is repeated three times within an eight-week period.

11 LRA S203(3)

12 Act 17 of 2002, S1 (xxi), hereafter referred to as the "MHCA"

13 S1(xxi)

14 S1(xvii)

15 S23(2)

Presently, a generally accepted diagnostic criteria in South Africa for the diagnosis of mental disorders, is the Diagnostic and Statistical Manual of Mental Disorders, 5th Edition.[16] The DSM-5 defines a mental disorder as *a syndrome characterised by clinically significant disturbance in an individual's cognition, emotion regulation, or behaviour that reflects a dysfunction in the psychological, biological, or developmental processes underlying mental functioning.*[17]

Can a mental disorder be classified as a disability for purposes of the LRA, EEA and BCEA? S1 of the EEA defines "people with disabilities" as *people who have long term or recurring physical or mental impairment which substantially limits their prospects of entry into, or advancement in, employment.* This definition has some obvious limitations, but South African labour legislation is otherwise silent on what constitutes a "disability". It is submitted that, for purposes of the LRA and BCEA, the common meaning of the word should be ascribed to it.[18] Commonly, the word "disability" means *a physical or mental condition that limits a person's movements, senses or activities.*[19] Thus, it requires little argument that a mental disorder can be referred to as a "disability". It follows that a mental disorder should qualify as a "disability" for purposes of the LRA and this has indeed been recognised in South African case law.[20]

Disability, unfair discrimination, and mental disorders

In terms of the MHCA, a mental health care user[21] may not be unfairly discriminated against on the grounds of his or her mental health status.[22] To do so constitutes an offence punishable with a fine, imprisonment or both.[23]

---

16 Diagnostic and Statistical Manual of Mental Disorders, 5th Edition, American Psychiatric Publishing, 2013 (hereafter referred to as the "DSM-5")

17 p.20. Metal disorders are usually associated with significant distress or disability in social, occupational, or other important activities. An expectable or culturally approved response to a common stressor or loss, such as the death of a loved one, is not a mental disorder. Socially deviant behaviour (e.g. political, religious or sexual) and conflicts that are primarily between the individual and society are not mental disorders unless the deviance or conflict results from a dysfunction in the individual, as described.

18 See for instance: Union Government v Mack 1917 AD 731 at 739; Sigcau v Sigcau 1941 CPD 344; Beedle & Co v Bowley 12 SC 401 at 402

19 https://en.oxforddictionaries.com/definition/disability

20 Also see Jansen v Legal Aid South Africa (JA121/2014) [2018] ZALCCT 17; (2018) 39 ILJ 2024 (LC) (16 May 2018) at par.43 - 44 where the Court held that a "mental impairment" (in this case, depression) qualifies as a "disability". This case was subsequently taken on appeal but the finding that depression can be classified as a disability, remains – Legal Aid v Ockert Jansen [2020] ZALAC 37, (2020) 41ILJ 2580 (LAC), [2020] 11 BLLR 1103 (LAC), 2021(1)SA 245(LAC); Also, in New Way Motor and Diesel Engineering (Pty) Ltd v Marsland, (2009) 30 ILJ 2875 (LAC) at par. 24, it was held that depression can be classified as a "disability" for purposes of the LRA

21 means, amongst others, a person receiving care, treatment, or rehabilitation services – S1(xix) of the MHCA

22 S10(1)

23 S70

The EEA[24] determines that no person may unfairly discriminate, directly or indirectly, against an employee in any employment policy or practice, on various grounds including disability.[25] In addition, the LRA[26] dictates that the dismissal of an employee is automatically unfair if the reason[27] for such dismissal is that the employer unfairly discriminated against an employee, directly or indirectly, on any arbitrary ground, including, but not limited to disability.[28] A dismissal would also be deemed to be unfair if the employer fails to prove that the reason for such dismissal is a fair reason related to the employee's conduct or capacity or is based on the employer's operational requirements and that the dismissal was conducted in accordance with a fair procedure.[29] The onus of proving a fair reason for a dismissal accordingly falls on the employer. Since mental disorders qualifiy as disabilities, a dismissal based purely on a mental disorder would constitute unfair discrimination and thus be an automatically unfair dismissal.

The reasons advanced for a person's dismissal can be numerous, suffering from a mental disorder being but one of these reasons. For this reason, it has been held that, for purposes of S187 of the LRA, the most probable or plausible inference to be drawn from the circumstantial evidence presented in a case would indicate the root or dominant cause for a dismissal.[30] This root- or dominant cause is normally taken to be the reason for a dismissal. When alleging dismissal based on a prohibited ground (such as disability), the onus for proving the reason for such dismissal does not fall squarely on the employee; the employee only needs to produce evidence that is sufficient to raise a credible possibility that an automatic unfair dismissal has taken place. Once the employee has established such evidence, the onus of proof falls on the employer to prove that the reason for the dismissal did not fall within a circumstance envisaged in S187 for constituting an automatic unfair dismissal.[31]

---

24 S6(1). However, note that in terms of S6(2) it is not unfair discrimination to promote affirmative action consistent with the Act or to prefer or exclude any person based on an inherent job requirement

25 The other grounds are race, gender, pregnancy, marital status, family responsibility, ethnic or social origin, colour, sexual orientation, age, religion, HIV status, conscience, belief, political opinion, culture, language, and birth

26 S187(1)(f)

27 What constitutes the reason for a dismissal is an important element that was authoritatively dealt with in Legal Aid Board v Ockert Jansen (supra)

28 Other grounds for unfair discrimination that would constitute an automatic unfair dismissal includes race, gender, sex, ethnic or social origin, colour, sexual orientation, age, religion, conscience, belief, political opinion, culture, language, marital status, or family responsibility. However, note that S187(2) states that, despite the provisions of S187(1)(f), a dismissal may be fair if the reason for dismissal is based on an inherent requirement of the particular job and that a dismissal based on age is fair if the employee has reached the normal or agreed retirement age for persons employed in that capacity.

29 S188

30 SACWU v Afrox Ltd (1999) 20 ILJ 1718 (LAC) par. 32; Jansen v Legal Aid Board supra at par. 47 - 48

31 Kroukam v SA Airlink (Pty) Ltd [2005] 12 BLLR 1172 (LAC) at par. 27 -28; Jansen v Legal Aid Board supra at par. 49 -53; LRA S192

It is important to take cognisance of the fact that the enquiry into the root-or dominant cause of a dismissal, is directed by the general principles applied in South African common law. An intricate part of this question is the element of "legal causation". This requirement stands alongside the factual enquiry regarding the cause of a dismissal and is, according to the Labour Appeal Court, a normative value judgment where the overriding consideration is what is fair and just in each set of circumstances.[32] Thus, in the judgment of Legal Aid Board v Ockert Jansen, the Labour Appeal Court held that the proximate cause for Jansen's dismissal were four instances of misconduct and not his depression which was viewed to be, at best a contributing or subsidiary causative factor.[33] It appears that the Labour Appeal Court was impressed by an employer's *"managerial prerogative of discipline where misconduct is committed by employees suffering all manner of mental difficulties such as depression, anxiety, alcoholism, grief and the like".*[34] This is in direct contradiction of the original finding that the true reason for the employee's dismissal was, in fact, his mental condition and not his alleged misconduct and that the two were inextricably linked.[35] It is submitted that if more evidence were led by the employee regarding the influence of his mental condition (depression), this judgment could have been different. S187(1)(g) of the LRA prohibits unfair discrimination against an employee on either a direct or indirect basis. It seems possible to argue, in appropriate circumstances, that a dismissal for misconduct resulting from depression is a form of indirect discrimination.

An employer cannot be said to have dismissed an employee on the ground of disability if the employer does not know about such disability. It is thus vitally important that employees suffering from some form of mental illness inform their employers of their condition as soon as it becomes apparent that the employee's work performance suffers as a result thereof.

Dismissal for ill health (including mental disorders)

Since a dismissal based on unfair discrimination resulting from a disability would constitute an automatic unfair dismissal, an employer cannot dismiss an employee purely on the grounds of a disability.[36] This does not mean that the employer cannot terminate such employee's employment if certain requirements are present. The LRA recognises three grounds on which a termination of employment might be

---

32 Legal Aid Board v Ockert Jansen (supra) par 48; The question of legal causation is essentially one of limiting the concept of causation to a factual relationship between conduct and harmful consequences which strikes a proper balance between the interests of the wrongdoer and of the innocent victim – per JC Van der Walt, Delict: Principles and Cases, Buttterworths,1979, par 53

33 Legal Aid Board v Ockert Jansen (supra) par 48

34 Legal Aid v Ockert Jansen (supra) par 43

35 Ockert Jansen v Legal Aid (supra) par 50 -51.

36 Supra; LRA S187(f);

legitimate. These are: the capacity of the employee, the operational requirements of the employer's business and the conduct of the employee.[37]

It is submitted that in an incapacity enquiry, an employer's operational requirements are automatically considered since part of the incapacity process is an enquiry into whether the employer can provide the incapacitated employee with alternative duties. Only where the employer is unable to do so can consideration be given to dismissal.

In establishing whether a dismissal because of incapacity based on ill health was fair under the prevailing circumstances, the following should be considered: firstly, whether the employee was, objectively measured, capable of performing the work required of them (poor work performance is not a directly relevant criteria). If so, the dismissal was clearly unfair and thus subject to sanction. If not, the enquiry should continue to consider the extent to which the employee was in fact able to perform their duties, the extent to which the employee's work circumstances and/or employment duties might be adapted to accommodate their disability and, lastly, the availability of suitable alternative work.[38] Thus, a dismissal based on the incapacity of an employee can only be justified if the employee is unable to fulfil their designated work function and the employee's work circumstances and or employment duties cannot be suitably adapted and the employer is unable to provide any suitable alternative employment.

The case of the *Standard Bank of South Africa Ltd v the CCMA & others*[39] is one of the leading judgments in South Africa on the topic of dismissals based on incapacity because of ill health.[40] In this judgment, the Labour Court expounded a four-pronged enquiry that an employer must observe before dismissal for ill health may be considered. These four focus points may be summarised as follows[41]:

- As a first step, the employer must enquire into whether an employee with a disability is able to perform their work. If so, that is the end of the enquiry and the employee cannot be dismissed on the ground of alleged incapacity;

- However, if the employee concerned is in fact unable to perform their duties and the employee's incapacity is of a permanent or long-term nature[42], the enquiry proceeds as follows:

  - Firstly, the employer must ascertain the extent to which the employee is

---

37 LRA Schedule 8 – Code of Good Practice: Dismissal, S2(2);

38 LRA Schedule 8 – Code of Good Practice: Dismissal S11

39 Standard Bank of South Africa v CCMA & Others [2008] 4 BLLR 356 (LC)

40 Another leading judgment on the same subject is IMATU obo Strydom v Witzenburg Municipality & Others (2012) JOL 28586 (LAC)

41 At par.70 and further

42 Std Bank v CCMA supra par.68

unable to perform their employment duties. This is a factual enquiry and will more than likely require medical or other expert advice;[43]

○ Secondly, the enquiry proceeds to determine the extent to which the employer can adapt the employee's work circumstances to accommodate their disability;

○ Thirdly, and only if no adaptation of the employee's position is possible, the employer must enquire if any suitable and alternative positions are available.

If the outcome of the complete enquiry as set out above leaves the situation unresolved, and only in this instance, can the employer consider dismissing the incapacitated employee.

Section 10 of Schedule 8 to the LRA (Code of Good Practice: Dismissal) deals with dismissals based on ill health. For further clarity, this section is quoted:

10. *Incapacity: Ill health or injury*

(1) *Incapacity on the grounds of ill health or injury may be temporary or permanent. If an employee is temporarily unable to work in these circumstances, the employer should investigate the extent of the incapacity or the injury. If the employee is likely to be absent for a time that is unreasonably long in the circumstances, the employer should investigate all the possible alternatives short of dismissal. When alternatives are considered, relevant factors might include the nature of the job, the period of absence, the seriousness of the illness or injury and the possibility of securing a temporary replacement for the ill or injured employee. In cases of permanent incapacity, the employer should ascertain the possibility of securing alternative employment, or adapting the duties or work circumstances of the employee to accommodate the employee's disability.*

(2) *In the process of the investigation referred to in subsection (1) the employee should be allowed the opportunity to state a case in response and to be assisted by a trade union representative or fellow employee.*

---

43 An Employer cannot assess on its own whether an employee is incapacitated because of ill health. This determination must be made by a medical practitioner, psychiatrist, or psychologist, usually in conjunction with an occupational therapist. It is the employer who is responsible for ensuring that the employee undergoes an assessment, and it is also the employer's responsibility to bear the costs of the assessment. Having said this, an employee cannot be forced to undergo a medical assessment or examination. Without a medical report prepared by a medical practitioner and/or occupational therapist, an employer cannot undertake investigations to determine whether it should accommodate an employee who is suffering from ill health and how it should do so.

(3)   The degree of incapacity is relevant to the fairness of any dismissal. The cause of the incapacity may also be relevant. In the case of certain kinds of incapacity, for example alcoholism or drug abuse, counselling and rehabilitation may be appropriate steps for an employer to consider.

(4)   Particular consideration should be given to employees who are injured at work or who are incapacitated by work-related illness. The courts have indicated that the duty on the employer to accommodate the incapacity of the employee is more onerous in these circumstances.

In *Standard Bank of South Africa Ltd v the CCMA & others*,[44] the facts can be summarised as follows: whilst in the employ of the bank, an employee sustained injury to her back in a motor vehicle accident. That necessitated the bank creating an alternative position for her as she could no longer perform her previous duties. However, some 2 years later, the bank dismissed the employee for incapacity which resulted from high absenteeism and low productivity. This was, however, only done after a long period during which the bank made continued efforts to accommodate the employee. These efforts included:

• The bank requested advice from a medical practitioner on how to help the employee;

• The bank looked for and found a series of alternative positions for the employee;

• Even though the alternative posts were more junior than her original job, the bank did not reduce the employee's pay; and

• When the employee was in pain, she would be sent home for the day. The bank went so far as to, on occasion, gave the employee 4 months' paid leave to allow her to get well.

The employee did not accept her dismissal and referred the dispute to the CCMA[45], where her dismissal was found to be unfair, and 6 months' salary was awarded. The bank then took the matter on review to the Labour Court. The Labour Court held, at the outset, that the employee was to be regarded as a person with a disability. The Labour Court then proceed to examine the steps which the bank took to accommodate the employee and found, in the main, that:

• The bank failed to act on the medical practitioner's recommendation to get advice from an occupational therapist on how to accommodate the employee;

• The bank failed to give the employee a telephone headset and a comfortable chair to assist her to work with less pain;

---

44 Supra – footnote 36

45 This is the Commission for Conciliation, Mediation and Arbitration, as established i.t.o. S112 of the LRA

- The bank failed to allow the employee to do the job of entering computer data out of fear that her medication might interfere with her concentration;

- The bank failed to consider the employee's request to work half-day;

- The bank failed to allow the employee to state a case for herself on her own behalf, before dismissing her; and

- The bank failed to consult technical experts before taking the dismissal decision.

The court concluded from the above that the employer had not really wanted to keep the employee but did acknowledge that the employer had genuine problems in keeping the employee on in its employ as the employee had been absent for 74 days in one year and 116 days in the following year. In addition, the employee admitted that she struggled to cope with the alternative jobs given to her and she often needed to go home early due to pain. In spite of this acknowledgement, the Labour Court held that the bank would have been able to accommodate the employee because the cost of doing so would have been affordable for the bank and that the employee's inability to cope with the new work was partly due to the employer's reluctance to give her headphones and a comfortable chair. The Labour Court accordingly found that the bank unfairly discriminated against the employee.

Whilst the employee in the Standard Bank matter above did not suffer from a mental illness, the judgment nevertheless serves as an example of how carefully an employer must evaluate a situation prior to taking the decision to dismiss a disabled employee on grounds of incapacity. The judgment confirms that an employer, dealing with the incapacity of a disabled employee, should[46]:

- Do everything it reasonably can to change the physical workstation of an injured employee if such injury interferes with the employee's ability to work;

- Endeavour to change the employee's tasks;

- Consult with the employee on these matters before dismissing them;

- Obtain and carry out the recommendations of medical experts, unless it can prove that this is truly not viable; and

- Before deciding that nothing more can be done to save the employee's job, get advice from a reputable labour law expert.

At present, the leading authority for the dismissal, because of misconduct, of an employee who suffers from a mental illness (depression), is the case of *Jansen v the*

---

46 See: https://www.labourguide.co.za/general/433-law-expects-employers-to-go-the-extra-mile

Legal Aid Board[47] and the subsequent judgment on appeal against this judgment, referred to as *Legal Aid Board v Ockert Jansen*.[48] The important facts pertaining to these judgments can be summarised as follows[49]: *Jansen was employed as a paralegal by the Legal Aid Board for a period of approximately 7 years when he was summarily dismissed. For approximately 4 years prior to his dismissal, Jansen was diagnosed as suffering from depression. During this time, Jansen handed several medical certificates to his employer certifying this fact. Jansen also informed his employer that his depression stemmed from both personal and professional difficulties.*

During the same period, Jansen was going through a divorce and his condition was exacerbated when he found out that his line manager represented his wife in domestic violence proceedings instituted against him. The situation was further aggravated by Jansen's children being financially prejudiced and deprived of necessities including food and clothing, a fact which Jansen found to be a bitter pill to swallow.

Against this background, the Legal Aid Board alleged that there were 4 acts of misconduct perpetrated by Jansen and he was called to attend a disciplinary enquiry to answer for these acts of misconduct. The misconduct charges are important for purposes of the outcome of the judgment on appeal. These were absence from work for a period of 17 days; transgression of the Legal Aid Board's policies by failing to inform his manager of his absence from work; insolence to superiors and failing to obey lawful and reasonable instructions given by a direct superior. Notably, this was an enquiry into misconduct and not incapacity.

At the disciplinary proceedings, Jansen admitted to the 4 acts of misconduct but maintained that he suffered from depression and that, because of this condition, he acted out of character. However, the chairperson at the disciplinary enquiry disregarded Jansen's claim of depression since Jansen did not lead any expert medical evidence to confirm his claim. The chairperson was, because the claim of depression was not taken into consideration, faced with the single fact that Jansen admitted to the various acts of misconduct. As a result, Jansen was dismissed.

Following his dismissal, Jansen referred a dispute to the CCMA and alleged that the Legal Aid Board unfairly discriminated against him since he was dismissed because of his mental illness. This appears to have been a claim based on the principles enunciated in the EEA since the CCMA found that it lacked jurisdiction to arbitrate the dispute. Hereafter, the matter was referred to the Labour Court. In his statement of claim before this court, Jansen based his claim purely on unfair discrimination. As will be seen later, this proved to be a fatal mistake.

---

47 Supra – footnote 20

48 Supra – footnote 20

49 Also see: https://www.golegal.co.za/psychological-disorders-ockert/

In its judgment, the Labour Court found that, because Jansen did not plead that his dismissal was substantively or procedurally unfair, such a claim could not be taken into consideration. Jansen's claim accordingly could only be decided based on an automatic unfair dismissal, because of unfair discrimination, in terms of S187(1)(f) of the LRA.

During the hearing before the Labour Court, Jansen produced expert medical testimony that convincingly showed that he was depressed. The Labour Court, based on this testimony, then held, firstly, that the true reason (or root cause) for the Jansen's dismissal was, in fact, his mental condition and not his alleged misconduct and that the two were inextricably linked. The Labour Court then proceeded to find that the Legal Aid Board should have followed an incapacity procedure and, since this was not done, Jansen's claim succeeded.

The Legal Aid Board took this judgment on appeal. In the Labour Appeal Court, the appeal succeeded for the single reason that the Labour Appeal Court did not agree with the Labour Court's finding that the root cause of Jansen's dismissal was his mental illness. The Labour Appeal Court held that, whilst the evidence did show that Jansen suffered from depression, there was no evidence to suggest that depression was the cause of Jansen's four acts of misconduct. The Labour Appeal Court held that the expert medical practitioner who testified on Jansen's behalf in the Labour Court, had not consulted with Jansen for approximately one year prior to his various transgressions.[50] There was accordingly no factual evidence before the Court that indicated the state of Jansen's mental health at the time he committed his transgressions. This, coupled with the concession of the medical expert that Jansen could still differentiate between right and wrong and that he could act in accordance with such appreciation, formed the factual basis for the Labour Appeal Court to conclude that Jansen was in fact dismissed because of his transgressions and not because of his mental illness.[51] Another important aspect of the Labour Appeal Court's judgment is the reference, in passing, to the fact that if Jansen had pleaded his case to include claims for substantive and/or procedural unfairness, it might have been possible to find that Jansen should not have been dismissed but rather be given a lesser punishment because of his suffering from a mental disorder.[52]

Remedies for unfair dismissal because of ill health

As stated before, the LRA permits three basic reasons for dismissing an employee. These are misconduct, incapacity, and operational requirements[53]. All these categories can find application where an employee with a mental illness is involved.

---

50 Legal Aid Board v Jansen (supra) at par 45

51 The rationale for this finding of the Labour Appeal Court is discussed under the heading Disability, unfair discrimination, and mental disorders

52 See par 48 -50 of Legal Aid Board v Jansen (supra)

53 LRA – S188(1) & 189; LRA - Schedule 8 – Code of Good Practice: Dismissal - Sections 10 and 11

In addition to the application of the LRA, the EEA can also provide protection to an employee with a mental disorder in the form of protection against unfair discrimination.[54]

The choice of type of claim is important since it affects the remedies available to the employee. A court can only consider what is before it on the pleadings in the matter and due consideration should be given to alternative claims that would cover all aspects of an employee's claims.[55]

Disputes pertaining to unfair discrimination under the EEA may be referred to the CCMA within 6 months after the act or omission allegedly constituting unfair discrimination, took place.[56] It is important to note that the CCMA can only attempt to resolve the dispute by means of a conciliation process.[57] If the attempt at conciliation is not successful, the matter can only be adjudicated upon by the Labour Court unless an agreement to arbitrate before the CCMA, is reached.[58] Whenever unfair discrimination in terms of the EEA is alleged, the employer bears the onus to prove that the act complained of, is in fact fair.[59]

A claim based on unfair discrimination in terms of the EEA, excludes disputes pertaining to unfair dismissals[60] i.e., substantive- or procedural unfair dismissals or labour practices. These latter disputes must be dealt with in terms of the relevant provisions of the LRA.

When faced with a claim in terms of the EEA, the Labour Court (and under certain conditions, the CCMA) has a wide discretion in so far as the appropriate sanction for unfair discrimination is concerned.[61] For present purposes, the most relevant sanctions include orders that compensation[62] and/or damages[63] be paid by the employer to the employee.[64]

---

54 EEA – S 5 & 6

55 See as an example Legal Aid v Ockert Jansen (supra) where the Labour Appeal Court held that, because Jansen based his claim on only the provisions of S187 of the LRA (automatic unfair dismissals), it could not assist Jansen by exploring the possibility that the sanction for his misconduct should have ameliorated by his mental illness i.e., depression. This would apparently have been possible if Jansen based his claim on the provisions of S191 of the LRA (unfair dismissals and unfair labour practices)

56 EEA – S10(2) Note that in terms of EEA – S10(3), the CCMA may at any time permit a party that shows good cause to refer a dispute after the 6 months' period has lapsed

57 EEA – S10(5)

58 EEA – S10(6); LRA – S141

59 EEA – S11

60 EEA – S10(1)

61 EEA – S50

62 EEA – S50(2)(a)

63 EEA – S50(2)(b)

64 "Compensation" in this context refer to payment of remuneration not received by an employee, whilst "damages" refer to compensation (or in legal parlance, contumelia,) for emotional suffering because of the unfair discrimination inflicted on the employee

If the sole reason for dismissing an employee, is the fact that the employee suffers from a mental illness, such dismissal would constitute an automatic unfair dismissal on the grounds of unfair discrimination.[65] When dealing with an employee with a mental illness in terms of the LRA, an employer initially has a choice to deal with the situation in accordance with the so-called "incapacity procedure"[66], alternatively, as an issue pertaining to the employer's operational requirements[67] and, thirdly, as misconduct[68] on the part of the employee. What procedure must be followed, is a factual question that will differ on a case-by-case basis.

When facing the question of what procedure to follow in the case of an employee with a mental illness, it is, firstly, important to note that a mental disability can impact on a person's state of mind (cognitive ability) and will (conative ability) to the extent that such person is unable to appreciate the wrongfulness of their conduct. In these circumstances, such a person would be unable to conduct themself in accordance with an appreciation of wrongfulness.[69] Where this is the case, dismissal for misconduct would be substantively unfair and such an action would be susceptible to legal sanction.[70] From an employer's perspective, an employee's actions under these circumstances should be approached from an incapacity[71] point of view or, in appropriate cases, from an operational requirement[72] perspective.

It seems probable that most cases involving mental illness in the workplace, would rather pertain to situations where an employee's cognitive and conative capacities have not been negated by the mental illness concerned and that the employee is in fact able to appreciate the wrongfulness of their conduct. Their culpability or blameworthiness might, however, still be diminished by the mental illness. In such a case, the employer can approach the situation as one of misconduct.[73] The employee's mental illness must still be taken into consideration when the appropriate sanction for misconduct is determined.[74] Thus, in cases that would normally warrant dismissal, mental illness might dictate that a lesser sanction be imposed.

---

65 LRA – S187(1)(f)

66 LRA – S188(1)(a)(i)

67 LRA – S188(1)(a)(ii)

68 LRA - S188(1)(a)(i) & S191

69 Similar situations, in other areas of South African law, would regard such person as "doli incapax" i.e., be deemed incapable of forming the intent to commit a crime or delict, such as in the case of a young child

70 Legal Aid v Ockert Jansen (supra) par 42

71 LRA – S188(1) & 189; LRA - Schedule 8 – Code of Good Practice: Dismissal - Sections 10 and 11

72 LRA – S189

73 LRA – S188(1)(a)(i)

74 Legal Aid v Ockert Jansen (supra) par 42

Whatever procedure the employer decides to follow, once the employee has made the employer aware that they suffer from a mental illness that affect their duties in one way or another, medical evidence regarding the existence of such mental illness, and the extent thereof, needs to be obtained. Such medical evidence can only be given by a suitably qualified medical practitioner that examined the employee during the relevant period. If the employer requests such evidence, the employer will be responsible for those costs. This does not, however, mean that the employee does not have to do anything. The employee must be able to, of their own accord, produce credible evidence of their mental illness and the effect it has on the performance of their duties. Only if the employee produces such evidence does the need arise for the employer to rebut such evidence and the conclusion of all the medical evidence will dictate the appropriate course of action to be taken in the circumstances.[75]

From an employee's perspective, if an employee wishes to dispute an employer's decision pertaining to their employment and the impact of their mental health on the fulfilment thereof, such employee can approach the CCMA and, in appropriate circumstances, the Labour Court. Whilst condonation for a late referral might be granted, a dispute pertaining to an unfair dismissal must be referred to the CCMA within 30 days[76] of the date of a dismissal or, if it is a later date, within 30 days of the employer making a final decision to dismiss or uphold a dismissal.[77] Due regard should be given to the fact that mental illness does not only provide a basis for a claim based on unfair discrimination, but that a mental illness can also provide a basis to claim extenuating circumstances that can influence the severity of disciplinary action to be imposed.

---

75 See, in general, the approach followed by the Labour Appeal Court in Legal Aid v Ockert Jansen (supra) regarding the procurement of evidence pertaining to mental illness.

76 Not 6 months as in the case of a dispute referred under the auspices of the EEA

77 LRA – S191(1)(b)(ii)

References

Chapter 1

Alvertis, I., Kokkinakos, P., Koussouris, S., Lampathaki, F., Psarras, J., Viscusi, G., & Tucci, C. (2015). Challenges laying ahead for future digital enterprises: a research perspective. In *International Conference on Advanced Information Systems Engineering* (pp. 195-206). Springer, Cham.

Beddington, J., Cooper, C.L., Field, J., Goswami, U., Huppert, F.A., Jenkins, R., Jones, H.S., Kirkwood, T.B.L., Sahakian, B.J. & Thomas, S.M. (2008). The mental wealth of nations. *Nature, 455*(7216), 1057-1060.

Docrat, S., Besada, D., Cleary, S., Daviaud, E., & Lund, C. (2019). Mental health system costs, resources and constraints in South Africa: a national survey. *Health policy and planning, 34*(9), 706-719.Kumar, A., & Nayar, K. R. (2020). COVID 19 and its mental health consequences. *Journal of Mental Health*, 1-2.

Harter, J. K., Schmidt, F. L., & Hayes, T. L. (2002). Business-unit-level relationship between employee satisfaction, employee engagement, and business outcomes: a meta-analysis. *Journal of applied psychology, 87*(2), 268.

Lund, C., Kleintjes, S., Kakuma, R., Flisher, A. J., & MHaPP Research Programme Consortium. (2010). Public sector mental health systems in South Africa: inter-provincial comparisons and policy implications. *Social psychiatry and psychiatric epidemiology, 45*(3), 393-404.

Schwab, K. (2017). *The fourth industrial revolution.* Currency.

World Health Organisation. (2001). *The World Health Report 2001: Mental health: new understanding, new hope.* World Health Organisation.

Chapter 2

American Psychiatric Association. (2013). *Diagnostic and statistical manual of mental disorders* (5th Ed). American Psychiatric Publishing, Washington DC.

American Psychiatric Association (2017). *What is Mental Illness?* Retrieved from: www.psychiatry.org/patients-families/what-is-mental-illness

Bryne, P. (1999). Stigma of mental disorders - changing minds, changing behaviour. *British Journal of Psychiatry,* 174, 1-2.

Buist-Bouwman, M. A., de Graaf, R., Vollebergh, W. A., & Ormel, J. (2005). Comorbidity of Physical and mental disorders and the effect on work-loss days. *Acta Psychiatrica Scandinavica,* 111(6), 436-443.

Constitution of the Republic of South Africa, 1996 - Chapter 2: Bill of Rights

Crawford, T.A. & Lipsedge, M. 2004. Seeking help for Psychological distress: the interface of Zulu traditional healing and Western biomedicine. *Mental Health Religion and Culture,* 7(2), 131-149

Crisp, A. H., Gelder, M. G., Rix, S., Meltzer, H. I., & Rowlands, O. J. (2000). Stigmatisation of people with mental illnesses. *The British Journal of Psychiatry,* 177(1), 4-7.

Day E.N., Edgren, K. and Eshleman, A. (2007). Measuring Stigma toward Mental Illness: Development and Application of the Mental Illness Stigma Scale. *Journal of Applied Social Psychology,* 37(10), 2191-2219.

Durojaye, E., & Agaba, D. K. (2018). Contribution of the Health Ombud to accountability: The life Esidimeni tragedy in South Africa. *Health and Human Rights*, 20(2), 161.

Evans-Lacko, S., & Knapp, M. (2016). Global patterns of workplace productivity for people with depression: absenteeism and presenteeism costs across eight diverse countries. *Social Psychiatry and Psychiatric Epidemiology*, 51 (11), 1525-1537.

Flisher, A. J., Lund, C., Funk, M., Banda, M., Bhana, A., Doku, V., ... & Petersen, I. (2007). Mental health policy development and implementation in four African countries. *Journal of Health Psychology*, 12(3), 505-516.

Frank, O. (2017). *Mental health and wellness aren't the same*. Retrieved from: https://work. qz.com/1115542/mental-health-and-wellness-are-not-the-same. Downloaded 22 September 2019.

Heginbotham, C. (1998). UK mental health policy can alter the stigma of mental illness. *The Lancet*, 352(9133), 1052-1053.

Helman, CG. (2007). "Cross-Cultural Psychiatry". *Culture, Health and Illness*, Fifth edition. London: CRC Press.

Hewson, M.G. (1998). Traditional Healers in South Africa. *Annals of Internal Medicine*. 128(1), 1029-1034.

Insel, T.R. (2008). Assessing the Economic Costs of Serious Mental Illness. *The American Journal of Psychiatry*. 165(6), 663-665.

Kubeka, N.P. (2016). The Psychological Perspective on Zulu Ancestral calling: a phenomenological study. Unpublished Masters dissertation: University of Pretoria.

Lund, C., Kleintjes, S., Kakuma, R., Flisher, A. J., & MHaPP Research Programme Consortium. (2010). Public sector mental health systems in South Africa: inter-provincial comparisons and policy implications. *Social psychiatry and psychiatric epidemiology*, 45(3), 393-404.

Mental Health America (2018). *Mind the Workplace Report*. Retrieved from: https://www. mhanational.org/mind-workplace-2018.

Murray, C.J.L., Vos, T., Lozano, R., Naghavi, M., Flaxman, A.D., Michaud, C. et al (2012) Disability-adjusted life years (DALYs) for 291 diseases and injuries in 21 regions, 1990–2010: a systematic analysis for the Global Burden of Disease Study 2010. *Lancet* 380:2197–2223. doi:10.1016/S0140-6736(12)61689-4.

National Alliance on Mental Illness. (2020). Mental Health by the Numbers. Retrieved from: www.nami.org/Learn-More/Mental-Health-By-the-Numbers

Ngubane, in Eagle, G. 2005. Therapy at the Cultural Interface: Implications of African Cosmology for Traumatic Stress Intervention. *Journal of Contemporary Psychology*, 35(2), 199-209

Niehaus, D.J., Oosthuizen, P., Lochner, C., Emsley, R.A., Jordaan, E., Mbanga, N.I., Keyter, N., Laurent, C., Deleuze, J., & Stein, D. (2004). A Culture-Bound Syndrome 'Amafufunyana' and a Culture-Specific Event 'Ukuthwasa': Differentiated by a Family History of Schizophrenia and other Psychiatric Disorders. *Psychopathology*. 37, 59-63.

Owen, P.R. (2012). Portrayals of schizophrenia by entertainment media: a content analysis of contemporary movies. *Psychiatric Services* 63(7), 655-659.

Parks, J., Svendsen, D., Singer, P., Foti, M. E., & Mauer, B. (2006). Morbidity and mortality in people with serious mental illness. *Alexandria, VA: National Association of State Mental Health Program Directors (NASMHPD) Medical Directors Council*, 25(4), 1-87.

Reavley, N. J., & Jorm, A. F. (2011). Stigmatizing attitudes towards people with mental disorders: findings from an Australian National Survey of Mental Health Literacy and Stigma. *Australian & New Zealand Journal of Psychiatry*, 45(12), 1086-1093.

Richardson, S., Shaffer, J. A., Falzon, L., Krupka, D., Davidson, K. W., & Edmondson, D. (2012). Meta-analysis of perceived stress and its association with incident coronary heart disease. *The American Journal of Cardiology*, 110(12), 1711–1716.

Schoeman, R. (2017). *Mental health problems cost SA's economy billions per year*. Retrieved from: https://www.businesslive.co.za/fm/features/2017-08-31-mental-health-problems-cost-sas-economy-billions-per-year

Sinason, Valerie (2002). "Dissociation and Spirit Possession". *Attachment, Trauma and Multiplicity: Working with Dissociative Identity Disorder*. Psychology Press. pp. 233–236.

Smook, Breggie, Ubbink, Marie, Ryke, Elma, & Strydom, Herman. (2014). Substance abuse, dependence and the workplace: A literature overview. *Social Work*, 50(1), 59-83.

The Standing Senate Committee on Social Affairs, Science and Technology (2006). Out of the shadows at last: transforming mental health, mental illness and addiction services in Canada. The Senate, Ottawa.

Train, B. (2007). *Fresh Perspectives: Introduction to Psychology*. Pearson South Africa.

UN General Assembly. (1948). *Universal declaration of human rights* (Article 23.1). Paris. Retrieved from http://www.un.org/en/universal-declaration-human-rights/

Wang, J., & Lai, D. (2008). The relationship between mental health literacy, personal contacts and personal stigma against depression. *Journal of Affective Disorders*, 110(1-2), 191-196.

Watson AC, Corrigan PW, Larson JE & Sells M. (2007). Self-stigma in people with mental illness. *Schizophrenia Bulletin*, 33, 1312–1318.

Weiss, M. G., & Ramakrishna, J. (2006). Stigma interventions and research for international health. *Lancet, 367(9509)*, 536 – 538.

World Health Organisation Depression factsheet [Internet]. 2013. Retrieved from: http://www.who.int/mediacentre/factsheets/f/en/

World Health Organisation (WHO). (2014). Factfiles Mental health: a state of well-being. Retrieved from: (updated 2014). https://www.who.int/features/factfiles/mental_health/en/

The World Health Organisation (WHO). (2020). *Towards a Common Language for Functioning, Disability and Health*. Retrieved from: https://www.who.int/classifications/icf/icfbeginnersguide.pdf

Chapter 3

American Psychiatric Association. (2013). *Diagnostic and Statistical Manual of Mental Disorders* (5th Ed.). American Psychiatric Publishing. Washington DC.

Blackmore, E. R., Stansfeld, S. A., Weller, I., Munce, S., Zagorski, B. M., & Stewart, D. E. (2007). Major depressive episodes and work stress: results from a national population survey. *American Journal of Public Health*, 97(11), 2088-2093.

Bowden, C. L. (2005). Bipolar disorder and work loss. *American Journal of Managed Care, 11*(3 Suppl), S91-S94.

Child, K. (2013). Bipolar disorder cases show 'staggering increase'. Retrieved from: www.timeslive.co.za/news/south-africa/2013-09-05-bipolar-disorder-cases-show-staggering-increase

Cuijpers, P., Sijbrandij, M., Koole, S. L., Andersson, G., Beekman, A. T., & Reynolds, C. F., 3rd (2014). Adding psychotherapy to antidepressant medication in depression and anxiety disorders: a meta-analysis. *World Psychiatry : Official Journal of the World Psychiatric Association*, 13(1), 56–67.

Czeisler MÉ , Lane RI, Petrosky E, et al. (2020). Mental Health, Substance Use, and Suicidal Ideation During the COVID-19 Pandemic — United States, June 24-30, 2020. MMWR Morb Mortal Wkly Rep 69, 1049-1057. DOI: http://dx.doi.org/10.15585/mmwr.mm6932a1external icon.

Dinsmoor, R.S & Odle, T.G (2015). Generalized Anxiety Disorder in *The Gale Encyclopedia of Medicine*. 4 (5), 2149–2150.

Ferrari, A. J., Stockings, E., Khoo, J. P., Erskine, H. E., Degenhardt, L., Vos, T., & Whiteford, H. A. (2016). The prevalence and burden of bipolar disorder: findings from the Global Burden of Disease Study 2013. *Bipolar Disorders*, 18(5), 440-450.

Foldes-Busque, G., Denis, I., Poitras, J., Fleet, R. P., Archambault, P., & Dionne, C. E. (2019). A closer look at the relationships between panic attacks, emergency department visits and non-cardiac chest pain. *Journal of Health Psychology*, 24(6), 717-725.

Freudenberger, H. J., & Richelson, G. (1981). *Burn-out: The high cost of high achievement*. Bantam Books.

Gallagher, M. W., Zvolensky, M. J., Long, L. J., Rogers, A. H., & Garey, L. (2020). The impact of covid-19 experiences and associated stress on anxiety, depression, and functional impairment in American adults. *Cognitive Therapy and Research*, 44(6), 1043-1051.

Ganster, D. C., & Rosen, C. C. (2013). Work stress and employee health: A multidisciplinary review. *Journal of Management*, 39(5), 1085-1122.

GBD 2015 Disease and Injury Incidence and Prevalence Collaborators (October 2016). Global, regional, and national incidence, prevalence, and years lived with disability for 310 diseases and injuries, 1990-2015: a systematic analysis for the Global Burden of Disease Study 2015. *Lancet*, 388(10053), 1545–1602.

Goetzel, R. Z., Hawkins, K., Ozminkowski, R. J., & Wang, S. (2003). The health and productivity cost burden of the "top 10" physical and mental health conditions affecting six large US employers in 1999. *Journal of Occupational and Environmental Medicine*, 45(1), 5-14.

Gray-Stanley, J. A., Muramatsu, N., Heller, T., Hughes, S., Johnson, T. P., & Ramirez-Valles, J. (2010). Work stress and depression among direct support professionals: the role of work support and locus of control. *Journal of Intellectual Disability Research*, 54(8), 749-761.

Hammar, Å., & Guro, Å., (2009). Cognitive functioning in major depression-a summary. *Frontiers in Human Neuroscience*, 3 (26).

Haslam, C., Atkinson, S., Brown, S., & Haslam, R. A. (2005). Perceptions of the impact of depression and anxiety and the medication for these conditions on safety in the workplace. *Occupational and Environmental Medicine*, 62(8), 538-545.

Hunt, G. E., Malhi, G. S., Cleary, M., Lai, H. M. X., & Sitharthan, T. (2016). Prevalence of comorbid bipolar and substance use disorders in clinical settings, 1990–2015: systematic review and meta-analysis. *Journal of Affective Disorders*, 206, 331-349.

Iacovides, A., Fountoulakis, K. N., Kaprinis, S., & Kaprinis, G. (2003). The relationship between job stress, burnout and clinical depression. *Journal of Affective Disorders*, 75(3), 209-221.

Jamison, K. R. (1996). *An Unquiet Mind: A Memoir of Moods and Madness*. New York: Vintage.

Kleinman, N. L., Brook, R. A., Rajagopalan, K., Gardner, H. H., Brizee, T. J., & Smeeding, J. E. (2005). Lost time, absence costs, and reduced productivity output for employees with bipolar disorder. *Journal of Occupational and Environmental Medicine*, 47(11), 1117-1124.

Lee, S. A., Jobe, M. C., Mathis, A. A., & Gibbons, J. A. (2020). Incremental validity of coronaphobia: Coronavirus anxiety explains depression, generalized anxiety, and death anxiety. *Journal of Anxiety Disorders*, 74, 102268.

Lerner, D., Adler, D. A., Rogers, W. H., Lapitsky, L., McLaughlin, T., & Reed, J. (2010). Work performance of employees with depression: the impact of work stressors. *American Journal of Health Promotion, 24*(3), 205-213.

Marwaha, S., & Johnson, S. (2004). Schizophrenia and employment: A review. *Social Psychiatry and Psychiatric Epidemiology, 39*(5), 337–349.

Merikangas, K. R., Jin, R., He, J. P., Kessler, R. C., Lee, S., Sampson, N. A., ... & Ladea, M. (2011). Prevalence and correlates of bipolar spectrum disorder in the world mental health survey initiative. *Archives of General Psychiatry, 68*(3), 241-251.

Michalak, E. E., Yatham, L. N., Maxwell, V., Hale, S., & Lam, R. W. (2007). The impact of bipolar disorder upon work functioning: a qualitative analysis. *Bipolar Disorders, 9*(1-2), 126-143.

Penninx, B. (2019). Examining the antidepressant scattergun approach. *The Lancet Psychiatry, 6*(11), 878-879.

Rajgopal, T. (2010). Mental well-being at the workplace. *Indian Journal of Occupational and Environmental Medicine, 14*(3), 63.

Rajagopalan, K., Kleinman, N. L., Brook, R. A., Gardner, H. H., Brizee, T. J., & Smeeding, J. E. (2006). Costs of physical and mental comorbidities among employees: a comparison of those with and without bipolar disorder. *Current Medical Research and Opinion, 22*(3), 443-452.

Romans, S. E., Tyas, J., Cohen, M. M., & Silverstone, T. (2007). Gender differences in the symptoms of major depressive disorder. *The Journal of Nervous and Mental Disease, 195*(11), 905-911.

Ruscio, A. M., Stein, D. J., Chiu, W. T., & Kessler, R. C. (2010). The epidemiology of obsessive-compulsive disorder in the National Comorbidity Survey Replication. *Molecular Psychiatry, 15*(1), 53.

Ruscio, A. M., Hallion, L. S., Lim, C. C., Aguilar-Gaxiola, S., Al-Hamzawi, A., Alonso, J., ... & De Almeida, J. M. C. (2017). Cross-sectional comparison of the epidemiology of DSM-5 generalized anxiety disorder across the globe. *JAMA Psychiatry, 74*(5), 465-475.

Ryder, A. G., Yang, J., Zhu, X., Yao, S., Yi, J., Heine, S. J., & Bagby, R. M. (2008). The cultural shaping of depression: somatic symptoms in China, psychological symptoms in North America? *Journal of Abnormal Psychology, 117*(2), 300.

Rydmark, I., Wahlberg, K., Ghatan, P. H., Modell, S., Nygren, Å., Ingvar, M., ... & Heilig, M. (2006). Neuroendocrine, cognitive and structural imaging characteristics of women on long-term sick leave with job stress–Induced depression. *Biological Psychiatry, 60*(8), 867-873.

SADAG. (2017). New SADAG Bipolar Disorder Survey. Retrieved from: www.sadag.org/images/pdf/New-Sadag-Bipolar-Disorder-Survey.pdf

Sajatovic, M. (2005). Bipolar disorder: disease burden. *American Journal of Managed Care, 11*(3), S80-84.

Schuch, J. J., Roest, A. M., Nolen, W. A., Penninx, B. W., & De Jonge, P. (2014). Gender differences in major depressive disorder: results from the Netherlands study of depression and anxiety. *Journal of Affective Disorders, 156*, 156-163.

Shirom, A., Westman, M., & Melamed, S. (1999). The effects of pay systems on blue-collar employees' emotional distress: The mediating effects of objective and subjective work monotony. *Human Relations, 52*(8), 1077-1097.

Stander, M. P., Bergh, M., Miller-Janson, H. E., Beer, J. C. D., & Korb, F. A. (2016). Depression in the South African workplace. *South African Journal of Psychiatry, 22*(1), 1-2.

Stein, D. J., Roberts, M., Hollander, E., Rowland, C., & Serebro, P. (1996). Quality of life and pharmaco-economic aspects of obsessive-compulsive disorder. A South African survey. *South African Medical Journal, 86*(12 Suppl), 1579-1582.

Substance Abuse and Mental Health Services Administration. (2017). *Key substance use and mental health indicators in the United States: Results from the 2016 National Survey on Drug Use and Health* (HHS Publication No. SMA 17-5044, NSDUH Series H-52). Center for Behavioral Health Statistics and Quality, Substance Abuse and Mental Health Services Administration. Retrieved from: https://www. samhsa.gov/data/

Sugarman, M.A. (2016) Are antidepressants and psychotherapy equally effective in treating depression? A critical commentary. *Journal of Mental Health*, 25 (6), 475-478.

Taylor, G., McNeill, A., Girling, A., Farley, A., Lindson-Hawley, N., & Aveyard, P. (2014). Change in mental health after smoking cessation: systematic review and meta-analysis. *British Medical Journal*, 348, p1151.

Tennant, C. (2001). Work-related stress and depressive disorders. *Journal of Psychosomatic Research*, 51(5), 697-704.

Vesga-López, O., Schneier, F., Wang, S., Heimberg, R., Liu, S. M., Hasin, D. S., & Blanco, C. (2008). Gender differences in generalized anxiety disorder: results from the National Epidemiologic Survey on Alcohol and Related Conditions (NESARC). *The Journal of Clinical Psychiatry*, 69(10), 1606.

Wardenaar, K. J., Lim, C. C., Al-Hamzawi, A. O., Alonso, J., Andrade, L. H., Benjet, C., ... & Gureje, O. (2017). The cross-national epidemiology of specific phobia in the World Mental Health Surveys. *Psychological Medicine*, 47(10), 1744.

Williams, D. R., Herman, A., Stein, D. J., Heeringa, S. G., Jackson, P. B., Moomal, H., & Kessler, R. C. (2008). Twelve-month mental disorders in South Africa: prevalence, service use and demographic correlates in the population-based South African Stress and Health Study. *Psychological Medicine*, 38(2), 211–220.

World Health Organisation. (2019). *Global status report on alcohol and health 2018*. World Health Organisation.

Yutzy, S. H., Woofter, C. R., Abbott, C. C., Melhem, I. M., & Parish, B. S. (2012). The increasing frequency of mania and bipolar disorder: causes and potential negative impacts. *The Journal of Nervous and Mental Disease*, 200(5), 380-7.

Chapter 4

American Psychiatric Association. (2013). *Diagnostic and Statistical Manual of Mental Disorders* (5th Ed.). American Psychiatric Publishing. Washington DC.

Bernardi, R., & Eidlin, M. (2018). Thin-skinned or vulnerable narcissism and thick-skinned or grandiose narcissism: similarities and differences. *The International Journal of Psychoanalysis*, 99(2), 291-313.

Blackburn, R. (2007). Personality disorder and antisocial deviance: comments on the debate on the structure of the psychopathy checklist-revised, *Journal of Personality Disorders*, 21 (2), 142-59

Campbell, W. K., Hoffman, B. J., Campbell, S. M., & Marchisio, G. (2011). Narcissism in organisational contexts. *Human Resource Management Review*, 21(4), 268-284.

Caligor, E., Levy, K., & Yeomans, F.E. (2015) Narcissistic Personality Disorder: Diagnostic and Clinical Challenges. *American Journal of Psychiatry* 172, 415-422

Chivers, T. (2014) Psychopaths: how can you spot one? https://www.telegraph.co.uk/books/ non-fiction/spot-psychopath/

Cleckley, H. M. (1951). The mask of sanity. *Postgraduate Medicine*, 9(3), 193-197.

Colligan, T. W., & Higgins, E. M. (2006). Workplace Stress. *Journal of Workplace Behavioral Health,* 21(2), 89-97.

Crompton, S., 2014. *All about me: Loving a Narcissist.* HarperCollins UK.

Franz, L., Chambers, N., von Isenburg, M., & de Vries, P. J. (2017). Autism spectrum disorder in sub-saharan africa: A comprehensive scoping review. *Autism Research,* 10(5), 723-749.

Goldman, A. (2006). High toxicity leadership: Borderline personality disorder and the dysfunctional organisation. *Journal of Managerial Psychology,* 21(8), 733-746.

Grandin, T. (2011). *The way I see it: A personal look at Autism & Asperger's.* Future Horizons.

Gunderson, J.G., Shea, M.T., Skodol, A.E., McGlashan, T.H., Morey, L.C., Stout, R.L, Zanarini, M.C., Grilo, C.M., Oldham, J.M., Keller, M.B. (2000). The Collaborative Longitudinal Personality Disorders Study: development, aims, design, and sample characteristics. *Journal of Personality Disorders.* 14(4), 300-15.

Hare, R.D. & Babiak, P. (2006). *Snakes in Suits: When Psychopaths Go to Work.* New York: HarperCollins.

Hedley, D., Uljarević, M., & Hedley, D. F. (2017). Employment and living with autism: Personal, social and economic impact. In *Inclusion, disability and culture* (pp. 295-311). Springer, Cham.

Hengartner, M. P., Müller, M., Rodgers, S., Rössler, W., & Ajdacic-Gross, V. (2014). Interpersonal functioning deficits in association with DSM-IV personality disorder dimensions. *Social Psychiatry and Psychiatric Epidemiology,* 49(2), 317-325.

James, O. (2013). *Office Politics: How to Thrive in a World of Lying, Backstabbing and Dirty Tricks.* Random House UK .

Juni, S. (2014). Diagnosing antisocial behavior and psychopathy. *Journal of Criminal Psychology,* 4(1), 76-96.

Kaufman, S. B., Yaden, D. B., Hyde, E., & Tsukayama, E. (2019). The Light vs. Dark Triad of Personality: Contrasting Two Very Different Profiles of Human Nature. *Frontiers in Psychology,* 10, 467.

Korzekwa, M. I., Dell, P. F., & Pain, C. (2009). Dissociation and borderline personality disorder: an update for clinicians. *Current Psychiatry Reports,* 11(1), 82-88.

Lugnegård, T., Hallerbäck, M. U., & Gillberg, C. (2012). Personality disorders and autism spectrum disorders: what are the connections? *Comprehensive Psychiatry,* 53(4), 333-340

Lyall, K., Croen, L., Daniels, J., Fallin, M. D., Ladd-Acosta, C., Lee, B. K., ... & Windham, G. C. (2017). The changing epidemiology of autism spectrum disorders. *Annual Review of Public Health,* 38, 81-102.

Maccoby, M. (2003). *The Productive Narcissist: The promise and peril of visionary leadership.* Broadway.

Markon, K.E., Krueger, F. Bouchard Jr., T. J. Gottesman I.I. (2002). Normal and Abnormal Personality Traits: Evidence for Genetic and Environmental Relationships in the 6-54 Minnesota Study of Twins Reared Apart. *Journal of Personality* 70 (5).

Meloy, J. R. (1988). *The psychopathic mind: Origins, dynamics, and treatment.* Rowman & Littlefield.

Montano, D., Reeske, A., Franke, F., & Hüffmeier, J. (2017). Leadership, followers' mental health and job performance in organisations: A comprehensive meta-analysis from an occupational health perspective. *Journal of Organisational Behavior,* 38, 327–350.

Office for National Statistics (2016) Dataset: A08: *Labour market status of disabled people* (20 July 2016). London: Office for National Statistics

Penney, L. M., & Spector, P. E. (2002, June). Narcissism and Counterproductive Work Behavior: Do Bigger Egos Mean Bigger Problems? http://onlinelibrary.wiley.com/doi/10.1111/1468-2389.00199/epdf

Rutter, M. (2005). Incidence of autism spectrum disorders: changes over time and their meaning. *Acta Paediatrica*, 94(1), 2-15.

Sansone, R. A., & Sansone, L. A. (2011). Gender patterns in borderline personality disorder. *Innovations in Clinical Neuroscience*, 8(5), 16.

Chapter 5

Africacheck. (2013). https://africacheck.org/reports/flawed-survey-claims-a-third-of-south-africans-are-drug-users/

American Society of Addiction Medicine. (2011). Public Policy Statement: Definition of Addiction. Retrieved from: https://www.asam.org/resources/definition-of-addiction

Andersson, L. M., & Pearson, C. M. (1999). Tit for tat? the spiraling effect of incivility in the workplace. *Academy of Management Review*, 24(3), 452-471.

Barling, J., Kathryne, E., Dupré, E., Kelloway, K. (2009). Predicting Workplace Aggression and Violence. *Annual Review of Psychology*, 60:1, p. 671-692

Bond, S.A., Tuckey, M.R., Dollard, M.F., (2010) Psychosocial Safety Climate, Workplace Bullying, and Symptoms of Posttraumatic Stress. *Organisation Development Journal* 28 (1), 37-56.

Faull, A. (2018) Police murder-suicide reveals South Africa's dark underbelly. Institute for Security Studies. https://issafrica.org/iss-today/police-murder-suicide-reveals-south-africas-dark-underbelly

Hoobler, JM., Rospenda, K.M., Lemmon G, & Rosa J.A. (2010). A within-subject longitudinal study of the effects of positive job experiences and generalized workplace harassment on well-being. *Journal of Occupational Health Psychology*, 15, 434–451.

Kardefelt-Winther, D., Heeren, A., Schimmenti, A., Rooij, A., Maurage, P., Carras, M., ... Billieux, J. (2017). How can we conceptualize behavioural addiction without pathologizing common behaviours? *Addiction*, 112(10), 1709-1715.

Khantzian, E. J., & Albanese, M. J. (2008). *Understanding addiction as self-medication: Finding hope behind the pain*. New York, NY: Rowman & Littlefield Publishers, Inc.

Lee, S., & McCrie, R. (2012). Mass Homicides by Employees in the American Workplace. *ASIS International*

Maluleke, R. (2018). Crime Statistics Series Volume V: Crime against Women in South Africa. Statistics South Africa.

Matzopoulos, R., Truen, S., Bowman, B., & Corrigall, J. (2013). The cost of harmful alcohol use in South Africa. *South African Medical Journal*, 104(2), 127-132.

Menéndez, C. C., Konda, S., Hendricks, S., & Amandus, H. (2013). Disparities in work-related homicide rates in selected retail industries in the United States, 2003–2008. *Journal of Safety Research*, 44, 25-29.

Mostofsky, E., Mukamal, K. J., Giovannucci, E. L., Stampfer, M. J., & Rimm, E. B. (2016). Key Findings on Alcohol Consumption and a Variety of Health Outcomes From the Nurses' Health Study. *American Journal of Public Health*, 106(9), 1586-1591.

Nielsen M.B., Einarsen, S. (2012). Outcomes of exposure to workplace bullying: A meta-analytic review. *Work and Stress*. 26, 309-332.

Olivier, L. Curfs,, LMG. and Viljoen, DL. (2016). Fetal alcohol spectrum disorders: Prevalence rates in South Africa. *South African Medical Journal*, 102(6 Suppl 1), S103-S106

Ortega A, Hogh A, Pejtersen J.H., Feveile H, & Olsen, O. (2009) Prevalence of workplace bullying and risk groups: a representative population study. *International Archives of Occupational and Environmental Health*. 82, 417-426.

Ortega A, Christensen KB, Hogh A, Rugulies R, Borg V. (2011). One-year prospective study on the effect of workplace bullying on long-term sickness absence. *Journal of Nursing Management*, 19, 752-759.

Pasche, S & Myers, B. (2012). Substance misuse trends in South Africa. Human *Psychopharmacology: Clinical and Experimental*. 27(3), 338-41.

Substance Abuse and Mental Health Services Administration (2018). 2017 NSDUH Annual National Report https://www.samhsa.gov/data/report/2017-nsduh-annual-national-report

Seggie, J. (2012). Alcohol and South Africa's Youth. *South African Medical Journal*, 102(7), 587.

Verkuil, B., Brosschot, J. F., Gebhardt, W. A., & Thayer, J. F. (2010). When worries make you sick: a review of perseverative cognition, the default stress response and somatic health. *Journal of Experimental Psychopathology*, 1(1), jep-009110.

Verkuil, B., Atasayi, S., & Molendijk, M. L. (2015). Workplace Bullying and Mental Health: A Meta-Analysis on Cross-Sectional and Longitudinal Data. *PLoS ONE*, 10(8).

World Health Organisation. (2019). World health statistics 2019: monitoring health for the SDGs, sustainable development goals. World Health Organisation. https://apps.who.int/iris/handle/10665/324835.

World Health Organisation. (2020). Towards an action plan to strengthen implementation of the Global Strategy to Reduce the Harmful Use of Alcohol. https://www.who.int/publications/i/item/action-plan-to-strengthen-implementation-of-the-global-strategy-to-reduce-the-harmful-use-of-alcohol

Chapter 6

Amato, P. R. (2010). Research on divorce: Continuing trends and new developments. *Journal of Marriage and Family*, 72(3), 650-666.

American Psychiatric Association. (2013). *Diagnostic and Statistical manual of mental disorders* (5th Ed). American Psychiatric Pub.

Cacioppo, J. T., & Patrick, W. (2008). *Loneliness: Human Nature and the Need for Social Connection.* WW Norton & Company.

Cacioppo, S., Capitanio, J. P., & Cacioppo, J. T. (2014). Toward a neurology of loneliness. *Psychological Bulletin*, 140(6), 1464.

Crenshaw, K. (1990). Mapping the margins: Intersectionality, identity politics, and violence against women of color. *Stanford Law Review.*, 43, 1241.

de Jonge, A. (2018). Corporate social responsibility through a feminist lens: Domestic violence and the workplace in the 21st century. *Journal of Business Ethics*, 148(3), 471–487. https://doi.org/10.1007/s10551-015-3010-9

Dickinson, E. (1976). The loneliness one dare not sound. *The complete poems of Emily Dickinson*, 379.

Eagle, Gillian. (2015). Crime, fear and continuous traumatic stress in South Africa: What place social cohesion? *Psychology in Society*, (49), 83-98.

Etzion, D. (1984). Moderating effect of social support on the stress–burnout relationship. *Journal of Applied Psychology*, 69(4), 615.

Eyetsemitan, F. (1998). Stifled grief in the workplace. *Death Studies*, 22(5), 469-479.

Ferguson, C.R., & Towhey, G.M., (2001). The Day After: Trauma in the Workplace. www.towhey.com/WorkplaceTrauma.htm

Freud, S. (1920). *A general introduction to psychoanalysis*. Boni and Liveright.

Gass, J. D., Stein, D. J., Williams, D. R., & Seedat, S. (2011). Gender differences in risk for intimate partner violence among South African adults. *Journal of Interpersonal Violence, 26*(14), 2764-2789.

Georganta, K., & Montgomery, A. (2016). Exploring Fun as a Job Resource: The Enhancing and Protecting Role of a Key Modern Workplace Factor. *International Journal of Applied Positive Psychology, 1*, 107-131.

Gerber, M., Brand, S., Elliot, C., Holsboer-Trachsler, E., Pühse, U., & Beck, J. (2013). Aerobic exercise training and burnout: a pilot study with male participants suffering from burnout. *BMC Research Notes, 6*(1), 1-9.

Groarke, J. M., Berry, E., Graham-Wisener, L., McKenna-Plumley, P. E., McGlinchey, E., & Armour, C. (2020). Loneliness in the UK during the COVID-19 pandemic: Cross-sectional results from the COVID-19 Psychological Wellbeing Study. *PloS one, 15*(9), e0239698.

Hall, D., Shucksmith, J., & Russell, S. (2013). Building a compassionate community: developing an informed and caring workplace in response to employee bereavement. *Bereavement Care, 32*(1), 4-10.

Heffernan, M. (2015). *Beyond measure: The big impact of small changes.* Simon and Schuster.

Herman, A. A., Stein, D. J., Seedat, S., Heeringa, S. G., Moomal, H., & Williams, D. R. (2009). The South African Stress and Health (SASH) study: 12-month and lifetime prevalence of common mental disorders. *South African Medical Journal, 99*(5).

Holt-Lunstad, J., Smith, T. B., & Layton, J. B. (2010). Social relationships and mortality risk: a meta-analytic review. *PLoS medicine, 7*(7).

Kaminer, D., & Eagle, G. (2010). *Traumatic Stress in South Africa.* NYU Press.

Keogh, O (2016). https://www.irishtimes.com/business/work/paying-attention-to-the-little-things-builds-better-businesses-1.2878248

Lazarus, R. S., & Folkman, S. (1984). *Stress, appraisal, and coping.* Springer publishing company.

Lazarus, R.S (1995). Psychological stress in the workplace. In R Crandall and L. Perrewe (eds). *Occupational Stress: A Handbook.* Washington: Taylor and Francis.

Leiter, M. P., & Maslach, C. (1988). The impact of interpersonal environment on burnout and organisational commitment. *Journal of Organisational Behavior, 9*(4), 297-308.

Leka, S., Griffiths, A., & Cox, T. (2004). Protecting workers' health series No 3: Work organisation & stress. Retrieved from the World Health Organisation website: *http://www. who. int/ occupational_health/publications/pwh3rev. pdf.*

Murthy, V. (2017). *Work and the loneliness epidemic.* Harvard Business Review, 9.

Naczenski, L. M., de Vries, J. D., van Hooff, M. L., & Kompier, M. A. (2017). Systematic review of the association between physical activity and burnout. *Journal of Occupational health, 59*(6), 477-494.

Naidoo, M. (2017). Challenging the status quo of an institutional culture in theological training. *Stellenbosch Theological Journal, 3*(2), 531-546.

Olivier, C. (2014) http://www.hrpulse.co.za/editors-pick/231789-domestic-violence-and-the-workplace

Ozcelik, H., & Barsade, S. G. (2018). No employee an island: Workplace loneliness and job performance. *Academy of Management Journal, 61*(6), 2343-2366.

Pentland, A. (2014). *Social physics: How good ideas spread-the lessons from a new science.* Penguin.

Perel, E. (2015). Rethinking infidelity ... a talk for anyone who has ever loved. TED.com https://www.ted.com/talks/esther_perel_rethinking_infidelity_a_talk_for_anyone_who_has_ever_loved?language=en

Perel, E. (2017). *The state of affairs: Rethinking infidelity-A book for anyone who has ever loved.* Hachette UK.

Perel, E. (2018) https://www.sxsw.com/interactive/2018/esther-perel-interactive-keynote-at-sxsw-2018-video/)

Preamble to the Constitution (1996). www.gov.za/documents/constitution-republic-south-africa-1996-preamble

Presidential Memorandum. (2012). The presidential memorandum—establishing policies for addressing domestic violence in the federal workforce. The White House. 18 April., http://www.whitehouse.gov/the-press-office/2012/04/18/presidential-memorandum-establishing-policies-addressing-domestic-violence.

Republic of South Africa. (1997). *Basic Conditions of Employment Act, No. 75 of 1997.* Pretoria: Government Printers.

Richter, L., Mathews, S., Kagura, J., & Nonterah, E. (2018). A longitudinal perspective on violence in the lives of South African children from the Birth to Twenty Plus cohort study in Johannesburg-Soweto. *South African Medical Journal*, 108(3), 181-186.

Rick, J., Young, K., & Guppy, A. (1999). From Accidents to Assaults: How Organisational Responses to Traumatic Events Can Prevent Post-Traumatic Stress Disorder (PTSD) in the Workplace. *HSE Contract Research Report 1995/98*

Selye, H. (1976). The stress concept. *Canadian Medical Association Journal*, 115(8), 718.

Statistics South Africa (2018a). *Victims of Crime Survey 2017/2018* www.statssa.gov.za

Statistics South Africa (2018b). *Marriages and divorces, 2016* http://www.statssa.gov.za/publications/P0307/P03072016.pdf

Steyn, M. (2013). Being different together: Case studies on diversity interventions in some South African organisations. http://opencontent.uct.ac.za/Humanities/Being-Different-Together-Case-studies-on-diversity-interventions-in-some-South-African-organisations

Sue, D. W. (2010). *Microaggressions in everyday life: Race, gender, and sexual orientation.* John Wiley & Sons.

U.S. Department of Health and Human Services, Substance Abuse and Mental Health Services Administration, Offi ce of Applied Studies. (2004). National Survey on Drug Use and Health, 2002. Research Triangle Park, NC: Research Triangle Institute.

Valdes-Dapena, C. (2018). Stop wasting money on team building. *Harvard Business Review*.

Vodacom Press Release (March 2019). www.vodacom.com/news-article.php?articleID=7377

Waber, B. N., Olguin Olguin, D., Kim, T., & Pentland, A. (2010). Productivity through coffee breaks: Changing social networks by changing break structure. Available at SSRN 1586375.

Waldinger, R., & Director, M. D. (2017). *Harvard study of adult development.*

Walker, P. (2018) https://www.theguardian.com/society/2018/jan/16/may-appoints-minister-tackle-loneliness-issues-raised-jo-cox

Whisman, M. A., Uebelacker, L. A., & Bruce, M. L. (2006). Longitudinal association between marital dissatisfaction and alcohol use disorders in a community sample. *Journal of Family Psychology*, 20(1), 164.

Wilson, C., & Moulton, B. (2010) *Loneliness among Older Adults: A National Survey of Adults 45+.* Prepared by Knowledge Networks and Insight Policy Research. Washington, DC: AARP

Wilson, T. D., Reinhard, D. A., Westgate, E. C., Gilbert, D. T., Ellerbeck, N., Hahn, C., ... & Shaked, A. (2014). Just think: The challenges of the disengaged mind. *Science*, 345(6192), 75-77. www.vodacomfoundationsa.co.za/gender-based-violence/ 2016

Zhong, C. B., & Leonardelli, G. J. (2008). Cold and lonely: Does social exclusion literally feel cold? *Psychological Science*, 19(9), 838-842.

Chapter 7

Blom, K and Vale, D. (March 2018). Cited in https://businesstech.co.za/news/internet/229009/ your-legal-rights-when-your-personal-data-gets-leaked-in-south-africa/

Brown, B. (2012). *Daring greatly: How the courage to be vulnerable transforms the way we live, love, parent, and lead.* Penguin.

Caton, C. L., Samet, S., & Hasin, D. S. (2000). When acute-stage psychosis and substance use co-occur: differentiating substance-induced and primary psychotic disorders. *Journal of Psychiatric Practice, 6*(5), 256-266.

Fleet, R. P., Dupuis, G., Marchand, A., Burelle, D., Arsenault, A., & Beitman, B. D. (1996). Panic disorder in emergency department chest pain patients: prevalence, comorbidity, suicidal ideation, and physician recognition. *The American Journal of Medicine, 101*(4), 371-380.

Hobfoll, S. E., Shirom, A., & Golembiewski, R. (2000). Conservation of resources theory. In Golembiewski, R (Ed.), *Handbook of Organisational Behavior.* (57-80) Marcel Dekker, New York.

Ingram, R. E. & Luxton, D. D. (2005). In B.L. Hankin & J. R. Z. Abela (Eds.), *Development of Psychopathology: A vulnerability stress perspective* (32-46). Thousand Oaks, CA: Sage Publications Inc.

Manderscheid, R., Delvecchio, P., Marshall, C., Palpant, R. G., Bigham, J., Bornemann, T. H., ... & Lubar, D. (2010). Attitudes toward mental illness-35 states, District of Columbia, and Puerto Rico, 2007. *Morbidity and Mortality Weekly Report, 59*(20), 619-625

Martins, N., & Ledimo, O. (2018). *Employee assistance programmes: a guide for the SA practitioner.* Knowledge Resources. Johannesburg.

Muller, R. A. E., Stensland, R. S. Ø., & van de Velde, R. S. (2020). The mental health impact of the covid-19 pandemic on healthcare workers, and interventions to help them: a rapid systematic review. *Psychiatry Research*, 113441.

National Department of Health, Republic of South Africa. (2011). Policy Guideline on 72-hour Assessment of Involuntary Mental Health Care Users.

Palmer, P. J. (2017). *The courage to teach: Exploring the inner landscape of a teacher's life.* John Wiley & Sons.

Republic of South Africa. (1996) Constitution of the Republic of South Africa, 1996 - Chapter 2: Bill of Rights

Republic of South Africa. (1997). Basic Conditions of Employment Act, No. 75 of 1997. Pretoria: Government Printers.

Republic of South Africa. (1998). Employment Equity Act, No.55 of 1998. Pretoria: Government Printers.

Republic of South Africa. (2000). The Promotion of Equality and Prevention of Unfair Discrimination Act, No.4 of 2000. Pretoria: Government Printers.

Chapter 8

Alderfer, C. P. (1969). An empirical test of a new theory of human needs. *Organisational Behavior and Human Performance, 4*(2), 142-175.

Arnetz, J. E., Goetz, C. M., Sudan, S., Arble, E., Janisse, J., & Arnetz, B. B. (2020). Personal protective equipment and mental health symptoms among nurses during the COVID-19 pandemic. *Journal of Occupational and Environmental Medicine, 62*(11), 892-897.

Bakker, A. B., & Demerouti, E. (2007). The Job Demands-Resources model: State of the art. *Journal of Managerial Psychology, 22*(3), 309-328. doi: 10.1108/02683940710733115

Bakker, A. B., Demerouti, E., & Euwema, M. C. (2005). Job resources buffer the impact of job demands on burnout. *Journal of Occupational Health Psychology, 10*(2), 170-180.doi: 10.1037/1076-8998.10.2.170

Barling, J. (2016) *Towards a psychologically healthy workplace.* Presentation to students at Wits University, Johannesburg.

Bedeian, A. G., & Armenakis, A. A. (1981). A path-analytic study of the consequence of role-conflict and ambiguity. *The Academy of Management Journal, 24*(2), 417-424.

Belkic, K. L., Landsbergis, P. A., Schnall, P. L., & Baker, D. (2004). Is job strain a major source of cardiovascular disease risk? *Scandinavian Journal of Work, Environment, & Health, 30*(2),85-128.

Boren, J. P. (2014). The relationship between co-rumination, social support, stress, and burnout among working adults. *Management Communication Quarterly, 28*(1), 3-25. doi: 10.1177/0893318913509283

Bowen, P., Edwards, P., & Lingard, H. (2012). Workplace stress experienced by construction professionals in South Africa. *Journal of Construction Engineering and Management, 139*(4), 393-403.

Brosnan, S. F. (2013). Justice-and fairness-related behaviors in nonhuman primates. *Proceedings of the National Academy of Sciences, 110*(Supplement 2), 10416-10423.

Cohen, D., & Prusak, L. (2001). *In good company: How social capital makes organisations work.* Brighton, MA: Harvard Business School Press.

Cranston, S. & Keller, S. (2013). Increasing the 'meaning quotient' of work. *McKinsey Quarterly,* January 2013.

De Vos, A., Akkermans, J., & Van Der Heijden, B. I. J. M. (2019). From occupational choice to career crafting. *The Routledge companion to career studies,* 128-142.

De Waal, F (2011). *Moral behavior in animals.* Retrieved from: https://www.ted.com/talks/frans_de_waal_moral_behavior_in_animals

De Waal, F. (2013). Two Monkeys Were Paid Unequally. Retrieved from: https://www.youtube.com/watch?v=meiU6TxysCg

Dijkstra-Kersten, S. M. A., Biesheuvel-Leliefeld, K. E. M., Van der Wouden, J. C., Penninx, B. W. J., & Van Marwijk, H. W. J. (2015). Associations of financial strain and income with depressive and anxiety disorders. *Journal of Epidemiological Community Health,* 1-6. doi: 10.1136/jech-2014-205088

Folger, R. G., & Cropanzano, R. (1998). *Organisational justice and human resource management* (Vol. 7). Sage.

Frankl, V. E. (1985). *Man's search for meaning.* Simon and Schuster.

Hall, D. T., & Nougaim, K. E. (1968). An examination of Maslow's Need Hierarchy in an organisational setting. *Organisational Behavior and Human Performance, 3*(1), 12-35.

Harter, J.K., Schmidt, F.L. and Hayes, T.L. (2002). Business-unit level relationship between employee satisfaction, employee engagement, and business outcomes: a meta-analysis. *Journal of Applied Psychology, 87,* 268-79

Heaney, C. A., Price, R. H., & Rafferty, J. (1995). Increasing coping resources at work: A field experiment to increase social support, improve work team functioning, and enhance employee mental health. *Journal of Organisational Behavior, 16, 335-352.*

Jorgensen, L. I., & Rothmann, S. (2008). Occupational stress, ill health and organisational commitment of members of the South African Police Service in the North West Province. *Acta Criminologica: Southern African Journal of Criminology, 21*(2), 1-15.

Kahn, J. R., & Pearlin, L. I. (2006). Financial strain over the life course and health among older adults. *Journal of health and social behavior, 47*(1), 17-31.

Kahn, R. L., Wolfe, D. M., Quinn, R. P., Snoek, J. D., & Rosenthal, R.A. (1964). *Organisational stress: Studies in role conflict and ambiguity*. Oxford, England: John Wiley.

Karasek, R. (1979). Job demands, job decision latittude, and mental strain: Implications for job redesign: *Administrative Science Quarterly, 24*(2), 85-308. doi:10.2307/2392498

Karasek, R. A., & Theorell, T. (1990). *Healthy work: Stress, productivity, and reconstruction of working life*. New York, NY: Basic Books.

Kelloway, E. K., & Day, A. L. (2005a). Building healthy workplaces: What we know so far. *Canadian Journal of Behavioral Sciences, 37*(4), 223-235.

Kelloway, E. K., & Day, A. L. (2005b). Building healthy workplaces: Where we need to be. *Canadian Journal of Behavioral Sciences, 37*(4), 309-312.

Kivimäki, M., Ferrie, J. E., Brunner, E., Head, J., Shipley, M. J., Vahtera, J., & Marmot, M. G. (2005). Justice at work and reduced risk of coronary heart disease among employees: The Whitehall II study. *Archives of Internal Medicine, 165*(19), 2245-2251.

Laundon, M., Cathcart, A., & McDonald, P. (2019). Just benefits? Employee benefits and organisational justice. *Employee Relations: The International Journal*.

Mangaliso, M., & Mphuthumi B. Damane. (2001). Building competitive advantage from "Ubuntu": Management lessons from South Africa [and Executive Commentary]. *The Academy of Management Executive (1993-2005), 15*(3), 23-34. Retrieved from http://www. jstor.org/stable/4165756

Marshall, M., & Marshall, E.I (2012). *Logotherapy Revisited: Review of the Tenets of Viktor E. Frankl's Logotherapy*. Ottawa Institute of Logotherapy. ISBN 978-1-4781-9377-7.

Milner, K., Russell, J., & Siemers, I. (2010). Friendship in socially isolating work environments. *South African Journal of Psychology, 40*(2), 204-213.

Myer, L., Stein, D. J., Grimsrud, A., Seedat, S., & Williams, D. R. (2008). Social determinants of psychological distress in a nationally representative sample of South African adults. *Social science & medicine, 66*(8), 1828-1840.

Nelson, B. (2004, January 27). Everything you thought you knew about recognition is wrong. [Magazine contribution]. Retrieved from www.workforce.com/2004/01/27/everything-you-thought-you-knew-about-recognition-is-wrong/

Ortlepp, K., & Friedman, M. (2001). The relationship between sense of coherence and indicators of secondary traumatic stress in non-professional trauma counselors. *South African Journal of Psychology, 31*(2), 38-45.

Ortlepp, K., & Friedman, M. (2002). Prevalence and correlates of secondary traumatic stress in workplace lay trauma counselors. *Journal of Traumatic Stress, 15*(3), 213-222.

Pentland, A. (2011) https://www.bbvaopenmind.com/en/articles/the-roots-of-innovation/

Pink, D (2009). https://www.ted.com/talks/dan_pink_on_motivation/transcript#t-1252944

Republic of South Africa. (1996). *Preamble to the Constitution of the Republic of South African*. Government Gazette. (No. 17678).

Republic of South Africa. (1997). *Basic Conditions of Employment Act, No. 75 of 1997*. Pretoria: Government Printers.

Sanne, B., Mykletun, A., Dahl, A. A., Moen, B. E., & Grethe, S. T. (2005). Testing the Job-Demand-Control-Support model with anxiety and depression as outcomes: The Hordaland Health Study. *Occupational Medicine, 55*, 463-473. doi:10.1093/occmed/kqi071

Schmidt, S., Roesler, U., Kusserow, T., & Rau, R. (2014). Uncertainty in the workplace: examining role ambiguity and role conflict, and their link to depression—a meta-analysis. *European Journal of Work and Organisational Psychology, 23*(1), 91-106.

Schnall, P. L., Landsbergis, P. A., & Baker, D. (1994). Job strain and cardiovascular disease. *Annual Review of Public Health, 15*, 381-411.

Stansfeld, S., Patel, C., North, F., Head, J., White, I., ... & Smith, G. D. (1991). Health inequalities among British civil servants: the Whitehall II study. *The Lancet, 337*(8754), 1387-1393.

Stevens, T (1994). Dr. Deming: 'Management Today Does Not Know What Its Job Is' (Part 1). *Industry Week*. Downloaded from https://www.industryweek.com/quality/dr-deming-management-today-does-not-know-what-its-job-part-1.

Taylor, F. W. (1911/1967). *The principles of scientific management*. New York, NY: Harper & Brothers.

Terkel, S. (1974). Working: People talk about what they do all day and how they feel about what they do. New York: The New Press.

Thatcher, A., & Milner, K. (2012). The impact of a 'green' building on employees' physical and psychological wellbeing. *Work, 41*, 3816-3823. doi: 10.3233/WOR-2012-0683-3816

Thatcher, A., & Milner, K. (2014). Changes in productivity, psychological wellbeing. *Work, 49*, 381-393. doi: 10.3233/WOR-141876

Warr, P. (1987). *Work, unemployment, and mental health*. New York, NY: Oxford University Press.

Warr, P. (1999). Well-being and the workplace. In D. Kahneman, E. Deiner, & N. Schwarz (Eds.), *Well-being: The foundations of hedonic psychology* (pp. 392-412). New York, NY: Russell Sage.

Xia, W., Fu, L., Liao, H., Yang, C., Guo, H., & Bian, Z. (2020). The Physical and Psychological Effects of Personal Protective Equipment on Health Care Workers in Wuhan, China: A Cross-Sectional Survey Study. *Journal of Emergency Nursing, 46*(6), 791-801.

Chapter 9

Aguinis, H., Gottfredson, R. K., & Joo, H. (2012). Delivering effective performance feedback: The strengths-based approach. *Business Horizons, 55*(2), 105-111.

Bakker, A. B., & Demerouti, E. (2007). The Job Demands-Resources model: State of the art. *Journal of Managerial Psychology, 22*(3), 309-328. doi: 10.1108/02683940710733115

Bandura, A. (1982). Self-efficacy mechanism in human agency. *American psychologist, 37*(2), 122.

Bandura, A. (1997). *Self-efficacy: The exercise of control*. New York: Freeman.

Csikszentmihalyi, M., & Seligman, M. E. (2000). Positive psychology: An introduction. *American Psychologist, 55*(1), 5-14.

Dickens, C. (1846). *A Christmas Carol in prose* (Vol. 91). Tauchnitz.

Emmons, R. A., McCullough, M. E., & Tsang, J.-A. (2003). *The assessment of gratitude*. In S. J. Lopez & C. R. Snyder (Eds.), *Positive psychological assessment: A handbook of models and measures* (p. 327–341). American Psychological Association. https://doi.org/10.1037/10612-021

Fehr, R., & Gelfand, M. J. (2012). The forgiving organisation: A multilevel model of forgiveness at work. *Academy of Management Review, 37*(4), 664-688.

Fredrickson, B. L. (2013). Positive emotions broaden and build. In *Advances in experimental social psychology* (Vol. 47, pp. 1-53). Academic Press.

Groopman, J. (2004). *The anatomy of hope*. New York: Random House.

Grossman, P., Niemann, L., Schmidt, S., & Walach, H. (2004). Mindfulness-based stress reduction and health benefits: A meta-analysis. *Journal of psychosomatic research, 57*(1), 35-43.

Harter, J.K., Schmidt, F.L. and Hayes, T.L. (2002), Business-unit level relationship between employee satisfaction, employee engagement, and business outcomes: a meta-analysis. *Journal of Applied Psychology*, Vol. 87, 268-79.

Hodges, T. D., & Clifton, D. O. (2004). Strengths-based development in practice. *Positive psychology in practice, 1,* 256-268.

Huber, G. (2019, July). Putting Humour to Work-A Complex Resource for Meaning Making. In *Academy of Management Proceedings,* 1, p. 13594). Briarcliff Manor, NY 10510: Academy of Management.

Kabat-Zinn, J. (2003a). Mindfulness-based interventions in context: past, present, and future. *Clinical psychology: Science and practice, 10*(2), 144-156.

Kabat-Zinn, J. (2003b). Mindfulness-based stress reduction (MBSR). *Constructivism in the Human Sciences, 8*(2), 73.

Kabat-Zinn, J. (2012). *Mindfulness for beginners: Reclaiming the present moment—and your life.* Sounds True: Boulder, Colorado.

Kabat-Zinn, J., Lipworth, L., & Burney, R. (1985). The clinical use of mindfulness meditation for the self-regulation of chronic pain. *Journal of behavioral medicine, 8*(2), 163-190.

Kahn, W.A. (1990), Psychological conditions of personal engagement and disengagement at work. *Academy of Management Journal,* 33, 692-724.

Langer, E. J. (1989). *Mindfulness.* Addison-Wesley/Addison Wesley Longman.

Langer, EJ, (2004). Harvard Business Review. https://hbr.org/2014/03/mindfulness-in-the-age-of-complexity

Langer, E. J., & Moldoveanu, M. (2000). Mindfulness research and the future. *Journal of social issues,* 56(1), 129-139.

Linley, A., & Dovey, H. (2015). *Technical manual and statistical properties for Realise2.* Coventry: Centre of Applied Positive Psychology.

Luthans, F., & Jensen, S. M. (2002). Hope: A new positive strength for human resource development. *Human resource development review, 1*(3), 304-322.

Luthans, F., Youssef, C. M., & Avolio, B. J. (2007). *Psychological capital: Developing the human competitive edge.* Oxford University Press: New York.

Luthans, F., Youssef, C. M., & Avolio, B. J. (2015). *Psychological capital and beyond.* Oxford: Oxford University Press.

Maslach, C., & Leiter, M. P. (2016). Understanding the burnout experience: recent research and its implications for psychiatry. World Psychiatry: official journal of the World Psychiatric Association (WPA), 15(2), 103–111.

Merriam-Webster (n.d.). Citation. In *Merriam-Webster.com dictionary.* Retrieved October 21, 2020, from https://www.merriam-webster.com/dictionary/citation.

Peterson, C., & Seligman, M. E. (2004). *Character strengths and virtues: A handbook and classification* (Vol. 1). Oxford: Oxford University Press.

Proctor, C., Tsukayama, E., Wood, A. M., Maltby, J., Eades, J. F., & Linley, P. A. (2011). Strengths gym: The impact of a character strengths-based intervention on the life satisfaction and well-being of adolescents. *The Journal of Positive Psychology,* 6(5), 377-388.

Santorelli, S. (Ed.). (2014). *Mindfulness-based stress reduction (MBSR): standards of practice.* Worcester: Center for Mindfulness in Medicine, Health Care & Society, University of Massachusetts Medical School.

Schaufeli, W. B. (2013). *The measurement of work engagement.* In R. R. Sinclair, M. Wang, & L. E. Tetrick (Eds.), *Research methods in occupational health psychology: Measurement, design, and data analysis* (p. 138–153). Routledge/Taylor & Francis Group.

Schneider, S. L. (2001). In search of realistic optimism: Meaning, knowledge, and warm fuzziness. *American Psychologist,* 56(3), 250.

Seligman, M. E. P., Steen, T. A., Park, N., & Peterson, C. (2005). Positive Psychology Progress: Empirical Validation of Interventions. *American Psychologist, 60*(5), 410–421. https://doi.org/10.1037/0003-066X.60.5.410

Sheldon, K.M. & King, L. (2001). Why Positive Psychology is Necessary. Retrieved from: https://www.researchgate.net/profile/Laura_King5/publication/12020093_Why_positive_psychology_is_necessary/links/02e7e525ef3a69b715000000/Why-positive-psychology-is-necessary.pdf

Sheldon, K. M., & Lyubomirsky, S. (2006). How to increase and sustain positive emotion: The effects of expressing gratitude and visualizing best possible selves. *The Journal of Positive Psychology, 1*(2), 73-82.

Snyder, C. R. (2002). Hope theory: Rainbows in the mind. *Psychological Inquiry, 13*(4), 249-275.

Strümpfer, D. J. W. (1990). Salutogenesis: A new paradigm. *South African Journal of Psychology, 20*(4), 265-276.

Tkachenko, O., Quast, L. N., Song, W., & Jang, S. (2018). Courage in the workplace: The effects of organisational level and gender on the relationship between behavioral courage and job performance. *Journal of Management & Organisation*, 1-17.

Winslow, C. J., Kaplan, S. A., Bradley-Geist, J. C., Lindsey, A. P., Ahmad, A. S., & Hargrove, A. K. (2017). An examination of two positive organisational interventions: For whom do these interventions work? *Journal of Occupational Health Psychology, 22*(2), 129–137. https://doi.org/10.1037/ocp0000035

Index

www.ingramcontent.com/pod-product-compliance
Lightning Source LLC
Chambersburg PA
CBHW080609270326
41928CB00016B/2973